Adventure Guide to the

Great Smoky Mountains

2nd Edition

Blair Howard

HUNTER

HUNTER PUBLISHING, INC.
130 Campus Drive
Edison, NJ 08818-7816
☎ 732-225-1900 / 800-255-0343 / fax 732-417-1744
Web site: www.hunterpublishing.com
E-mail: hunterp@bellsouth.net

IN CANADA:
Ulysses Travel Publications
4176 Saint-Denis, Montréal, Québec
Canada H2W 2M5
☎ 514-843-9882 ext. 2232 / fax 514-843-9448

IN THE UNITED KINGDOM:
Windsor Books International
The Boundary, Wheatley Road, Garsington
Oxford, OX44 9EJ England
☎ 01865-361122 / fax 01865-361133

ISBN 1-55650-905-7
© 2001 Blair Howard

Cover photo by Kennan Ward
Maps by Kim André, © 2001 Hunter Publishing, Inc.

4   3   2   1

Contents

Maps

Introduction

Mention the Great Smoky Mountains to most people and they immediately think of the Great Smoky Mountains National Park. And so they should, for each year more than nine million people make it the most visited national park in the United States. But the park is not the be all and end all of the Smokies. In fact, it's just a small part of the whole.

The Smokies, for the purposes of this book, encompass an area that runs from the Virginia state line, straddling the Tennessee/North Carolina border, all the way down into northern Georgia. Along the way they embrace the great Nantahala, Pisgah, Cherokee and Chattahoochee national forests – four vast outdoor tracts of wilderness.

Although civilization came here in colonial times, the area is, for the most part, still a very primitive domain that hasn't kept pace with the outside world. Great pockets of unspoiled wilderness exist within the Smokies; some areas still don't have electricity, and there are places where the locals are downright suspicious of strangers. Many people here live out their lives much as their ancestors did almost 100 years ago.

A visit to the national park will take you to the famous mountain city of Gatlinburg, to Dollywood and Pigeon Forge, but the land where Davy Crockett was born and raised has much more to offer. Over a dozen ski resorts are tucked away among the hills and valleys; there are plenty of unspoiled fishing spots and hundreds of backcountry camping grounds offer thousands of sites, from primitive to full-service. Then there are the tiny towns, some no more than a couple of clapboard shacks and a country store; towns like Tellico Plains, Sylva, Highlands, Sweetgum and Rainbow Springs. A network of backcountry roads, narrow and winding, join one small woodland colony to the next. Hundreds of miles of narrow trails, pathways and bridleways interlace the forest and criss-cross one another in a bewildering spider's web of footpaths. It's an area where careless travelers can get easily get lost, and stay lost for days on end.

The Great Smoky Mountains are also home to a diverse assortment of wildlife. Black bear, white-tailed deer and wild boar roam

free; wild turkeys, eliminated from eastern Tennessee by generations of hunters, have returned to the Cherokee National Forest.
And each year in the fall, the great hardwood forests provide visitors with spectacular displays of color.

The Smoky Mountains represent one of the last real opportunities
for great adventure in the southeastern United States.

■ The Nature Of Adventure

 Adventure means different things to different people.
To some it means the far-off jungles of Africa, the snows
of Antarctica, or the peaks of the mighty Himalayas. To
others it means beachcombing, hiking or horseback riding. Adventure in the Smokies means an excursion into the great
outdoors – hiking, rock climbing, snow skiing, fishing, hunting,
and boating. The *Adventure Guide to the Great Smoky Mountains*
covers all those activities and more. It takes you to the historic
sites in the area, and to the hundreds of antique stores, gift shops
and craft fairs. It covers fine dining and luxury hotels, and details
afternoon drives on country roads.

We have taken three separate approaches to the order of this book.

First, each type of adventure is briefly covered on pages 27 to 43.
There, you will find out what's available and where.

Second, each geographical region is described in depth, along with
a detailed report of attractions and adventures within that particular region.

Lastly, we have included three separate directories at the back of
the book – one for camping, one for accommodations, and one for
information services. The listings in the camping and accommodations directories are not recommendations, but they do include
short descriptions of the facilities.

So, if you want to spend a few days snow skiing, you'll turn to that
particular activity on page 34, and there you'll find that snow skiing is available in upper eastern Tennessee and upper western
North Carolina. From there, it's simply a matter of turning the
pages to your region of choice where you'll find a list of resorts and
all the information you'll need to make an educated choice.

■ Geography

The Appalachian Highlands are generally grouped into five geographic regions: the Piedmont; the Blue Ridge; the Ridge & Valley; the Appalachian Plateau; and the New England-Acadian Region.

- The **Piedmont Region** begins in the north near New York City and extends southward all the way into central Alabama. It lies between the Coastal Plain and the eastern fringes of the mountains. Most of the region consists of undulating farmland and forests with low-lying hills and ridges of 1,000 to 2,000 feet in altitude.

- The **Blue Ridge Region** is a long line of heavily forested mountains and ridges that stretch from Pennsylvania into northern Georgia. From the low country in the north, the ridge grows ever more lofty and much wider as you follow it south. Many of its peaks, especially in western North Carolina and the Great Smoky Mountains National Park, tower above 6,000 feet.

 Mount Mitchell, at almost 6,700 feet in the Black Mountains of western North Carolina, is the highest point east of the Mississippi.

- The **Ridge and Valley Region** lies just west of the Blue Ridge. It's an area of long, narrow valleys separated by ridges that run roughly parallel to one another. The Hudson-Champlain Valley, a broad, fertile section of the region, begins in central Alabama and continues northward through New York.

 In Pennsylvania, one section of the great valley contains nearly all the anthracite coal in the United States.

- The westernmost section of the highlands is the **Appalachian Plateau Region**, where narrow valleys divide the steep hills and level uplands. It's a region of great geological wealth where most of the world's largest deposits of bituminous coal are found. At the southern end of the region lies the Cumberland Plateau, the

Catskill Mountains and, in the center, the Allegheny Plateau.

■ The heavily forested **New England-Acadian Region** extends northward from Pennsylvania into Newfoundland. The Taconic, Green, and White mountains are its best-known ranges, and Mount Washington (6,288 feet) is the highest peak in the region.

The Great Smoky Mountains incorporate the highest mountain ranges in the entire Appalachian system. Within the boundaries of the Great Smoky Mountains National Park alone, 16 peaks rise to more than 6,000 feet.

According to geologists, the rocks exposed in the Great Smoky Mountains are among the oldest in the world. They were formed long before the separation of the continental plates from sediments that were deposited in the shallow seas to the west, which later formed most of the interior land surface of the United States. When the earth began to cool and contract, great sections of these seas were thrown upward and the area now known as **Appalachia** was elevated. At first, its rocks were folded and compressed into a series of sharp peaks and mighty gorges. Then came the wind and storms, with millions of years of erosion that carved and shaped them into the gentle, rounded contours with which we are familiar today.

The Piedmont, Blue Ridge and New England-Acadian regions are predominantly granite – very old formations of tilted, crumpled, broken strata. The Ridge and Valley region is built upon underlying beds of limestone, shale, and sandstone, thrown upward and folded one on top of another. The Appalachian Plateau is tilted slightly toward the northwest.

In the beginning, the Blue Ridge and Piedmont regions were part of a very large island or group of islands. The rocks were broken and changed in a great upheaval of the Earth's crust. Molten material from the Earth's interior produced the granite and other crystalline rocks.

The Ridge and Valley settled and became a region of shallow seas between the Blue Ridge and Piedmont regions and the mainland. Some geological deposits of the plateau were formed in the sea, but the coal deposits were formed in the swamps that came later.

More than 200 million years ago, as the Earth continued to cool and the plates to move, so the island moved slowly westward. As it did, forces beneath the Earth's surface squeezed and folded the thick formations to such an extent that fault lines collapsed and the rocks were pushed upward, creating the first Appalachian Mountains. Scientists think they were once probably as high and steep as the Rocky Mountains, which were formed much later.

By the time the Appalachian Mountains had formed, the Plateau Region lay far inland. There, the cataclysmic events had raised and tilted the strata but had not folded it. It was a hostile environment of volcanoes, wind and water. The sand and mud settled in the valleys and the Earth's surface continued to move. The land slipped and broke into narrow blocks that sank or tilted upward in long mountains.

All through the Mesozoic period and into the Cenozoic, the action of wind and water eroded the mountains of the plateau until the surface became almost level. Rivers in the plateau flowed westward to the interior. Those in the eastern sections found their way to the Atlantic Ocean.

In late Cenozoic times, the Appalachian region continued its wild transformation. Mountains continued to rise and the constant uplift gave speed to rivers swollen by the heavy rains of the era. The rivers eroded the land, carving and dividing the great plain into a series of irregular hills and long ridges.

The rivers and streams of the Plateau Region were in a state of flux, often changed course, and traced an intricate network. The larger rivers of other regions remained true to their courses. And, since most of them flowed southeast to the sea, they often crossed the ridges and valleys, carving new channels, called water gaps. Their tributaries bypassed the great ridges of resistant rock. They flowed between them, cutting narrow, parallel valleys.

The modern Appalachian Mountains are less than 25 million years old, the result of the final upheaval and erosion that took place late in the Cenozoic era. The highest peaks are all that remain of the mountains formed more than 200 million years ago in the Permian period.

Today, the peaks, ridges, hills, and valleys of the highlands form a great natural belt almost 2,000 miles long and, in some places, up to 360 miles wide.

The region we are concerned with, the Great Smoky Mountains, is, in fact, a section of two central regions of the Appalachian Highlands that separate the Eastern Seaboard from the Midwestern United States – the Piedmont and the Blue Ridge. The Piedmont extends southward from New York all the way into central Alabama; the Blue Ridge, from Pennsylvania into Northern Georgia.

The Appalachians have played a significant role in the history and development of the United States. They were the first great barrier faced by the early settlers. It wasn't until the first intrepid explorers found passes through the highlands and blazed the first trails westward that pioneers were able to move on from Jamestown and the colonies to settle the West.

Coal from the Appalachians was the essential ingredient for the foundation of industrial development. And coal it was that made American manufacturing the most productive in the world. The Appalachians also furnished stone, oil, gas, timber and iron ore. And they provided necessary power when the tumbling rivers were harnessed to produce electricity.

Today, the mountains offer unparalleled scenic beauty and plenty of opportunities for outdoor recreation. There are facilities for summer and winter sports; trails and parkways that serve hikers and motorists; national forests and parks, as well as numerous parks and historic sites.

■ Flora & Fauna

 Deviate only a few yards from the beaten path, away from the hoards of visitors, and you'll enter a world that remains essentially untouched by humans. Combine that with a heavy annual rainfall that can go as high as 80 inches and some of the most fertile soil in the world, and it's no wonder the area's plant life developed in greater variety here than anywhere else in the temperate zone.

 Botanists claim that this region is the original home of all modern-day Eastern vegetation. About 150 species of trees have been found in the highlands. Europe has fewer than 100.

The Appalachians have the largest virgin hardwood and red spruce forests in the United States, and there could be as many as 2,000 species of plant life. In the Smokies, many attain rates of growth found only in the rainforests of the tropical regions. Some tulip trees reach heights of almost 200 feet, with diameters in excess of nine feet; one species of wild grapevine has been known to grow a main stem more than five feet in circumference, and some laurel shrubs grow more than 40 feet tall.

Sometimes you'll find treeless areas on the rounded mountain tops. These are known as **balds**, and are often covered with dense undergrowth, grass and shrubs. Some claim they are the result of ancient windfalls, some say the trees were destroyed by fires from which they never recovered, and still others claim the balds are the remains of ancient Indian campsites.

In many areas the lower slopes of the mountains and the walls of deep ravines carved by rushing streams are blanketed by hundreds of acres of rhododendron, laurel, azalea, and myrtle. In some places the growth is almost impenetrable. These areas are known as **slicks**, or **hells**.

ANIMALS

The Smokies are home to more than 50 species of mammals and 120 species of birds. There are at least 30 different reptiles, including 19 species of snakes and nine lizards, and there are at least 46 amphibians.

The mammal community includes black bears, wild hogs, white-tailed deer, foxes, bobcats and raccoons. The coyote is present in some areas, mainly in the Cherokee National Forest, and there are plans to reintroduce the red wolf into the Great Smoky Mountains National Park.

The animal with the highest profile, and one you are likely to see in the forests of the Smokies, is the **black bear**. Outside the Great Smoky Mountains National Park, the black bear is a timid creature. Hunted throughout the forests, except in the park, it keeps very much to itself, although it does sometimes stray from the cover of trees into populated areas where it forages for food in garbage cans.

The **wild boar** or hog, found mostly in the Cherokee National Forest, is a wily creature. It, too, is a popular prey for hunters. The boar, now present in ever-increasing numbers, is not native to the region and is regarded as something of a problem, doing a great deal of damage in the forest by rooting for tubers. It also competes with native wildlife for food; each adult will consume some 1,400 pounds of acorns a year, the principal source of food for much of the wildlife. Many would like to see the animal eliminated from the Smokies.

The **white-tailed deer** can be found throughout the Smokies, but is most plentiful in the Cherokee National Forest. It's often possible to see deer in the early morning or late afternoon, on the edge of the woodlands or in the bordering fields.

Wild animals should not be a problem provided you stay away from them. Of the bigger and more exotic animals, only the black bear and the wild boar are really dangerous.

To see a bear, even at a distance, is a rare thrill. To see one close up and angry is something else. The cubs are most delightful creatures, and will wander up to you, curious and playful. Be careful. Wherever there's a cub, you can be sure its mama is close by with her ears cocked, and she will defend her young with her life.

Though rarely seen, wild boars are a fierce and ferocious adversary, apt to charge when cornered, intent on inflicting a nasty wound if he can.

Don't feed wild animals, and don't give them the opportunity to feed themselves – a scrounging bear is a clever and resourceful creature. Somehow they identify with the brightly colored backpack, and will have no hesitation about raiding your pack if you leave it within easy reach. Hang packs and food containers from a high branch, at least six feet off the ground, and make sure that the branch will not support the weight even of a small bear. Small animals, too, will invade your pack or food supply if you leave it lying on the ground.

Always remember, the woods and forests are their home, not yours. You are the visitor.

INSECTS

The Smokies are home to all sorts of winged, crawling and stinging creatures, which are attracted to the flowers and foliage of the forests, rivers and lakes. Unfortunately, they will also be attracted to you. Check with your doctor or pharmacist for any allergy medication or insect repellent you may need.

Mosquitos are common during the summer, especially in the evenings. Wear a lightweight, long-sleeved shirt or blouse and pants along with your insect repellent and you should be okay.

Other venomous insects you're likely to encounter are the **fire ant**, the **honeybee**, the **yellow jacket** and the **hornet**. Only in cases where there's an allergy will emergency room treatment be required if you are bitten or stung; calamine lotion will usually help ease pain.

More annoying than dangerous are the **deerflies** that live in the forests; **chiggers**, the nasty little red bugs that inhabit dense bushy areas in summertime; and the ubiquitous **horseflies** that are especially prominent in the open woods and grasslands.

Ticks

Unfortunately, ticks are a fact of life here and some of them carry diseases.

Lyme disease is rapidly becoming a problem in the Smokies, and Rocky Mountain spotted fever has been around for a long time. Both are carried by ticks, and both can have a devastating effect. Anyone venturing into heavily wooded areas should take the precautions listed below.

Rocky Mountain spotted fever is the result of toxins secreted when an American dog tick – one of the family of wood ticks found in vast numbers here – bites you. This fever can be fatal if not treated quickly.

Lyme disease is a tick-borne viral infection for which there is no cure or vaccination. It need not, however, be fatal. A program of antibiotics will keep the disease in check until the immune system can build up antibodies to cope with it.

The symptoms of Lyme disease are similar to many other illnesses: low-grade fever, fatigue, head and body pain. The tick bite itself may at first go unnoticed but, within a month of being bitten, a red rash will appear around the bite. Sometimes the rash is a solid red, sometimes it has a brighter outer edge with little or no color in the middle. Although it can vary in size and even cover an entire arm or thigh, it usually is about four inches in diameter.

A blood test will usually confirm the disease by detecting antibodies in the immune system, but it can take as long as two months before those antibodies begin to appear.

The deer tick, which can carry Lyme disease, lives in wooded areas as well as on dogs. You can decrease the chances of your pet carrying ticks by using a tick spray, dip, powder or a tick collar.

Observe the following basic rules to reduce your chances of infection.

- Wear long-sleeved shirts, long pants and, especially, a hat when venturing out into the woodlands. Use repellents and tuck your pants into high socks to keep ticks from crawling under your clothes.

- Keep shoes and boots tightly laced.

- Wear light-colored clothing; it will not only be cooler, but will make it easier to spot ticks before they can crawl into an open neck or button hole.

- Wear collared shirts to help stop ticks crawling onto your neck.

- Check your clothing after an outing. The deer tick is small, often no bigger than a large pinhead.

If you find a tick attached to your skin, use fine-jawed tweezers and grip the tick as gently as you can, and as close to your skin as possible. Do not squeeze the tick's body or you will inject its fluids into the bite, which can cause infection.

There are many good repellents on the market. The most effective contain an agent called DEET. Use only repellents with a DEET content of less than 20%; in stronger concentrations the chemical can cause itching and burning.

Best of all are the proprietary brands of skin softener such as Avon's Skin-So-Soft, a product that was used extensively against flying bugs and pests during the Gulf War. It smells nice and won't cause burning or itching.

Spiders

Many spiders live in the Great Smoky Mountains, and some of them bite. But there are only two venomous spiders you'll need to watch out for: the brown recluse and the black widow. Most spider venoms are not harmful to humans, but the brown recluse is the most deadly of all North American spiders.

The black widow's venom contains neurotoxins that affect the transmission of nerve impulses. That produced by the brown recluse is necrotic. It produces a local swelling and death of tissues around the area where the poison was injected, similar to the flesh-eating virus that made headlines a few years ago, but on a lesser scale.

The **black widow** lives in old wooden buildings, on dead logs, wooden benches and picnic tables. They are easily recognized by their jet black color, large bulbous body and a distinctive red, hourglass-shaped mark on their underside.

The **brown recluse** makes its home in out-of-the-way nooks and crannies; in the roofs of old buildings, garages, shelters, outhouses and such. It's slightly smaller than the black widow, but has the same characteristic long legs. Its color varies from a light fawn to a dark chocolate brown.

If you are bitten by either spider, go to the nearest emergency room for treatment. Many national park and forest ranger stations can offer immediate first aid, but expert treatment is essential.

SNAKES

There are a limited number of poisonous snakes living in the Great Smoky Mountains. Of these, there are four members of the pit viper family that you should avoid: the **copperhead**, the **water moccasin**, the **cottonmouth** and the **timber rattlesnake**. The copperhead and the timber rattlesnake are fairly common throughout the Smokies. The cottonmouth, although quite rare, can be found almost anywhere, but it particularly likes the water (swamps, riverbanks, lakes). The water moccasin inhabits the same areas as the cottonmouth.

To avoid a snakebite, watch where you step; never put your hands into nooks and crannies or other rocky places; never go barefoot; sleep up off the ground.

If you or someone in your party is bitten, administer first aid (do not apply a tourniquet) and transport the victim immediately to the nearest hospital emergency room. If you are by yourself, go immediately for help, but avoid exerting yourself.

PLANTS

Many poisonous plants are indigenous to the Great Smokies. At least a dozen of them, including some species of mushroom, are deadly if ingested; and many more will cause nasty skin rashes. Especially deadly is **jimson weed**, which can cause coma and even death, and the members of the **nightshade** family.

Poison oak and **poison ivy**, along with several other varieties of poisonous creeper, grow in profusion throughout the forests. They can cause a nasty rash. You should learn to recognize their most distinctive feature, a three-leaf arrangement.

To be safe, assume that everything is poisonous. Don't put anything into your mouth and don't touch plants you can't identify. Don't pick flowers.

Despite all precautions, even the most experienced adventurer will sometimes fall victim to curiosity or mis-identification. A victim of poisoning should quickly drink two or three glasses of water to dilute the poison. Vomiting should then be induced – syrup of ipecac works well – and the victim transported to the nearest emergency room, along with a sample of the plant.

■ The People

 These mountains are the ancestral home of the Cherokee Indians. They called them "Great Smoky" for the blue-gray mists that often shroud the peaks. Scattered throughout the remote hills, valleys and bottomlands are families that still live in the self-sufficient, primitive fashion of their ancestors more than 100 years ago. Most people who once lived in the Great Smoky Mountains National Park have been moved out, but a few still hold life leases. They are the descendants of English, Scottish, and Irish settlers who moved west from Jamestown shortly after its founding.

These backwoods families, isolated for generations, have kept alive the speech, ballads, and customs of 17th- and 18th-century Britain. They are a solitary people and keep very much to themselves, rarely venturing far from the primitive small-holdings they call home. Some have never ventured beyond the trees. A few have no conception of modern society. In some places, electricity has not yet arrived, let alone the telephone. They are a wary, suspicious people who don't take kindly to strangers.

■ History

De Soto & the First Settlers

 The recorded history of the Great Smoky Mountain region is a short one compared with the great age of the mountains. **Hernando De Soto**, the first white man to visit the area, arrived in 1540 and encountered the Indian tribes that lived in the forests. Archaeological evidence suggests that by then Indians had already lived in the mountains for more than 12,000 years.

De Soto and his men raped, pillaged and looted, then left. For more than 100 years afterward, the Indians continued to exist peacefully, having no further contact with the white man. It wasn't until the late 1600s that English colonists in Virginia found their way into the Southern Appalachians, made contact with the Cherokee, and established a number of scattered settlements in the area.

Settlers vs. Cherokees

During the French and Indian War, the English built Fort Loudoun in the western reaches of the Smokies. At the time, it was the westernmost outpost in the British Empire; it was also a thorn in the side of the Cherokee Nation. In 1760 they attacked the fort and massacred its garrison. The English retaliated by destroying many Cherokee villages.

White settlers put down their roots along the banks of the Nolichucky, Watauga and Holston rivers, to the great annoyance of the Cherokees.

The American Revolution

When the American War of Independence started, the Indians took advantage of the upheaval and attacked the white settlements. It was a great mistake. The hardened backwoodsmen retaliated and, again, the Cherokee villages were destroyed.

Following the defeat of the Cherokee, the backwoodsmen turned their attention to the war against the English. From Sycamore Shoals, now a state historic park in Elizabethton, Tennessee, the frontiersmen marched east along the Overmountain Victory National Historic Trail and helped defeat the British at the Battle of King's Mountain.

Westward Migration

Following the end of the War of Independence, the white man moved west, bringing a new civilization to the mountains and valleys west of the Appalachians. Vast as the new land was, however, there was never enough. Greedy eyes now turned to the lush territory held by the Cherokees. During the late 1830s, most of the tribes were forced from their lands. They headed westward along what was to become known as the "Trail of Tears."

Red Clay State Park (see page 67-68) on the western edge of the Cherokee National Forest is the site of the last tribal council held before the great exodus.

As the plains and valleys of the interior of the American continent offered more fertile land, so the westward migration of the white settlers pretty much bypassed the remote and inaccessible areas of the Southern Appalachians. In some areas, however, the rugged mountains reminded the new Americans of their abandoned homes across the seas. Men and women from the Scottish highlands felt very much at home there, as did many German and Irish immigrants. Their descendants still farm remote areas here today.

The Civil War

During the Civil War, the inhabitants of the mountains in east Tennessee and western North Carolina were of divided sympathies. Some areas became hotbeds of Union activity – a refuge for runaway slaves or a haven for escaped federal prisoners of war. The war became an excuse to settle old scores. Families sympathetic to one cause or another turned to violence against their neighbors. In some places, the animosities engendered in those far-off days still linger today.

The Smokies Today

By the end of the late 19th century, the area was beginning to develop and new industries arrived. The railroad came and the lumber and mining industries flourished. Large corporations laid the mountain tops bare in search of copper and other minerals, but even then the conservationists were taking a hard look at the Great Smoky Mountains.

President Roosevelt's New Deal and the Civilian Conservation Corps brought order and access to the mountains and forests. The Tennessee Valley Authority (TVA) built a series of dams, creating huge lakes, fast-flowing whitewater rivers and, along with them, vast recreation areas that opened the wilderness to the weekend outdoorsman.

Today, much of the area is administered and maintained either by the National Forest Service or the National Parks Service. Millions of people visit the mountains every year. Tourism is the new industry now; conservation is its watchword.

■ Climate

Often, especially after a rainfall, dawn washes over mountain gorges filled with white cloud-like mists through which the peaks and ridges peep like rocky islands set in a sea of cotton candy. In the evenings, spectacular sunsets set the mountains afire.

Spring fills the air with the scent of fresh flowers. Crocuses and daffodils bloom in February, and from May until June dogwoods, wildflowers, mountain laurels, azaleas and rhododendrons blossom all across the Smokies.

In **summer**, the mountains turn lush and green. The forests are covered with a blanket of fern, snakeroot, black and blue cohosh, jewel weed, wood nettle, strawberry bush, chickweed, foamflower and heart-leafed aster. Summer in the Smokies is a time to take things easy, to spend quiet hours in a boat, drifting on the still waters of a mountain lake. It's a time for strolling the riverbanks at the canyon bottom, to sit and listen to the roar of a mountain waterfall, or the tinkling, tumbling waters of a meandering stream. It's a time to just sit quietly on the rocks high above the valleys, or on a canyon rim, where the air is invigorating, the view breathtaking, and only the dull buzz of the insects and the sounds of the birds singing in the trees disturb the silence of a warm and hazy afternoon.

In October, the air turns crisp in the early morning, and the advent of autumn paints the mountains in a riot of color: bronze, amber, yellow, gold and red. **Fall** in the Great Smoky Mountains is a busy time. Thousands of visitors crowd the main roads and parkways, sightseeing, leaf-peeping and picnicking. There's a fair almost every weekend. In the backcountry, fall means hiking, horseback riding, boating, fishing and hunting.

Winter comes as early as mid-November and turns the hardwood trees into stark woodland skeletons. By Christmas the first snows have fallen and transformed the Blue Ridge into a winter fairyland reminiscent of the fabled Narnia made famous by C.S. Lewis. It's a magical kingdom of ice and snow, and a time for warm woolly clothing, crackling campfires, fishing for trout in cold mountain streams, or skiing the soft white powder at the mountain resorts.

Rainfall in the Smokies is a year-round occurrence and can vary in intensity from a fine mist to a full-blown thunderstorm. Rain is the lifeblood of the mountains and forests. The wilderness, during and after a rainfall, takes on a new vitality. The forests fill with sounds of life, rivers and streams swell and gather new strength, waterfalls are a little more spectacular, and the woodland flowers are always a little brighter in color. A sudden downpour can lower the temperature in summer by more than 10°.

The average rainfall is 55 inches, except in Cascade Country – along the North Carolina/Georgia border – where it often exceeds 80 inches. This rainbelt offers magnificent waterfalls and rushing mountain rivers; Transylvania County alone has more than 150 waterfalls.

Snow falls mostly during the months December through February, although it has been known to fall in early May. Seldom does it exceed more than a foot in depth, and rarely does it snow for more than a few days at a time, except, of course, on the ski slopes in the northern section of the mountains.

Temperatures range from below zero in the depths of winter to a high in the mid-90s during the summer months. In higher elevations, however, they stay mostly in the 70s and 80s. At night, summertime temperatures drop into the 60s, and even the 50s. In winter, they can plummet to minus 20 or 30.

Basics

■ Getting Around

Getting around in the Smokies can be something of a trial. Much of the area is wilderness and virtually inaccessible. Civilization has, however, made inroads into what once was a land of unmarked narrow roads that petered out into pot-holed dirt roads leading nowhere – or so it seemed. Today, the Blue Ridge is criss-crossed by a network of four-lane highways and interstates.

Driving Tips

- Stay off the high mountain roads in winter. They are often snow-covered and impassable. And even if they are clear of snow, they can be icy and extremely slippery. In places, the road's edge drops away 100 feet.

- Always observe the speed limits posted on mountain roads, and especially on side roads, which can be narrow, making passing difficult even at slow speeds.

- Don't park on blind bends to go sightseeing. If the view is good, you can bet there will be a pull-off a little farther along where the view is even better.

- Exercise patience while driving in the mountains, especially on side roads and in the very busy resort towns of Gatlinburg, Pigeon Forge and Helen. In summer and fall, the colorful scenery causes traffic to slow dramatically. Don't sound your horn if you find someone dawdling along in front of you.

- Watch out for falling rocks and flash floods. Never try to cross a flooded bridge or road; the waters travel swiftly and the currents can be strong enough to sweep away a good-sized truck.

- Fog can be a problem, often patchy and unpredictable. Be especially careful on foggy mountain roads. Slow your vehicle to no more than 15 miles per hour and put on your lights and hazard warning signals.

- Don't pick up hitch-hikers, no matter how respectable they may appear. The mountains attract some strange, and often dangerous, characters. If you have a cellular phone, carry it with you at all times.

THE REGIONS

For our purposes the Great Smoky Mountains can be divided into five geographical regions: southeastern Tennessee, northern Georgia, southwestern North Carolina, upper east Tennessee, and northwestern North Carolina. These five regions, along with the four great national forests that overlap them – Cherokee, Pisgah, Nantahala and the Chattahoochee – are as diverse as they are vast. In some areas commercial tourism is king. In others, it's the great outdoors and the wilderness. There are theme parks, historic areas, national and state parks, metropolitan cities, and vast tracts of virtually unexplored backcountry.

MAJOR CITIES

There are three major metropolitan areas in the Great Smoky Mountain region as covered in this book: Chattanooga; the Tri-Cities region of upper east Tennessee; and Asheville, in North Carolina. Each is covered within the text of its own geographic region.

MAJOR ROADS

From the north and northwest, the area is served by I-81, I-40, and US 441, 321 and 129 in Tennessee, and by I-40 and US Highways 23, 70, 221 and the Blue Ridge Parkway in North Carolina.

To the south and west, I-24, I-59 and I-75 converge in Chattanooga, and from there US Highways 60, 64, and 68 intersect with I-75 and US 58 and 411. Drive east on these into the mountains and join with US 129, US 441 and the Blue Ridge Parkway.

From the east you'll take I-26 and I-40 and US Highways 21, 70, 221, 321 and 421.

From Georgia and the southeast the area is served by I-75 to the south, and from there by US Highways 129, 411 and 441.

Basics

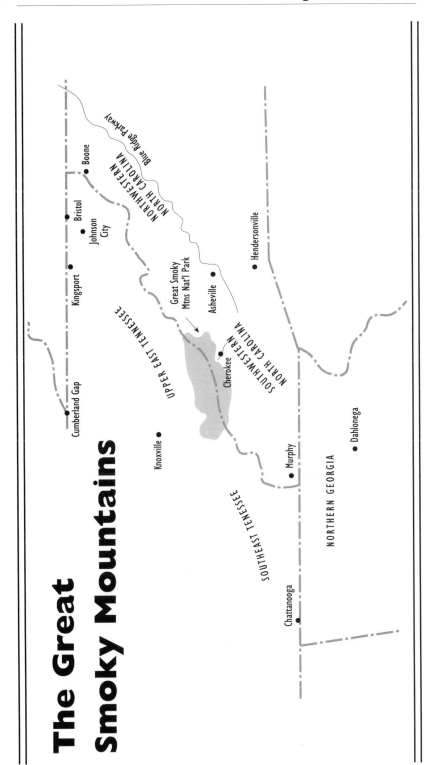

The Great Smoky Mountains

Blue Ridge Parkway

NORTHWESTERN NORTH CAROLINA

Boone

Bristol

Johnson City

Kingsport

Hendersonville

Great Smoky Mtns Nat'l Park

Asheville

UPPER EAST TENNESSEE

SOUTHWESTERN NORTH CAROLINA

Cumberland Gap

Cherokee

Knoxville

Murphy

Dahlonega

NORTHERN GEORGIA

SOUTHEAST TENESSEE

Chattanooga

AIRPORTS

The region is served by four major airports: **Asheville Regional Airport** in North Carolina; **Tri-Cities Regional Airport** in upper east Tennessee; **MaGee-Tyson Airport** in Knoxville; and **Loval Field** in Chattanooga. National carriers serve these facilities, but not necessarily with large jets.

BUS LINES

Service into all major cities in the Great Smoky Mountain area, including Asheville, Chattanooga, Knoxville and the Tri-Cities, is provided by **Greyhound-Trailways**, ☎ 800-231-2222.

RENTAL CARS

The airports listed above are served by most national car rental companies.

Rental Car Toll-Free Numbers
Alamo 800-327-9633
Avis 800-831-2847
Budget 800-527-7000
Enterprise 800-736-8222
Hertz 800-654-3131
National 800-227-7368

RV & CAMPING TRAILER RENTALS

Cruise America has a fleet of trailers and RVs that range in size from 15 to 36 feet.

In the low season, you can rent a 23-foot RV to sleep five people for as little as $650 per week, including insurance. A 31-foot, top-of-the-line luxury motorhome to sleep six will cost you about $765 per week. You'll be required to leave a refundable deposit of either $100 or $500, depending upon the rental package you choose. Cruise America (☎ 800-327-7778) has branches in most major cities throughout the country.

MAPS

You'll find it mentioned many times throughout this book that a good, detailed map is essential for adventuring in the Great Smoky Mountains. This is particularly true if you plan to hike. The popular road atlases and "Official State Maps" are fine if you intend only to travel the main highways. But adventuring means leaving the beaten path.

We recommend you go to your local bookstore and purchase either one or both of **DeLorme's _North Carolina Atlas and Gazetteer_** and **_Tennessee Atlas and Gazetteer_**. These are highly detailed, topographical atlases of 80 or 90 pages, size 15½ x 11 inches. Many hiking trails, most smaller forest roads, canoe trails and some fishing locations are shown, along with state parks, national parks, historic sites and areas of great natural beauty. If you can't find the atlases, contact Delorme Mapping direct at PO Box 298, Freeport, ME 04032, ☎ 207-865-4171. They will take your order over the telephone and you can charge it to your Visa or MasterCard. At the time of writing, the cost per atlas was $16.95, plus shipping.

The second type of map we recommend is the "**quad**" **map**, available only from the National Forest Service. These are more detailed than DeLorme atlases, but they are not as handy and they don't give any consumer information. If you are a hiker, the quad sectional map soon will become an essential part of your equipment.

Quad maps can be purchased from any National Forest Service Supervisor's Office (see _Information Directory,_ page 327-330, for listings).

■ Safety

PERSONAL SECURITY

Personal security in the mountains is very much a matter of common sense. Mugging and other crimes of violence are not unheard of. Stay alert at all times. Never travel alone in the forests or on the backcountry roads on foot, bicycle or horseback. Stay away from isolated, backcountry homes; the owners can be suspicious and may act first and ask questions later. If you need directions, ask at a gas station or convenience store. Carry one of the propri-

Basics

etary personal protection systems: mace, pepper spray and/or a personal siren. Firearms are prohibited in most national and state parks, but are permitted, provided you have the proper licenses, in the national forests.

Car-jacking can be a problem in the big cities of Chattanooga and Knoxville. Keep your doors locked at all times when driving, especially at stop lights. Never pick up hitch-hikers. At rest stops and welcome centers, keep a sharp lookout for suspicious characters; stay securely locked inside your car until they are gone, and then report them to the staff inside the facility. If you have a cellular phone, keep it handy. Emergency 911 service is available almost everywhere.

Be careful inside public restrooms. Don't leave wallets, pocketbooks, bags or any other tempting articles beside the washbasins. Snatch thieves are opportunists and move like lightning.

DRIVING SAFETY

As vast as the Smokies are, there's no doubt that you'll do a lot of driving, so you should do a little planning. Know what you want to do, where you want to go, and how to get there.

Get a good map. The big road atlases are okay, but you really need something a little more detailed, such as the DeLorme atlases already mentioned. The roadside welcome center can supply you with an Official State Map and the ranger stations and state and national park visitor centers often have maps that are even better. Carry your map with you at all times.

- Observe all traffic regulations and speed limits, especially within park boundaries.

- Make sure your vehicle is in good mechanical shape. Break down on one of the remote mountain backroads and you'll be in for a very long wait.

- Keep your gas tank topped up. Gas stations are few and far between in the wilderness areas.

- If you have a cellular telephone, carry it with you. Help is only a phone call away.

- Make sure your spare tire is good and fully inflated.

- Have your brakes and headlights checked before you start your vacation. The mountainous backroads are often narrow, with tight turns, steep grades, and room only for one-way traffic.

■ Pack a first aid kit and include a compass, flashlight, tools, a change of clothing, and plenty to drink.

■ Dress for the season. It might be warm in the car, but get stuck in deep snow, or break down, and you'll have some walking to do.

■ Finally, always tell someone where you're going and what time you expect to arrive or return.

BOATING

■ Obey all boating regulations, especially speed limits and motor restrictions, and pay particular attention when maneuvering around other boats.

■ Handle boat fuel and oil properly.

■ Don't drink and drive. The laws that apply to drinking and driving a car also apply on the water. More than 50% of all boating fatalities are alcohol-related.

■ Clear water weeds from boats, motors and trailers immediately after returning to the ramp so that you won't spread them to other lakes and rivers.

■ Wear a life jacket. Four out of five deaths on the water are caused by drowning. Federal law now requires that every boat carry one personal flotation device (PFD) per passenger. It takes only one unexpected wave from the wake of another boat or a water-logged branch to throw you into the water. A bang on the head or the sudden shock of cold water can render you helpless.

During my writing of this book there was an incident in Alabama that graphically illustrated the importance of the warnings offered here. An entire family of five was wiped out when their boat capsized on a lake in Jackson County. None of them could swim, and none was wearing a life jacket. Alcohol was the main cause of the accident.

Fashionable Life Jackets

Manufacturers have come a long way in their quest to build a more comfortable, better-looking life jacket. Some are now being made with specific activities in mind, such as waterskiing or kayaking. They come in all sorts of colors and patterns and are lighter and more comfortable than the old vests. Some are even made for anglers, with numerous pockets for tackle and lures.

STREAMS & CREEKS

This is a land of beautiful streams, creeks and rivers. Unfortunately, they can also be the cause of injury, or even death. Mountain streams are almost always fast-flowing waterways, more so after a rainfall. Water levels rise quickly and can turn a burbling stream into an impassable torrent. Always remember that water-worn rocks are smooth and slippery, often overgrown with a fine layer of moss or algae.

Here are a few tips that will help keep you out of trouble when crossing a waterway:

- Always test your footing before attempting to cross. Either do it yourself or, if you can't swim, have some other sure-footed member of your party do it. If you can, use a rope to loop members of the party together and cross one at a time.

- Stay away from large rocks in the middle of rushing water; the water around them is often deep and the currents strong.

- Try to step only on dry rocks, or sections of rock, and be careful of green-colored rocks; dry or not, they can be extremely slippery.

- If someone does take a bath, especially in winter, dry them off quickly and have them change into dry clothing. Many mountain streams and creeks are icy cold, even during the summer months, and hypothermia can set in.

FOREST FIRES

Forest fires are a big problem here. Every year, thousands of acres of woodland are lost to fires. Some are the result of arson, some of lightning strikes, but most are caused by careless humans. A campfire left smoldering or a carelessly tossed match or cigarette can do an untold amount of damage. Make sure fires are dead. Dowse them with water and then cover them with dirt. It's better not to smoke at all in the forest (or anywhere) but, if you must, use a cigarette lighter and carry your butts out with you.

THUNDERSTORMS

Lightning should be taken seriously. If you get caught in a storm, get off the high ground. If you are on a ridge or a bald, try to move off the trail and down into the woods; the lower you can go the better. If you are caught in open country, keep moving. Don't stand still. Static electricity can build in your body. Never shelter under a large tree or in a metal-roofed trail shelter.

SUNBURN

It's essential that you wear a good sunscreen. Check with your pharmacist to ensure the proper SPF (sun protection factor) for your type of skin.

Basics

Adventures

■ Camping

Camping is very much a part of the Great Smoky Mountain experience, and a number of options are available.

First, there are the commercial campgrounds. These vary in size and quality of service and amenities. Then there are the state and national park campgrounds. While these might not offer all the bells and whistles available in the large commercial operations, some offer facilities and recreational opportunities that rival those offered by their privately owned competitors. These include some things that the commercial grounds don't offer at all: group camping, youth camping and primitive camping.

You'll find listings of all three types of campground, by region and in alphabetical order, in the *Camping Directory* at the back of this book.

COMMERCIAL CAMPGROUNDS

Profit, obviously, is the motivating force at all commercial campgrounds. Large or small, they are in business to make money, and that's good for the camper. Competition – and there's more than many of them would like – means the commercial campgrounds are constantly striving to improve facilities and services. Generally, commercial campgrounds are clean, tidy and well cared for. Security in smaller campgrounds often leaves a lot to be desired, but is taken much more seriously at larger establishments, where gates are manned 24 hours a day and on-site personnel patrol the grounds.

Most of the larger campgrounds are self-sufficient, offering all sorts of amenities, from laundromats to full-service shops, to marinas and restaurants. Some do not allow tents, catering only to campers with RVs or trailers. Many have rental units available: RVs, trailers, cabins, etc. Many more rent bicycles, boats, paddleboats, and canoes. Larger campgrounds will have staff on hand to look after your needs around the clock; smaller ones might have staff available only for checking in during the daylight hours.

Most have a list of rules and regulations that restrict noise and activities after dark, pets and alcohol.

KOA KABINS

KOA offers rustic wooden cabins that provide some of the comforts of home and all the fun of camping out. Each Kabin sleeps at least four, has an outdoor grill and picnic table, and campers have full use of the campground's amenities and services: hot showers, flush toilets, laundry, convenience store and recreational facilities. Contact KOA at Kampgrounds of America, Inc., PO Box 30558, Billings, MT 59114, ☎ 406-248-7444; or visit their website at http://www.koa.com.

NATIONAL FOREST CAMPGROUNDS

There are a lot of campgrounds in the four national forests that make up most of the Smoky Mountain region. Facilities are rarely as extensive as in state park units, and some are downright basic – no hookups, hand-pumped water, and so on. If you're one of those die-hard primitive campers who likes to get down and dirty, you'll find yourself very much at home.

Most of the campgrounds are fairly small, but they are well kept, clean, and tend to be far away from the busy highways and noisy commercial attractions. Fees are very reasonable and, if you don't mind roughing it a little, the national forest campgrounds offer great value.

 Be sure to take all you need with you; service outlets can be many miles away.

STATE PARK CAMPGROUNDS

Dozens of state parks and forests are scattered across the three-state region covered in this book. Their campgrounds offer all you would get at a privately operated facility, plus group, youth and primitive camping, hiking trails, lakes, fishing, and boating. Although many state parks are close to major cites, camping at one of them is almost always a wilderness experience, deep in the forest and far from civilization.

Park Fees

Admission to state parks in Tennessee and North Carolina is free. In Georgia a one-day pass costs $2 per vehicle (maximum of eight people).

Camping fees vary from park to park, from state to state, and with the extent of facilities. You'll find fees listed along with the individual campgrounds in the *Camping Directory* at the back of this book. As always, fees are subject to change without notice.

Full-service facilities offer water and electric hookups (on individual campsites) for tent, trailer and RV campers. Restrooms and hot showers are accessible to all registered campers in these areas. There is usually a dump station, too.

Group camping and **youth camping** is offered at most state parks in all three states. These designated areas are reserved for youth organizations, groups of families, or gatherings of friends. Facilities in group camping areas vary throughout the park system, from full-service group cabins to basic sites.

Primitive camping is available at most of the Smoky Mountain national and state parks. Overnight backpacking and canoeing into these areas is only for the physically fit, experienced and self-sufficient outdoor enthusiast.

Cabins are for the camper who likes a roof overhead. Many state parks offer a variety of rustic cottages and cabins that sleep from four to six persons. These are given in the individual park listings. Some of the cabins feature the rustic appeal of the original Civilian Conservation Corps construction, while other contemporary cabins have modern amenities.

- **Vacation cabins** are a little more luxurious than camping cabins. Usually, they provide all the comforts of home, including private baths and kitchens. Facilities in these cabins vary from park to park, but may offer fireplaces and/or air conditioning. Typically, the cabins sleep six people.

- **Private cabins** offer private sleeping quarters that are sometimes, but not always, convenient to other park facilities.

■ **Group cabins** are accommodations in groups of units, or in large, single-unit sleeping quarters. They usually feature fully equipped kitchens, dining rooms, and/or meeting spaces.

Reservations for cabins are usually accepted up to one year in advance and a deposit equal to a two-night stay is required for confirmation of the booking. Calls for reservations should be made between 8 am and 5 pm, Monday through Friday.

Like camping fees, charges for renting a cabin vary from park to park according to season and the type of facilities offered, and are subject to change.

Personal checks, Visa and MasterCard are accepted.

LIVING HISTORY PROGRAMS

Many state parks in the Smoky Mountains offer living history programs where visitors can learn what life might have been like for the Civil War Soldier or early pioneer.

FESTIVALS & EVENTS

The Smoky Mountain region seems to maintain a continuous schedule of festivals and events, interpretive and environmental demonstrations, and volunteer opportunities. State parks have interpretive get-togethers, nature programs, organized walks and hikes, lectures and more.

ACCESSIBILITY

Most campgrounds – state, national and commercial – are easily accessible. Reaching some of the more primitive locations does, however, require lengthy and often strenuous hikes. Campers going primitive should be sure they are in the best physical condition.

AVAILABILITY

This area is rapidly becoming one of the premier camping destinations in the United States and the availability of some sites can be limited, especially in the spring and early fall. Be sure to book far enough in advance to ensure your stay at the campground of choice.

The high season for camping begins when the first blooms of spring appear and ends when the last leaf has fallen in early November, although die-hard campers can still be found roughing it when the snow is two feet deep in the forests.

The most popular campgrounds stay heavily booked throughout spring, summer and fall. When schools are out and on most major holidays, especially Easter, Labor Day and Christmas, it's almost impossible to find a berth at any of the larger commercial grounds. Choice sites at the state parks, allocated either by reservation or on a first-come, first-served basis, will almost always be occupied.

If you're looking for a cabin, you should reserve as far in advance as possible; many cabins are booked solid up to a year ahead.

COSTS

Commercial Campgrounds: Costs vary, starting at around $18 per night for a basic site with few frills. The high, depending very much upon location, runs around $55 for a site with all the amenities, including private deck, table and chairs, and so on.

State Parks: You'll pay between $10 and $16 per night for a site, depending upon the location and the season. A waterfront site may cost an extra $2 per night; use of the boat ramp could cost $2 to $4 more. The state park cabins can cost anywhere from $20 to $100 per night.

Senior or **disabled** visitors are usually discounted, often as much as 50%.

Primitive camping costs from zero to $5 per person per night ($2 for persons under 18).

National Forests: Rates vary. Generally, the lower the fee, the fewer the facilities. Most national forest campgrounds do not have warm water showers; some do not have piped water, in which case you must use a hand pump; most do have flush toilets, but some have only chemical toilets.

- **Cherokee National Forest** fees range from a low of $5 in the Nolichucky Ranger District to a high of $20 for a double-size site at some campgrounds in the Unaka and Ocoee districts. Individual family sites without electricity are $5 per night; with electricity $10 per night. Tent camping for single units of up to five people is $10 per night. Where group camping is available, the fee for a minimum group of at least 30 people is $30

- **Pisgah National Forest**: $0 to $15.
- **Nantahala National Forest**: $0 to $15.
- **Chattahoochee National Forest**: $0 to $15.

Credit cards are accepted at most commercial and some state park campgrounds.

TIME RESTRICTIONS

Commercial: You can visit for as long as you like, or for as long as you have money enough to pay the bill.

State Parks: Maximum of two weeks.

National Parks: 14 days in any 30-day period.

PETS

Pets may not be allowed in the camping areas at some state parks, but are welcome in national park campgrounds provided they are quiet and kept on a leash.

Pets are welcome at some commercial campgrounds. Check individual listings.

 It is unlawful in all three states to leave pets in your vehicle, locked or not.

SECURITY

Most campgrounds in this book maintain good security and have the safety of their guests very much in mind. This is especially true at state parks, which are generally gated and locked at night.

Many commercial campgrounds are not gated, but do have on-site staff working security around the clock.

■ Caving

 The Appalachians are riddled with caves and caverns. Some were carved out of solid rock by mighty underground rivers; some are the result of Earth movement. All are millions of years old. None is alike.

Most commercial caves are garish, unnatural places where the ancient formations have been transformed into glitzy fairylands of colored lights and mystical music. They are places where official-looking, but privately employed, traffic marshals wave the unwary off the main road, into a parking lot, and from there into a gift shop and the entrance to a hole in the mountain and an underground world that should exist only in the world of science fiction. Unless you like that sort of thing, you'll find them a total waste of money.

A few commercial cave systems, however, have been left very much in their natural state and are worth seeing. The fantastic formations have been illuminated, but only to the point where they are visible. Visitors wander the dimly lit corridors far below, step on the shores of vast underground lakes where huge trout live, and clamber through tiny openings to emerge into huge underground chambers. These are the worlds you imagined when you read of the adventures of Tom Sawyer, Becky Thatcher, Injun Joe and all the other wonderful characters immortalized by Mark Twain.

For the spelunker – the dedicated caver with ropes, pitons, helmet and flashlight – there's plenty. Your caves are generally not open to the public, but some of the commercial caves offer what they call "wild cave tours." What that might mean is a matter of interpretation. For sure, they will not let you loose on your own. Commercial cave owners are very nervous about people getting injured on their property.

Commercial cave systems, good and bad, can be found in the upper east Tennessee region in Bristol, Townsend and Sevierville; in southeastern Tennessee you'll find them in Sweetwater and Chattanooga. Each system is described in detail in its appropriate chapter within this book.

■ Fall Color

 Autumn, when the days are clear and sunny and the nights cool and crisp, lures millions of visitors to the Great Smoky Mountains. They come to view the spectacular colors of fall that bring a new enchantment to the mountains. The woodland trails are a riot of gold, amber, yellow, copper and red; the Blue Ridge Parkway turns into a ribbon of color, while the reflections on the surface of the still mountain lakes turn the world upside down for everyone to enjoy. Even the streets of the big cities and tiny mountain communities blaze with the colors of fall.

Throughout the Smokies, a number of locations provide special views at this time of year. They are individually listed by location throughout the book.

■ Spring Wildflowers

Each year, from late March through early June, the forests and woodlands burst with new life in a riot of pink and white.

The air fills with the scent of dogwood, honeysuckle, foamflowers, trillium, lady's slipper and a thousand others. Roan Mountain puts on a spectacular display when more than 700 acres of rhododendron cover it in a blanket of pastels.

■ Snow Skiing

The Great Smoky Mountain ski resorts are among the best in the nation. Most have multiple slopes that cater to skiers of all levels of expertise. Some have snow-making equipment that significantly extends the season. Skiing is available in northwestern North Carolina and, to a lesser extent, in upper eastern Tennessee and southwestern North Carolina.

■ Hiking

Hiking is the major pastime here, with hundreds of trail systems threading through the region. Thousands of miles of foot trails lead through rolling pine forests, beside fast-moving mountain rivers, waterfalls and along country lanes and backroads; all are available for backpackers and nature lovers, and all are open year-round for public use. This book describes the most popular trails, as well as some of the smaller ones, along with their locations, length, entry and exit points, and their degree of difficulty.

There are more trails listed here and more practical hiking information than you'll find in many of the so-called hiking manuals. Even this book, however, doesn't cover everything. For more detailed guides to the thousands of smaller trails, visit any one of the national forest or state park ranger stations.

SAFETY

Although hiking in the Great Smoky Mountains is always a delightful experience, it can also be a hazardous one. The Great Smoky Mountain Wilderness is a vast, forested area, some of it largely uncharted territory. The four national forests cover some 2.5 million acres, all of it within the scope of this text. It's not unusual for hikers to get lost, and stay lost for days, especially in winter. Rescue squads are frequently called out to scour the forests and ridges in search of a lost hiker. More often than not, the victim is a child that's wandered away from a campsite, or simply lagged behind on a woodland trail and strayed away from the path.

It's important that you behave responsibly, which means not only must you exercise basic common sense, you must also adhere to the rules of safety and woodland law.

If you're new to hiking, there is a lot to learn. There are, however, a number of excellent books in the shops and at your local library that will get you started. Several come readily to mind, including *The New Complete Walker III*, by Colin Fletcher; *Backpacking, One Step at a Time*, by Harvey Manning; and *Walk Softly in the Wilderness*, by John Hart. In the meantime, here are some basic rules.

- Purchase a **good map**. Maps of the better-known hiking trails are readily available at ranger stations, state parks, bookstores and gift shops. Better yet are topographical "quad" maps, described on page 21. If you can read a road map, you can read a topographical map.

- **Stay on the trail**. The well-maintained trails are marked and easy to follow. Even so, it's easy to take a wrong turn and find yourself on a less-developed trail, and then onto something that's barely a trail at all. You may not be able to find your way back without a map and compass. Plot your progress as you go; take notes and always know your position on the map.

- **Bring a compass**. It goes without saying that if you need a map, you must surely need a compass. If you stray away from the trail it might be five or six miles before you stumble onto another one, and that's only if you walk in a straight line. Maintain your sense of direction at all times.

- **File a hiking plan** with someone you know, or at a ranger station, just in case you do get lost. Don't forget to call and let them know you've arrived at your destination; otherwise they'll be out looking for you.

- Carry a **first aid kit**. Keep it simple: band aids, elastic bandage, butterfly closures, adhesive tape, aspirin or something similar, antihistamines for bee stings, bug repellent.

- Take along a good **hunting knife** with either a fixed or folding blade. Buck makes some great outdoor knives, as do Schrade and Case. Forget the much-vaunted (but basically useless) Swiss Army knives with all their bits and pieces. A heavy knife with a strong, sharp blade is all you'll need.

- **Flashlight**. Not generally needed if you're on a day hike, right? Wrong. If you get lost at dusk, a four-hour hike can quickly turn into an all-night experience as wooded areas grow dark far quicker than open terrain. Trails become difficult to see, let alone follow. Carry at least one spare set of batteries.

- **Wet-weather gear**. You don't need to carry a full set of rain gear – a large, three- or four-ply garbage bag will do quite nicely in an emergency. Don't laugh. A garbage bag will fold almost to nothing, and it's better to stay dry than to struggle through the undergrowth soaked to the skin, to suffer even further when the rain stops and the sun comes out to turn your wet clothing into something a medieval torturer would have been proud to own. For extended hikes, you'll need to take a poncho or a lightweight rain suit.

- Take **waterproof matches** in addition to your lighter. Lighter flints sometimes get wet and refuse to work. A small fire, especially in winter, can save your life.

- Always wear a good **hat**. It will keep the bugs out of your hair and your body heat in. You lose up to 35% of body heat through your head. In winter a good warm hat could save your life.

- **Snacks** aren't essential, but they can do wonders for your disposition. A candy bar will give you extra energy and a feeling of well-being. Take along more than you think you'll need; you won't be sorry.

- Carry plenty of **water**. The mountain streams look pure and inviting, but some, especially in the mining districts, can be polluted. It's best not to take chances.

- A **camp stove** is recommended for overnight trips. You should avoid lighting campfires if you can. Forest fires are a real problem in the mountains, often destroying thousands of acres at a time. Almost all are started by careless hikers.

- **Waterfalls** are always beautiful and there are literally hundreds of them throughout the Great Smoky Mountains. Everybody wants to get a better look. But keep in mind that rocks surrounding a fall are smooth, worn away by fast-flowing water, covered in algae or moss, and thus extremely slippery. One wrong step can send you plummeting to the rocks below or into the cold, raging waters. It's best to view waterfalls from the bottom and stay off nearby rocks.

Finally, if you do get lost, don't panic. Stay where you are; conserve energy and food. If you feel you must move on, stay on the trail and travel by compass in one direction only.

■ Mountain Biking

One of the fastest growing sports in the Great Smoky Mountain Region is mountain biking. It provides an adventure like no other; it's great for the cardiovascular system too. The trails are as diverse as you can imagine. You'll encounter everything from long flat trails through the woods to tough mountain climbs. Some trails follow mountain streams, while others wend their way along quiet, pastoral riverbanks. All offer a new type of challenge in one form or another. Wilderness campsites along the way are numerous. National forest trails, and most state park biking trails, are marked with a bicycle symbol.

■ Bird Watching

 More than 120 species of wild birds make their homes in the Great Smoky Mountains. Bird lovers can expect to see red-tailed hawks, ruffed grouse, wild turkey, five types of owl, vultures, ravens, blue herons, a wide variety of warblers, and seven species of woodpecker. If you're lucky, you may see such rare birds as the Eastern screech owl, the endangered red-cockaded woodpecker, the hooded warbler, golden eagle, peregrine falcon or even a bald eagle.

Birding is best done in the early morning. Find a spot and remain still. Be sure to take along a good field guide, binoculars and a notebook. The best months are April, May, September and October; May is best of all.

■ Hunting

 Hunting is a major sport. From late fall through early spring one hunting season or another is usually in force, encompassing a variety of weapons from the bow and arrow through the black powder rifle and modern, high-powered hand gun. Deer, as always, are popular quarry, but there's also a rare breed of mountain man that will pursue wild boar into the heavy undergrowth armed only with a pistol, and there are stories of a man who lives in Polk County, Tennessee, who goes after them armed only with a large hunting knife.

■ Horseback Riding

 Horseback riding is available throughout the Smokies, in most state parks, the Great Smoky Mountains National Park and all four national forests. Well-marked equestrian trails take riders through some of the most scenic portions of the Blue Ridge, and there are staging areas/corrals and overnight camping for horses and riders in many of the parks.

Be sure to call ahead when planning your ride, especially when organizing a group event. Contact the National Park Service or the National Forest Service (see Information Directory*) to learn about trail conditions and any special regulations that may be in effect.*

The following rules and regulations for equestrians are in effect throughout the year in all four national forests:

- Horse trails are marked with a sign like the one you see to the right. If a trail is unmarked, or if the sign has a red slash through the horse, then horses are not allowed. Open and gated forest service roads are open for horseback riding, unless they are signed otherwise. Obey trail and road closures.

- Stay on the trail. Taking shortcuts causes erosion and skirting wet areas widens trails.

- Travel in small groups, preferably six or fewer.

- Do not tie horses to trees, even temporarily.

- Plan your trip to avoid the spring thaw and extended wet weather.

- Pack it in and pack it out. Leave no trash in the forest.

- Communicate with other trail users, and tell them how to safely pass your horse.

- Hikers and mountain bikers should yield to horses, unless riders have a better place to pull off.

- When camping, use a line with tree-saver straps to tether your horse. Keep your horse 100 feet away from streams and creeks and a fair distance from trails and campsites.

- Pack some grain, since grazing is limited. Break up and scatter manure.

- Fill in pawed holes when breaking camp.

- Horses are not permitted in developed campgrounds or picnic areas.

■ Rock Climbing

Fast becoming one of the most outdoor popular sports, even for beginners, rock climbing is an adventure you might want to consider, though not without taking some professional instruction first. The degree of difficulty, of course, depends a great deal on the terrain. Difficulty ratings are based upon two nationally accepted systems: the Yosemite Decimal System and the Aid System.

The Yosemite Decimal System
Easy 5.0-5.3
Moderate 5.4-5.6
Difficult 5.7-5.9
Very difficult 5.10-5.13

The **Aid System** rates climbs in degrees of difficulty from A1 through A5, A1 being the easiest of climbs.

In most state parks rock climbing is permitted in designated areas only, and you must register with the park authorities before making a climb. National Park and Forest areas do not require registration; even so, it's best to let someone know where you going in case of accidents.

■ Gliding

Gliders, or sailplanes, are just like a regular aircraft with a cockpit, instruments and controls, but rely on thermals rather than engine and propeller. The sport is available in southeastern Tennessee at a small rural airport near Benton. Light aircraft tow sailplanes high into the thermals over the mountains where they float for up to 90 minutes, never achieving more than 30 miles an hour before drifting gently back to earth. Lessons are available in two-seater aircraft at **Chilhowee Glider Port**, Highway 441, Benton, TN 37307. ☎ 423-338-2000.

■ Watersports

BOATING

 Boating is allowed on most of the larger lakes through-out the region and, to a lesser extent, on smaller lakes, where motor restrictions may apply.

TUBING

To some, the ultimate in fun is tubing. You'll have to supply your own truck inner-tube, but there's nothing quite so exciting, or re-laxing (depending on the state of the water), as riding the surging river on a tube. Not all rivers are suitable for tubing, and it's defi-nitely not recommended on the whitewaters of the Ocoee and Nolichucky; the water is too fast, and the rocks and currents much too dangerous. Before you embark on a tubing run down any river, check first with the local ranger station to make sure that it's safe to do so. You'll find listings of all national forest ranger stations, with phone numbers, in the directories at the back of this book. Rafting companies and outfitters are also listed in that section.

FISHING

Trout fishing in the mountain rivers is at its best in the Smokies. There are many good locations – Citicoe Creek Wilderness in the Cherokee National Forest and the Hiwassee River, both in Ten-nessee, are particularly good, but almost every creek and river in the mountains of western North Carolina provides opportunities that are just as good.

Lake fishing is best in eastern Tennessee, but northern Georgia and, to some extent, western North Carolina offer some fine op-portunities too.

Adventures

Fishing Licenses

Licenses are required in all three states for all persons aged 16 and older. They can be obtained at any local bait or tackle shop, and at any State Wildlife Resources Agency Office. Contact them at ☎ 615-781-6500 for Georgia; ☎ 888-248-6834 for North Carolina; and ☎ 615-781-6500 for Tennessee. It's also a good idea to check for specific local regulations.

The fishing spots listed in each regional section of this book have been selected because they are areas where we think you will do well. Some are popular and often crowded, but others are little-known hideaways. Some are easily accessible, while others are off the beaten path. There are, of course, a great many more places to fish in the Great Smoky Mountains than are listed in this book, but to find them you'll have to do some exploring.

WHITEWATER CHALLENGES

Rafting and kayaking are available on a great many mountain rivers, especially at the southern end of the region. The Ocoee River, the home of the 1996 Olympic kayaking events, is especially popular for rafting, as are the Hiwassee and Nolichucky rivers. In North Carolina there are opportunities on the French Broad River in the northwestern section of the state, but most of the action takes place in the southeast. Literally dozens of outfitters and backcountry adventure companies vie for attention. A five-mile run down the Ocoee will last about two hours and can cost anywhere from $35 to $40, depending upon season; a wild ride down the Nolichucky will last for up to five hours and cost upwards of $50. You ride under the supervision of a qualified guide, usually six or eight to a raft, and no experience is necessary.

Whitewater Classification

Class I.	Easy
Class II	Intermediate
Class III.	Difficult
Class IV.	Very Difficult
Class V	Exceptionally Difficult
Class VI.	Impossible

CANOEING

Tennessee, North Carolina and, to some extent, northern Georgia offer varied paddling opportunities, ranging from quiet mountain lakes to wide-open rivers or fast-running whitewater. Some of the routes pass through parks, some through national forests. Some are in controlled waters. Almost all of the canoe trails described in this book are in scenic country. For water gauges in Tennessee, ☎ 865-632-6065. In North Carolina and Georgia, call the TVA (☎ 423-632-2264).

Rentals

Canoes and kayaks, along with basic instruction, are available for rent at most whitewater outfitters. Many offer vacation packages that include not only rafting or kayaking, but horseback riding and hayrides too. You'll find a list of outfitters with a brief description of their services on page 331.

While the lakes, streams and rivers of the Great Smoky Mountains offer hundreds of miles of canoeing possibilities, many of the waters open to canoes are also open to other users, including anglers, motor-boaters, and waterskiers. In most areas, the waterways are publicly owned, but in some places the riverbanks belong to private individuals. Canoe and adventure outposts throughout each region will equip you for a canoe trip, pick you up at your exit point, and shuttle you back to your car (see page 331).

Adventures

Shopping

■ Antiquing

 The antique business is very big all over the Smoky Mountain region. You'll find stores on every street in every small town, and on almost every corner of every mountain road. If antiquing means adventure to you, then you won't be disappointed. Check the pages of each region for the best opportunities.

■ Craft Hunting

 Country crafts are another big business in the mountains. The old skills have been preserved from one generation to the next, and everything from handmade furniture to tiny wooden gifts are available at very reasonable prices. Opportunities are boundless. Goodies can be bought anywhere and everywhere; at festivals, roadside stores, flea markets and even garage sales.

Southeastern Tennessee

History

Hernando De Soto, the first white explorer to visit the southeastern Tennessee area, dropped by in 1540 and claimed it for Spain. For more than 100 years after De Soto and his men left, life was quiet in the area. But, in 1663, things turned ugly. The English (not to be outdone by their Spanish rivals) petitioned the area and their new colony for Britain; so did the French (operating out the Mississippi Valley).

> *The history of **Chattanooga Valley** – the name is derived from a Cree Indian word meaning "rock coming to a point," a fair description of Lookout Mountain – goes back long before the Europeans began squabbling. The American Indian had lived and hunted here for more than 7,000 years by the time De Soto arrived.*

The valley was the last capital of the **Cherokee Nation**. And it's to this legacy that the city must turn to find its roots. **John Ross**, the last great chief of the nation, was the well-educated grandson of Indian trader John McDonald. In 1815 he established a trading post on the banks of the Tennessee River on what is today known as Ross' Landing. The trading post became the nucleus from which the city of Chattanooga evolved.

By the mid-1800s the city had become an important railroad center and, located as it is in a gap between two mountain ranges, the gateway to Georgia and the south. In 1863, at the height of the Civil War, two battles were fought for control of the railhead and the mountain pass. The **Battle of Chickamauga** was the bloodiest two days of the entire Civil War. The result was an expensive victory for the Confederacy. Losses on both sides totaled more than 34,000. The Union army was driven from Chickamauga into

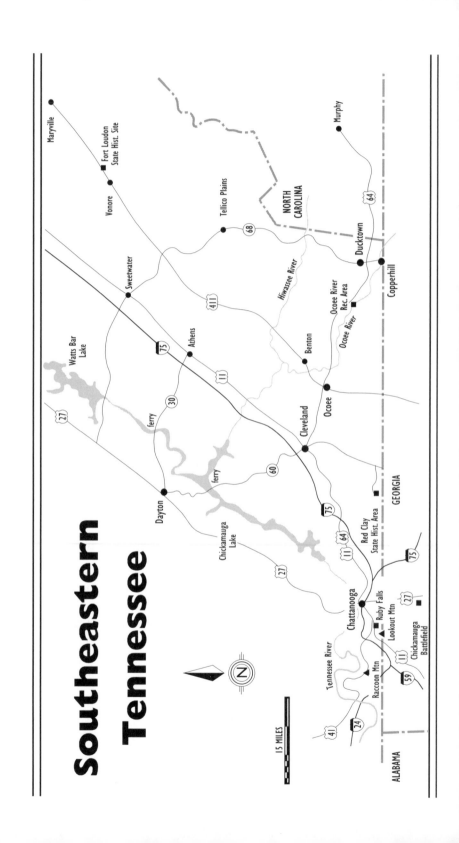

Southeastern Tennessee

N

15 MILES

ALABAMA

Tennessee River

Raccoon Mtn

41
24

Chattanooga

Ruby Falls
Lookout Mtn
27

Chickamauga
Battlefield
111
59

75

GEORGIA

Red Clay
State Hist. Area

111
64
75

Cleveland

Ocoee

60

ferry

Dayton

Chickamauga
Lake

27

Watts Bar
Lake

27

30

ferry

75

Athens

111

411

Sweetwater

Benton

Ocoee River

Ocoee River
Rec. Area

Hiwassee River

68

Tellico Plains

Ducktown

Copperhill

64

Murphy

**NORTH
CAROLINA**

Vonore

Fort Loudon
State Hist. Site

Maryville

Chattanooga, and Confederate forces occupied the heights of Lookout Mountain and Missionary Ridge.

The **Battle of Chattanooga** – some call it the Battle Above the Clouds – on November 24, 1863, resulted in victory for General US Grant, and was a deathblow to the Confederacy. In the years that followed, the battlefield at Chickamauga became the first of our National Military Parks.

Sightseeing

■ Chattanooga

 Today, Chattanooga is a major tourist center. The "Scenic City" is a convenient stop for snowbirds en route from northern states to Florida. It entertains millions of visitors each year, and more new attractions are conceived and built to keep them coming.

Although the city is best known for its historical heritage and surrounding scenic beauty, it also ranks high as a cultural center. It offers two major theaters, a large symphony orchestra, a couple of dedicated dramatic groups, and a half-dozen or so museums.

BOOKER T. WASHINGTON STATE PARK

This park, just north of Chattanooga, is named for the famous educator, Booker Taliaferro Washington. Sited on the shores of the Chickamauga Reservoir, the 353-acre park is a popular get-away for city dwellers.

There are no individual campsites, but there's still plenty to see and do. There's a swimming pool, playgrounds, several picnic areas with tables and grills, and a group campsite. Boats are available for rent, and there's a public-access boat ramp. The group lodge, available year-round, has a fully equipped kitchen and can accommodate up to 40 people. All this is set among acres of rolling fields, and hiking and nature trails.

Booker T. Washington State Park, 5801 Champion Road, Chattanooga, TN 37416. ☎ 423-894-4955.

Take State Highway 58 north from Chattanooga to Harrison Bay. The park is on your left.

Southeastern Tennessee

CHATTANOOGA AFRICAN-AMERICAN MUSEUM

This museum reflects the heritage and identity of black Americans in and around Chattanooga Valley. Housed in the brand new Bessie Smith Hall, it boasts a rare collection of artifacts from original sculptures to music to African-American newspapers. The museum provides a public center for education, research and entertainment. The Bessie Smith Hall is on Martin Luther King in downtown Chattanooga. ☎ 423-267-6053.

CHATTANOOGA CHOO CHOO

No visit to Chattanooga would be complete without a stop at the famed Chattanooga Choo Choo. Unfortunately, it has become something of a commercial giant, oriented more toward making money than its historical heritage. It's located in a particularly seedy district, although the city is working hard to refurbish the area.

First opened in 1909, the terminal station was once the heart of the Southern railway system. However, by the late 1960s railways were rapidly being replaced by faster and more convenient modes of transportation. And so, in 1970, the terminal was closed. The last train left on August 11th of that year.

Fortunately, that was not the end. The station and its terminal building were re-opened in 1973 as a hotel and convention center. Today, it is the centerpiece of the 30-acre Chattanooga Choo Choo Holiday Inn Resort (☎ 800-HOLIDAY).

The old station has been restored and, along with its dining and sleeping cars and great domed restaurant – claimed to be the highest in the world. It's well worth a visit. Take I-24 west through Chattanooga and follow the signs.

CHATTANOOGA SYMPHONY

The Tivoli Theater (see page 57) is home to the Chattanooga Symphony and Opera Association. And it's at this famous old theater that the 90-member symphony orchestra, under the direction of Robert Bernhardt, performs 25 concerts each year, including two fully staged operas, seven symphony concerts, and four pops concerts. ☎ 423-267-8583.

CHICKAMAUGA NATIONAL BATTLEFIELD PARK

Shortly after dawn on September 19, 1863, on the banks of small creek near Jay's Mill in northern Georgia, a brigade of Federal infantry encountered a large force of Confederate cavalry. Thus began a bloody battle that raged back and forth for two days. The result was a victory for the Confederate forces. Losses on both sides totaled more than 34,000 and General George H. Thomas earned for himself the nickname "Rock of Chickamauga."

Today you can hike more than seven miles of historic trails and private roads, stand on Snodgrass Hill and let your imagination wander back to those terrible days when General Thomas' heroic few held back the might of an entire Confederate army. After a tour of the battlefield, you can visit the park headquarters for an interpretive film show and a number of interesting exhibits, including a large collection of vintage firearms.

The visitor center is open daily from 9 am to 9 pm. Admission is free. From Chattanooga, take I-75 and drive east to the Battlefield Exit and follow the signs. ☎ 706-866-9241.

CREATIVE DISCOVERY MUSEUM

This is a hands-on educational experience for children and adults that promotes learning and discovery through sight, sound and exploration. The 42,000-square-foot facility features the Little Yellow House for pre-schoolers, an optics tower, a 120-seat theater, and several exhibits that require active participation by the visitor. These include the Field Scientist's Laboratory and dinosaur dig where children discover bones buried in the sand; an Inventor's Workshop, where participants crank up a series of ingenious gadgets; and an Artist's Studio, where you can try your hand at painting, print making and sculpting.

The museum, on the corner of 4th and Chestnut streets in downtown Chattanooga, is open from 10 am until 5 pm daily, May through August, and on Tuesday through Sunday the rest of the year. Admission is free. ☎ 423-756-2738.

HARRISON BAY STATE PARK

Harrison Bay is the result of the Tennessee Valley Authority's recreation demonstration site project of the 1930s. Just a few miles north of Chattanooga, the 1,200-acre park, along with more than 40 miles of Chickamauga Lake shoreline, provides many outstanding recreational opportunities, including camping, fishing, hiking, boating and picnicking. There's a public pool, a fully developed campground with extensive facilities, a marina nearby where you can rent boats and canoes, and a camp store for supplies. The park can become extremely crowded during the summer months.

Harrison Bay State Park, 8411 Harrison Bay Road, Harrison, TN 37341. ☎ 423-344-6214. The park is open year-round from 8 am until sundown.

From Chattanooga, take US 58 northbound for eight miles. The park is on the left.

HUNTER MUSEUM OF ART

Of the city's many museums, this one is housed in an elegant mansion (the one-time home of Coca-Cola magnate and philanthropist George Thomas Hunter). It has a fine collection of modern and classical paintings and sculpture. The collection is regarded as one of the most important gatherings of American art in the Southeast. Open 10-4 weekdays except Monday, and 1-4 on Sunday. Admission is $5. 10 Bluff View, Chattanooga, TN 37403. ☎ 423-267-0968.

LOOKOUT MOUNTAIN

From almost anywhere in the city you can look up at the mountain and see the New York Monument, a tiny speck against the skyline that marks the position of **Point Park**.

Following the Battle of Chickamauga on September 19 and 20, 1863, the Union army was driven north into the Chattanooga Valley. Confederate forces occupied the heights of Lookout Mountain and Missionary Ridge and for two months they laid siege to Chattanooga. And it was at Lookout Mountain on November 24 that Federal troops, newly reinforced by General Ulysses S. Grant, claimed the victory was the beginning of the end for the Confederacy.

The view from Point Park is spectacular, though often hazy. You'll see the city of Moccasin Bend and the Tennessee River. A flight of stone steps leads a short way down to a small museum, which

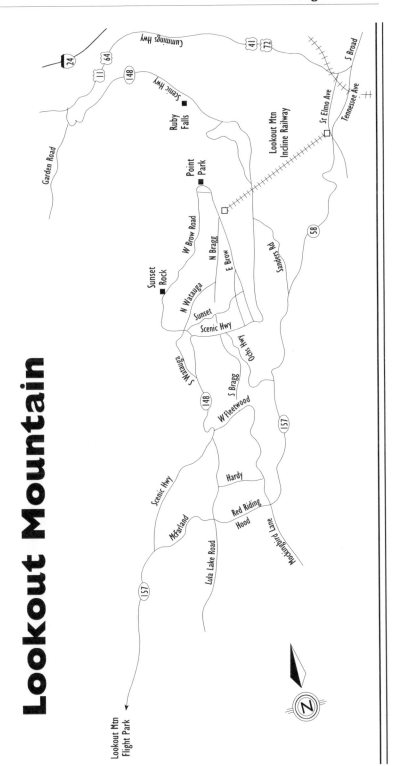

Lookout Mountain

houses a number of interesting Civil War-era artifacts. On summer weekends re-enactors give military demonstrations, such as loading and firing a rifle. In fall, the colors here are a sight to behold.

There are plenty of quiet roads to walk. If you're hungry, stop at the mountaintop café for a soft drink or a cup of coffee and a bite to eat. There are several gift shops, too, including one at the terminal of the Incline Railway.

Point Park, open from 8 am until sundown, is part of the Chickamauga National Battlefield. Admission to Point Park is free. ☎ 706-866-9241.

From Chattanooga, take the Broad Street Exit off I-24, follow the signs and drive to the top of the mountain. Alternatively, use the Incline Railway and walk to the park.

From I-24 west of the city, take the Browns Ferry Exit and follow the signs up the mountain.

If you decide to drive up the mountain from either direction, take no notice of the official-looking people you will see waving you off the road into the Ruby Falls parking lot, unless you would like to visit the falls, that is. These people are not associated with the park.

INCLINE RAILWAY

Known as "America's Most Amazing Mile," this incline railway ascends almost 3,000 feet to the top of Lookout Mountain at a grade approaching 73°. From the summit of Lookout, it's a short walk to Point Park National Battlefield where, on a clear day, you can enjoy breathtaking views over five states. The temperature on the mountain is often 10° cooler than it is in the city and makes a welcome change on a hot summer's day. The incline is both the steepest and the safest passenger railway in the world.

From Chattanooga, take the Broad Street Exit off I-24 to Lookout Mountain and follow the signs. From I-24 west of the city, take the Browns Ferry Exit and follow the signs. ☎ 423-821-4224.

RACCOON MOUNTAIN ADVENTURE PARK

Raccoon Mountain is something of an adventure playground, offering hang-gliders and ultra-light aircraft, an alpine slide and go-carts, horseback riding, hiking and walks in underground caverns.

Raccoon Mountain is west of Chattanooga on I-24 at the Tiftonia 174 Exit on Cummins Highway. ☎ 423-825-0444.

Raccoon Mountain Cavern

Raccoon Mountain Cavern, part of the Raccoon Mountain Adventure Park, is another of Chattanooga's major commercial attractions. The cave system itself is unique, the rock formations fabulous, even breathtaking, and the attraction well ordered. Unfortunately, the owners have gone a bit overboard with the colored lights inside the caves.

If you want to take the kids on a fantastic journey, this is the place for you. Although the rock formations are among the best in the eastern United States, you'd better go elsewhere if you want to see the underground world in a more natural state.

The cavern is open from Memorial Day through Labor Day. Tours lasts about 45 minutes and costs $3. ☎ 423-821-2283.

ROCK CITY

Rock City, like Ruby Falls and the Incline Railway, is a part of the Lookout Mountain experience. It is also a commercial enterprise. The attraction is a small but high-profile theme park on the cliff's edge atop the mountain.

Your tour will take you on a long winding trail between rocks and along a series of natural stone walkways to scramble through narrow fissures with names like Fatman's Squeeze. Along the way, you'll cross the Swingalong Bridge to finally emerge on a scenic overlook high above the Chattanooga Valley called Lover's Leap. From there, it's into a series of small man-made caverns to view special exhibits such as Fairyland Caverns and Mother Goose Village. It's very well done and very commercial.

The view from Lover's Leap is spectacular and well worth the price of admission. But, then, so is the view from Point Park, just a mile or so away near the Incline Railway, and that's free.

Rock City is one of Lookout Mountain's most popular attractions and is almost always extremely crowded, especially at the height of the tourist season, April through October.

From I-24 eastbound, take Exit 175 and follow the signs up the mountain. From I-24 westbound, take Exit 178, then follow the signs to Highway 58 and on up the mountain.

The attraction is open daily from 8 am until sundown, except Christmas. Admission is $10.95 for adults and $5.95 for children age three to 12. ☎ 706-820-2531.

ROSS' LANDING PARK & PLAZA

This $10 million park, surrounding the Tennessee Aquarium, was built on land that has played a significant role in Chattanooga's development. It is the fifth phase of the Chattanooga Riverpark system, a time capsule that depicts the evolution of Chattanooga and eastern Tennessee. It's a unique and elaborate piece of art and history rolled into one and really has to be seen to be fully appreciated.

The ribbons are actually part of a new concept that encourages exploration. The idea is that you become a part of the story as you wend your way among the trees, pools, and gardens from one significant spot to the next, and thus discover for yourself the heritage of the city and the surrounding countryside.

RUBY FALLS

Ruby Falls is the second of Chattanooga's underground attractions, and it's one of the most famous cave complexes in the nation. For 100 miles in every direction as you approach the city, you will see giant signs, mostly painted atop barns and every other type of agricultural building, exhorting you to "Visit Ruby Falls."

The cave was discovered in 1928 by accident when engineers excavating an elevator shaft to another cave stumbled upon it. Mr. Joe

Lambert, a local adventurer, decided to explore. For more than 16 hours he crawled through the pitch black darkness.

Unfortunately, it has become a commercial attraction, another underground world of light and magic. Nowhere in the entire complex will you see a rock formation in its natural state. It has been turned into a subterranean fairyland of red, green, blue, and a hundred other colors. Essentially, Ruby Falls is a narrow underground passageway that leads eventually to a vaulted cavern. Here, there is a very thin stream of water falling about 100 feet (they say it's 145 feet) into a small, rocky pool.

Your tour begins with an elevator ride down into the mountain. When you reach the bottom you'll be entertained for several minutes, parrot fashion, by a supposedly knowledgeable guide, usually a youngster, and then taken along the narrow passage through the rocks, accompanied by a running commentary on the various rock formations along the way, to the cavern, which is always in total darkness when you arrive. Then, to the theatrical sounds of Also Sprach Zarathrustra – the theme from *2,001, A Space Odyssey* – the lights slowly come up and you're treated to a tacky presentation of constantly changing colored lights. Even so, the kids seem to like it, and so do many adults. For what it is, the experience is an expensive one.

Open from May 1st until Labor Day. Located high on the slopes of Lookout Mountain in Chattanooga, Ruby Falls is easily reached from I-24; just follow the signs. Admission is $9.50; $5 for kids under 16. ☎ 423-821-2544.

SOUTHERN BELLE

This is Chattanooga's answer to the Mississippi riverboats that ply the waters from Memphis to New Orleans. Though smaller than those on the Mississippi, the *Southern Belle* is just as appealing. Cruisers can enjoy an evening meal of prime rib and shrimp Creole, and dance to the sounds of live country music. The company offers a number of special cruises, including a Valentine's Dinner Cruise, Mother's and Father's Day Cruises, Christmas Carol Cruises and many more. The riverboat operates out of Ross' Landing near the Tennessee Aquarium. ☎ 423-266-4488 for rates, reservations and information.

Southeastern Tennessee

TENNESSEE AQUARIUM

Perhaps the grandest of Chattanooga's attractions is the new $45 million Tennessee Aquarium, designed by Peter Chermayeff. It was completed in the spring of 1992 and became an instant success. Billed as the first major freshwater-life center in the world, it averages some 20,000 visitors per week.

Those numbers mean crowds, which, on hot summer days, can also mean frustration and frayed tempers. On weekends you can expect to stand in line for an hour or more. Even so, the aquarium is well worth a visit.

More than 4,000 animals from rivers all over the world inhabit the 130,000-square-foot facility. It is arranged into five great galleries: The Appalachian Cove Forest, which recreates the source of the Tennessee River; The Tennessee River Gallery; Discovery Falls, where one can examine Tennessee's animals and ecosystem; The Mississippi Delta Gallery, with its swamplands, bayous, and saltwater exhibit from the Gulf of Mexico; and the Rivers of the World Gallery, which features replicas of six of the world's great rivers.

A visit to the aquarium takes you from the source of the Tennessee River high in the Appalachians, down through the mid-waters of the river and on to the Mississippi Delta. From there, it's onward through a number of natural living environments that accurately recreate the habitats of the fish, birds, amphibians, reptiles, mammals, and insects of Africa, South America, Siberia and Asia. The highlight of the journey is the 60-foot-high central canyon, touted as the "mysterious, watery world of the river." Time and again you will enter and re-enter the canyon as a series of bridges and ramps connect the galleries. 1 Broad Street, ☎ 423-265-0695.

TENNESSEE VALLEY RAILROAD

The T.V.R. museum was founded in 1961 by a group of local enthusiasts determined to save the old steam passenger trains. Today the T.V.R. is the largest operating historic railroad in the South. From Grand Junction Station to the Chattanooga Choo Choo, the trains run a daily timetable much as they did more than three decades ago. It's a neat and interesting diversion, a rolling time machine and a rare and unusual experience. 419 Cromwell Road, ☎ 423-894-8028.

TIVOLI THEATER

Known as "The Jewel of the South," the magnificent Tivoli Theater has been a part of Chattanooga's cultural heritage since 1921. It was renovated to its former glory over a two-year period at a cost of more than $6 million, and re-opened in 1989 and is now a grand playhouse.

The interior is decorated in baroque style, complete with elegant foyer, high domed ceilings, a grand lobby, and magnificent crystal chandeliers. Designed to "transport its patrons to a world of regal splendor," the Tivoli is second to none in style and comfort, offering the finest in cultural entertainment – from the best of Broadway to grand opera, ballet, and classical music and from great American movies to country music. 709 Broad Street, ☎ 423-757-5050.

■ Cherokee National Forest

This forest is spread over a vast area of eastern Tennessee. Outdoor recreational facilities within the forest are plentiful and lean toward the primitive, with an emphasis on hiking, hunting, fishing and swimming. Overall, the area is divided into six sections or USDA Forest Service Ranger Districts, each administered by a regional office. Each district has roughly the same type of outdoor activities to offer, although the topography of the regions varies considerably. Each is covered, in some depth, within its own particular geographic region later in this book.

There are three USDA Forest Service Ranger Districts in the southeastern region of the forest: Ocoee, Hiwasee and Tellico.

OCOEE RANGER DISTRICT

Located in extreme southeastern Tennessee, this district offers a variety of recreational activities.

Camping of a fairly primitive nature is offered in six separate locations: Chilhowee, Parksville Lake, Thunder Rock, Sylco, and Tumbling Creek (see *Camping Directory*).

There are literally hundreds of trail and woodland footpaths for **hiking** in this section of the forest. Many of them are described in detail under *Hiking*, starting on page 81.

Boating is available on Parksville Lake, with public boat ramps at King Slough on the western side of the lake, Parksville Lake to the east, and at East Parksville Lake. There is a $1 usage fee and restrooms can be found at all three locations. Parksville Lake has two man-made beaches for **swimming**, one at Mac Point and one at Parksville Beach. Drinking water and restrooms are available at both locations. There is a usage fee of $2 per car at Mac Point and $2 at Parksville Beach.

HIWASSEE RANGER DISTRICT

Hiwassee offers **camping** at two locations: Quinn Springs and Lost Creek (see *Camping Directory*).

There are 12 excellent **hiking** trails within this district. You'll find them described in the Adventures section, page 77.

Once again, you'll find extensive opportunities for **boating** and other watersports described in some detail in the Adventures section beginning on page 62.

There are nine **horse trails** totaling more than 31 miles in the Hiwassee Ranger District. For more details, check with the District Office at ☎ 423-263-5486.

There are several designated **Scenic Routes** to drive in this district. These include Forest Roads 23, 44, 68, 103, 108, 220 and 297. These popular and often busy routes, especially during the summer and fall, also offer a number of outdoor opportunities, including picnicking, swimming, and photography.

Facilities for **off-road vehicles** are extremely limited in the Hiwassee Ranger District. There are two motorcycle trails and one jeep trail totaling almost eight miles. For details and rules and regulations, contact the office at ☎ 423-263-5486.

TELLICO RANGER DISTRICT

Tellico has nine developed **campgrounds**: three at Indian Boundary, one at Spivey Cove, Holly Flats, Big Oak Cove, State Line, Davis Branch, North River, Jake Best and McNabb Creek. See *Camping Directory* for listings.

More than 105 miles of **hiking** trails are within the Tellico District. See *Hiking* section for southeastern Tennessee on page 74.

Twenty-one miles of **horse trails** lace the district. For information, contact the Tellico Ranger District Office at ☎ 423-253-2520.

There's lots to see and do in the Tellico District, and **driving** is one of the most pleasurable pastimes. Of the many miles of scenic routes available, especially beautiful, though often very busy, are the Tellico River Road, Tellico-Robbinsville Road and Citico Creek Road. These offer lots of opportunities for picnicking, swimming, walking, bird and nature watching, and photography.

■ Ocoee

HIWASSEE STATE SCENIC RIVER & OCOEE RIVER

The Hiwassee was the first river to be managed under the Tennessee State Scenic River Program. A 23-mile stretch of the river winds its way from the North Carolina state line to Highway 411 just north of Benton. This section of the river, famous for its trout fishing, offers a variety of watersports, including canoeing. Hikers and photographers, too, will find the area a haven for animal and plant life. There are numerous public access boat ramps and a several picnic and swimming areas.

From Cleveland, Tenessee, take Highway 64 east to its junction with Highway 411 and turn north. Go 12 miles to Highway 30 and turn east, following the river to Reliance, Tennessee.

The Ocoee River, from the North Carolina state line to the Ocoee Dam near Reliance, is one of the premier whitewater rivers in the southeastern United States. The fast-running river winds its way down from the Copper Basin high on the mountain, through the Cherokee National Forest and a scenic natural gorge, passing a number of public access sites, picnic areas, and swimming beaches, until finally it widens, becomes tranquil, and enters Parksville Lake just above the Ocoee River Dam 10 miles east of Cleveland.

From Cleveland, take Highway 64 to the junction with Highway 411, turn north and proceed to the river.

■ Fort Loudoun State Historic Park

This 1,200-acre park was one of the earliest British fortifications on the Western frontier. The original fort was built in 1756 near some of the principal villages of the Cherokee Nation, including Tenase, from which the Volunteer State derives its name, and Tuskegee, the birthplace of the great Sequoia, one of the Cherokee Nation's most famous members.

Today, the fort and the Tellico Blockhouse overlook the TVA's 16,500-acre Tellico Reservoir and the foothills of the Great Smoky Mountains not far to the east.

Fort Loudoun is a day-use park, but its historic significance make it well worth a visit. Facilities include a visitors center offering historical and interpretive programs, a museum and gift shop, a picnic area, boat launching facilities into Tellico Lake, and several hiking trails. Activities center mainly around Tellico Lake and include all sorts of watersports: fishing, swimming, waterskiing, boating, sailing and canoeing.

Fort Loudoun State Historic Park, 338 Fort Loudoun Road, Vonore, TN 37885. ☎ 423-884-6217. The park is open during the summer months from 8 am until 10 pm, and from 8 am until sundown during the winter. Fort Loudoun is at Vonore, off US 41.

■ The Lost Sea

The Lost Sea is a part of a vast system of caves and caverns on the edge of Cherokee National Forest near Sweetwater. This, too, is a commercial operation, but one far different from the glitzy caves in and around Chattanooga. It has not been enhanced or manipulated. One of the nation's Registered Natural Landmarks, today it remains in much the same condition as it was when re-discovered by two small boys more than 50 years ago. This is the cave that will most remind you of the underground adventures of Tom Sawyer and Becky Thatcher.

The Lost Sea is a lake at the end of a vast series of caverns. It's in *The Guinness Book of World Records* as the world's largest underground lake. The emphasis at the Lost Sea has been to keep everything as natural as possible. A certain amount of necessary lighting has been installed, but it is minimal, and no unnatural colors have been used. The result is a walk along dimly lit stone corridors, up and down stone steps, and across vast open caverns. Along the way you'll see a Tennessee moonshine still and what little remains of a Confederate saltpeter mine. Overhead, you'll see graffiti burned onto the rock walls by Confederate soldiers more than 130 years ago – the oldest is dated 1863. As you return toward the entrance, you'll visit the Cherokee Indian council room where Chief Craighead met with his followers prior to their mass exodus along the Trail of Tears.

The air beneath the mountain is still and cool. When they turn out the lights, as they do for part of the tour, the dark clings like a black velvet blanket.

The highlight of the hour-long tour is a boat ride across the lake. There, you'll watch as your guide feeds a school of giant rainbow trout, some of which weigh in at more than 20 lbs.

The attraction is open year-round from 9 am each day. Closing times vary with the seasons: 5 pm, November through February; 6 pm, March, April, September and October; 7 pm, May, June and August; and 8 pm in July. Admission is $10 for adults and $5 for children.

The Lost Sea is in Sweetwater, 30 minutes south of Knoxville, or an hour north of Chattanooga. From Sweetwater, take I-75 to Sweetwater, Exit 60, then take Highway 68 east and follow the signs.Lost Sea, 140 Lost Sea Road, Sweetwater, TN 37874, ☎ 423-337-6616.

■ Red Clay State Historic Area

Red Clay is a 260-acre park dedicated to the memory of the Cherokee Indians who died on the infamous Trail of Tears. After the Cherokees were banned from their nearby capital of New Echota, it became the site of the last Tribal Council meetings prior to the exodus. Today, the park is a quiet sanctuary of rolling green fields, sparkling streams, and lush parkland – a place where you can spend a few quiet hours on a sunny afternoon.

Facilities are limited to day use, and there is a visitors center, a museum and gift shop, a picnic area, and several hiking trails.

From Cleveland, take US 60 south for 10 miles. The park sign is on the right, close to the Georgia state line. Red Clay is open daily year-round from 8 am until sundown. Admission is free. Red Clay

State Historic Park, 1140 Red Clay Road SE, Cleveland, TN 37311. ☎ 423-478-0339.

Adventures

■ Boating

FORT LOUDOUN LAKE

 Fort Loudoun Lake is easily accessible from Knoxville, Lenoir City and all points west and south via I-75 and I-40. It's one of the most popular outdoor areas in the Knoxville vicinity. It's also a popular spot for anglers, and becomes especially busy in the early mornings and over weekends, when the boating fraternity turns out in force, even during the late fall and early spring. But the waters are wide and long, and there seems to be room for everyone. There are at least 15 public boat ramps, most of them on the west side.

From the south, take I-75 to Highway 321 at Lenoir City, turn east onto 321 and follow it to the lake.

From Knoxville and the west, take I-40 to its junction with I-75, follow I-75 south to Highway 321 and proceed as indicated above.

From Maryville and the east, take Highway 321 west to the lake.

HIWASSEE RIVER

The Hiwassee is a fast-moving river more suited to trout fishing than to boating. There are, however, a couple of places where the locals go to spend time on the water, river running and waterskiing.

At **Reliance**, just north of Benton in Polk County on Highway 30, there's a small recreation area just off the highway next to Webb's Country Store by the bridge. Take the dirt road just to the right of the store and go 100 yards or so. There, you find a picnic area and public-access boat ramp.

At **Agency Creek** in Meigs County, just northwest of Cleveland on Highway 58 going north, you'll find a public access ramp into the Hiwassee next to the Iron Bridge on both sides of the river. And, just before you get to the bridge, also on Highway 58, you'll find **B&B Marina**, which also has an access ramp. This little recreation area can become very crowded on weekends, but is quiet during the week, even in summer.

The river at Agency Creek is much better for boating and skiing than farther upstream at Reliance. In places it can be as much as a half-mile wide, resembling a lake rather than a river. Here, you find numerous small tributaries, narrow and often shallow. A little farther downstream to the west, the Hiwassee joins the Tennessee River. Again, the river is wide and deep here. Turn south and it leads to Harrison Bay, Chickamauga Lake and Chattanooga. Go north and it leads to Knoxville. B&B Marina also has a restaurant where you can eat lunch and dine on Tennessee catfish.

LITTLE TENNESSEE RIVER

The Little Tennessee is part of the Tennessee River system, such an extremely large part that the word "little" is inappropriate. From Fort Loudoun Lake, the river runs east for many miles until, eventually, it enters Tellico Lake, and then Chilhowee Lake. A boat ride from Fort Loudoun to Chilhowee is an interesting trip of more than 60 miles. If that's too much, you can follow the riverside roads and you'll find dozens of places to park with public-access ramps into the river.

The river is best approached from I-40 and I-75 via Lenoir City. From there, follow the Tellico Highway along the south shore, and take Highway 72 eastward to its junction with Highway 411. Turn north on 411 to the junction with Highway 360, which follows the south shore east into the mountains.

PARKSVILLE LAKE

From Cleveland, take Highway 64 east toward Copper Hill, Ducktown and North Carolina and go seven miles to the entrance of Cherokee National Forest at Parksville on the Ocoee River, next to Ocoee Dam Number One at Sugarloaf Mountain.

This a vast expanse of quiet water at the foot of the raging whitewaters of the Ocoee – the site of the 1996 Olympic whitewater events is just a few miles up the road. Situated as it is in the Cherokee National Forest, and a part of the TVA's Wilderness Recreation Program, the area has become a very popular weekend boating resort.

Along with several public access boat ramps, the TVA has provided a number of other recreational facilities along the lakeshore. These include several roadside and lakeside picnic areas with tables (bring your own grill), a swimming beach, and a shooting range where you can practice with handguns, rifles and shotguns.

Just a few miles farther on Highway 64 you'll find the **Ocoee Inn and Restaurant** nestled on the shore of a small, secluded bay. It has an access ramp, as well as a parking area for boat trailers. Better yet, the restaurant is open for lunch and dinner. The food is good and the menu features catfish and hush puppies.

A mile or so beyond the Ocoee Inn, at its junction with Greasy Creek, you'll find a second public access boat ramp with ample parking for vehicles and trailers. Beyond Greasy Creek, the lake narrows and eventually turns shallow as it joins the controlled waters of the Ocoee River.

You are advised not to proceed upriver past this point for two reasons. First, you may get stuck on the muddy river bottom. Second, you may fall victim to the TVA when they shut or open the weir gates at Ocoee Dam Number Two, thus lowering or raising the level of water in the river.

The Ocoee River, especially the public access areas at Parksville Lake, become very crowded during the summer months and boating on weekends can be a trial, even hazardous.

TENNESSEE RIVER

There's plenty of boating action on the Tennessee south from Knoxville to Chattanooga, and beyond. There are public access ramps at a number of places, many of which have already been mentioned. Others can be found at Watts Bar, Old Washington on Highway 30 west of Athens, Highway 60 at the old Dayton ferry landing, and from the Hiwassee at B&B Marina on Highway 58.

If you take Highway 312 from the junction at Highway 60 at Birchwood and travel south, you'll find side roads leading to more ramps at Johnson Road, Grasshopper Creek, Thatch Ware, Ware Branch and Skull Island. All are quiet, little-used, and all have ample parking for vehicles and boat trailers.

Beyond Skull Island, Highway 312 rejoins Highway 58, and from there it's only a mile or two to the access points at Harrison Bay and then Chattanooga.

WATTS BAR LAKE

Watts Bar Lake is the result of yet another of the TVA's commercial enterprises on the water. This time they have harnessed the waters of the Tennessee River. The great dam and the huge nuclear reactor, when it comes fully on line, will provide electricity for cities as far as way Knoxville and Chattanooga. Watts Bar Lake itself now covers thousands of acres of what once was prime farm land. Today, it's fast becoming the outdoor recreation capital of eastern Tennessee and, as always, the TVA has gone out of its way to turn the manmade lake to good use. Campers, fishermen, boaters and refugees from the cities in search of a quiet hour or two in the country arrive on the weekends in droves. At the last count there were more than 30 public boat ramps; all have ample parking for vehicles and trailers.

Watts Bar is perhaps the most popular boating spot in eastern Tennessee. Over the weekend the lake can become a circus, with people waiting in line to use the ramps. The water almost boils as hundreds of boats criss-cross the lake, sometimes at speeds in excess of 50 miles per hour. If you want to get away from it all and enjoy a quiet hour or two on the water, to be alone with your thoughts and the wonders of nature, you'd better look elsewhere.

■ Canoeing Trails

FRENCH BROAD RIVER

 The route here covers some 25 miles of scenic river from the Highway 70 bridge all the way to Douglas Lake. The terrain along the way is mostly wooded and can be spectacular in the fall. The put-in is at the Highway 70 bridge; the take-out at Rankin Bridge on Douglas Lake, or at any of the other access points along the lake shore. The going is mostly easy, but there are one or two intermediate sections. To reach the access point, follow Highway 70 east from Newport to the bridge.

Southeastern Tennessee

HIWASSEE RIVER AT RELIANCE

This is an 11-mile route through some of the prettiest country in the Smokies. The river, in places, is fast. Put in at the Appalachia Power Plant and paddle downstream through the Cherokee National Forest, along the State Scenic River, to the Highway 411 bridge north of Benton where you'll find the exit point.

From Cleveland, take Highway 64 east to its junction with Highway 411 and turn north. Go 12 miles to Highway 30. Turn east on 30 and follow the river to Reliance. Cross the river there by way of the bridge next to Webb's Country Store, then turn right along the river bank and drive on to the Appalachia Power Plant where you'll find the entry point.

OCOEE RIVER

This five-mile section of the Ocoee River is considered a Class IV rapid and is recommended only for canoeists with considerable experience. This is your chance to try your hand and skills against the same waters as did the Olympic kayak squads. Put in at the parking area at Ocoee Dam Number Two and exit at the Powerhouse parking area.

From Cleveland, take Highway 64 east toward Copper Hill, Ducktown and North Carolina and go for 10 miles. About seven miles out from Cleveland you enter the Cherokee National Forest at Parksville on the Ocoee River, next to Ocoee Dam Number One at Sugarloaf Mountain. Drive on until you come to the TVA Powerhouse; from there go to Ocoee Dam Number Two; the entry point is five miles farther.

TELLICO RIVER

The **Tellico River Canoe Trail** is a 44-mile route that passes through the Cherokee National Forest, Red Mountain and Notchy Creek Knob. It's a Class I trail with easy going for most of the way. Even so, it's best canoed during spring, summer and fall. Put in at the Tellico Ranger Station and exit the river at the Tellico Dam Recreation Area.

From Tellico Plains, follow Highway 165 east along the riverbank for three miles to Indian Boundary Road. Highway 165 and Indian Boundary turn north; you will fork to the right and stay with the Tellico River all the way to the ranger station.

■ Camping

For camping information and locations within the Cherokee National Forest and state parks, consult the *Camping Directory,* page 275.

■ Fall & Spring Colors, Scenic Drives

NICKAJACK LAKE TO CHATTANOOGA

This scenic loop involves a drive of about 54 miles and is especially colorful from late September into early October. The drive begins at the Tennessee Welcome Center on I-24, 17 miles west of Chattanooga. From the center, take Highway 27 at the first exit north and go to Powell's Crossroads. From there, head east, still on 27, over Walden's Ridge until you arrive in Chattanooga, north of the river on Cherokee Boulevard. Cross the river via the Market Street Bridge, turn west on M.L. King and go to Broad Street. Continue on along Broad Street, which eventually becomes Highway 41, and follow it all the way along the banks of the Tennessee River to Nickajack Lake where you'll rejoin I-24 on the south side of the river. You can return to Chattanooga via I-24. The trip should take about two hours, depending upon whether you stop along the way.

TRAIL OF TEARS STATE SCENIC ROUTE

The Trail of Tears pays tribute to the 13,000 Cherokee Indians that were forcibly removed from their hunting grounds during the 1830s. From Red Clay they were herded west through Tennessee to the new reservation in Oklahoma. It was a trip that cost many lives. Red Clay State Park was the site of the last Cherokee Council before the exodus. The Trail of Tears follows the entire route from Red Clay to Oklahoma, more than 900 miles. The short stretch from Red Clay to Cleveland, about 12 miles or so, is a pleasant excursion. Red Clay in the fall is a riot of color, and so is the route from the park into Cleveland. At the end of the short drive, Cleveland provides another pleasant day out. There's a modern shopping mall, a lively downtown business area, dozens of restaurants and a small park.

Southeastern Tennessee

From Red Clay State Park on Blue Springs Road, take the Weatherly Switch Road to Highway 60, or Dalton Pike as it's known locally, turn north and follow the road into Cleveland.

HIGHWAY 64 – CLEVELAND TO COPPER HILL

The drive from Cleveland to Copper Hill is one of the prettiest in southeastern Tennessee. From Cleveland, Highway 64 leads eastward toward North Carolina. It's not a loop, but a two-lane road and you'll have to return the same way. The round-trip of about 60 miles will take a morning or afternoon to complete, depending upon side trips along the way. In the fall the entire route is ablaze with autumn color. In spring the wildflowers bloom and fill the air with a delicate fragrance. The **Ocoee River Gorge**, through which you'll pass along the way, is an area of great natural beauty.

Take Highway 64 from Cleveland and proceed east to Ocoee Dam Number One on the edge of **Parksville Lake**. There you'll find a scenic overlook. Go a few miles more to the **Ocoee Inn** on your left. If it's open you might like to stop in for some catfish. For the next several miles the road skirts Parksville Lake. There are a number of picnic spots, several boat ramps, and a sandy swimming beach. On the far side of the lake the river narrows and the road begins to climb up the mountain. It winds its way ever upward, hugging the riverbank, with steep cliffs that rise right from the edge of the road to the top of the mountain, to Copper Hill. As you drive slowly through the gorge, look upward and to your right. Among the trees, about halfway up the steep mountainsides on the far side of the river, you'll see a wooden flume that runs for several miles from Ocoee Dam Number Two to the Powerhouse, where two large pipes connect it to the turbines. The TVA controls the flow of the river, either through the flume to make electricity, or down the river gorge to allow for whitewater rafting and kayaking.

Beyond Ocoee Dam Number Two the road climbs ever more steeply to **Copper Hill**. The sleepy little community nestles in a small valley on top of the mountain. As you approach the town you'll see that the mountain has been scarred by many years of mining. Today, the mines are almost all closed, and the mountain is slowly returning to its natural state. While you're in Copper Hill, stop in at the **Museum of Mining**, where you can see some interesting exhibits that interpret the industry in the Copper Hill area over the past 100 years.

Your return journey takes you back down Highway 64 to Cleveland. Even though you've already seen the route, you'll find it different when traveling down the mountain.

■ Fishing

CHATTANOOGA AREA

 You can fish year-round at several places in the Chattanooga area. At **Chickamauga Lake**, you'll find boat ramps in the city park close to its junction with Amnicola Highway and Highway 153. Public boat ramps are also available at **Nickajack Lake**, off I-24 about 10 miles east of the city on both sides of the lake; at **Harrison Bay** on Highway 58 northbound; and just a few miles farther at both Booker T. Washington and Harrison Bay state parks. Year-round fishing is excellent for largemouth bass, striped bass, crappie, bream, bluegill, and catfish.

CHILHOWEE LAKE

Chilhowee Lake, not to be confused with the lake often called by the same name at the top of Chilhowee Mountain farther south, is set on the Little Tennessee River at the edge of Great Smoky Mountains National Park, east of Lenoir City and south of Maryville in Monroe County. It's a rather small lake, but the fishing is good and the waters are well stocked with smallmouth and largemouth bass; brook, lake and rainbow trout; bluegill; catfish; and walleye. It's a little remote, but that keeps the lake fairly quiet.

From Maryville, take Highway 411 south to its junction with Highway 115 and follow that to the river, then onward to Chilhowee Lake.

From I-75, take Highway 68 east to Sweetwater and from there to Madisonville and its junction with Highway 411. Drive north on 411 and cross the Little Tennessee River. When you reach the other side, you'll have a couple of options. You can take the small side road and travel east along the river bank to Chilhowee Lake, a long and tortuous trip. Or you can drive on along 411 to its junction with Highway 115, turn east and follow it to the lake.

From the Great Smoky Mountains National Park, the ride is somewhat easier. Just follow the Foothills Parkway south until you reach the lake.

FORT LOUDOUN LAKE

This lake is actually part of the Tennessee River. The fishing here is considered fair, and the lake is kept stocked with smallmouth, largemouth, spotted and white bass. Crappie, bluegill, catfish, and sauger are also present in fairly good numbers.

There are at least 15 public access ramps into the lake, most of them on the west side of the river.

From the south, take I-75 to its junction with Highway 321 at Lenoir City, turn east onto 321 and follow it to the lake. From Knoxville and the west, take I-40 to I-75. Follow I-75 south to the junction with Highway 321 and proceed as indicated above. From Maryville and the east, take Highway 321 west.

HIWASSEE RIVER

The Hiwassee is a fast-moving river well suited to trout fishing, and, indeed, it's famous as such. Other than trout there's little else of interest to anglers.

The trout fishing grounds are not easy to find. From Cleveland, take Highway 64 east to Highway 411 and turn north. Go 12 miles to Highway 30 and turn east, following the river to Reliance. Now you have a couple of options. First, you can take the dirt road to the right of Webb's Country Store, park your vehicle in the recreation area parking lot and go the rest of the way on foot, under the railroad bridges and down to the river bank. From there, walk east as far as you can go. Fishing here as excellent.

Your second option is to cross the river via the bridge next to the store, then turn right along the riverbank and drive several miles to the Appalachia Power Plant. There are parking spaces and access to the water all the way along the trail (the road along the water's edge deteriorates to dirt-road status) from the bridge to the powerhouse. Once again, depending on the level of the river, the trout fishing in the Powerhouse area is excellent.

LITTLE TENNESSEE RIVER

This tributary of the Tennessee River offers anglers good sport and a wide variety of species, including smallmouth, largemouth, spotted, striped and white bass, as well as crappie, bluegill, catfish, walleye and sauger.

For directions, see page 63. Along the way you'll find dozens of places with public access points and ramps into the river.

OCOEE RIVER

Probably the best spot to fish the Ocoee is a small stretch of river running from the Hiwassee in the north to Parksville Lake south of Benton and east of Cleveland. The fishing here is fair, and you can expect to catch smallmouth, largemouth, spotted and white bass, as well as crappie, bluegill, catfish and sauger. The river can be accessed at its junction with Highway 411 just south of Benton.

From Cleveland, take Highway 64 to Highway 411. Turn north and proceed to the river.

Parksville Lake

Fishing in Parksville is not recommended. For many years the waters of the Ocoee that tumble down the mountain from the small mining town of Copper Hill have been polluted by the industry that gave the town its name. Today, things are improving a little, but there's a long way to go. And, although a dauntless, stubborn few continue to fish the waters of the lake, the catches are few and far between.

TENNESSEE RIVER

The Tennessee River has always been known for its good fishing. Tennessee catfish are renowned throughout the South as the very best of good eating, and the lakes are filled with bass, crappie, walleye and bluegill. Aside from Harrison Bay and Booker T. Washington state parks and Watts Bar Lake, there are any number of access points to the river that will provide you with a host of good fishing opportunities.

You can take Highway 58 north from Chattanooga, or you can join it via Highway 60 from Cleveland, Highway 30 from Athens, or

Southeastern Tennessee

Highway 68 from Sweetwater. Once on Highway 58, try one of the many side roads that lead to the river, or follow the road until you find a spot that looks good to you. You can also continue westward from Cleveland along Highway 60 toward Dayton until you reach the river, which is more than a half-mile wide at that point. Here you'll find an access ramp close to the old ferry landing.

In Chattanooga, access to the river is available at the Tennessee River Park on Amnicola Highway.

WATTS BAR LAKE

Watts Bar, a vast man-made lake some 60 miles north of Chattanooga, is one of the premier fishing spots in eastern Tennessee. The sport is good and the area highly recommended. Unfortunately for anglers, it is also extremely popular with the weekend boating crowd. Often very busy, the lake has more than 30 public boat ramps. Largemouth, smallmouth, spotted and white bass, crappie, bluegill, and sauger are all here. The sport's "Big Game" hunters come from around the country in search of the mighty hybrid striped bass that also inhabit the lake. These freshwater fish are routinely caught at weights in excess of 20, 30 and, on rare occasions, even 40 lbs. If that's not tantalizing enough, the waters below the weir gates of the dam also provide good sport. Experienced anglers frequent the lakeshore and roadside restaurants and tell tales of great catfish, monsters of six feet or more and weighing in at over 100 lbs. Are the stories true? Many locals swear that they are. The fish simply lie on the bottom of the river below the weir gates and gorge themselves, year after year, on fish chopped up and thrown out from the great turbines. Many of the big cats are caught "foul-hooked" by fishermen working the bottom of the lake illegally with weighted line.

Warning

Fishing the river below the dam can be extremely dangerous. Little warning is given before the engineers open the weir gates. When they do, millions of gallons crash through into the river below, causing the waters to rise very quickly and creating currents that can capsize a boat. Get caught in such a situation and the chances are you'll end up in the water, where even the strongest swimmer is not capable of overcoming the currents and undertow. Rarely a year goes by without someone dying as a result of fishing too close below the dam gates.

■ Hang-Gliding

 Hang-gliding is possible in several places around Chattanooga, but most notably on Lookout and Raccoon mountains.

RACCOON & LOOKOUT MOUNTAINS

Lookout Mountain is perhaps the best hang-gliding spot in the nation. The sheer cliff, wide-open spaces, swift-rising thermals and crisp mountain air make this an ideal place for this most exhilarating high adventure sport.

Lookout Mountain Flight Park & Training Center

Located high above Lookout Valley at an elevation of almost 3,000 feet, this is one of the oldest and best-known hang-gliding facilities in the nation. Adventurers of all skill levels use this center to hone their skills.

Beginners can take courses of instruction that range from $599 to $899, depending upon the rating the student wishes to achieve.

For the would-be adventurer who's not quite sure of the sport but wants to give it a try, there's the chance to fly tandem with a qualified instructor. The flight lasts from 20 to 30 minutes and achieves an elevation of more than 2,000 feet.

Rental gliders are available at $55 per day.

Each spring the center hosts an annual hang-gliding competition, which is attended by the best from around the world.

Contact Lookout Mountain Flight Park, Route 2, Box 215H, Rising Fawn, GA 30738. ☎ 706-398-3541.

From Chattanooga, take the scenic parkway up the mountain and follow the road toward Covenant College. The center is on the right at the edge of the mountain.

High Adventure Sports, Inc.

For beginners, this company on Raccoon Mountain near Chattanooga has something different. The Adventure Park has one of only two hang-glider simulators in the country. It's a strange-looking contraption, but it works, and it does give beginners some idea of what to expect from the real thing.

You climb to a ledge about 100 feet above the park where you strap yourself into what looks like a real hang-glider. And it is, except that it's fixed to a long cable that stretches away from the ledge for 400 or 500 feet to the park below.

After a certain amount of basic instruction, you'll launch yourself from the ledge and the glider will travel down the cable at a speed just sufficient for it to make use of the airlift provided by its wings. The glider flies straight and true, down the cable to the landing field. A couple of rides and you're ready for the real thing, so they say.

High Adventure Sports is next to Raccoon Mountain on Cummins Highway. From Chattanooga, take I-24 to the Tiftonia Junction with Cummins Highway, and then follow the signs. ☎ 423-825-0444.

■ Hiking

CHEROKEE NATIONAL FOREST: TELLICO RANGER DISTRICT

 BALD RIVER TRAIL: This route is officially designated Forest Trail (FT) 88 and is an easy walk through the forest.

The trail begins close to the parking lot near Bald River Falls. From there it runs for five miles along the length of the Bald River Gorge, heads through upland hardwood forest and then goes on to the Cantrell Parking Area at Holly Flats. During the spring season, the pathway is lined with blooming wildflowers and rhododendrons. Bring a camera if you come at this time of the year.

The Bald River Trail is one of the busiest trails in the area. It will not provide solitude or peace and quiet.

Side trails off the Bald River Trail include **Cow Camp** (FT 173), a short woodland trail of less than a mile that leads to Bald River; and **Henderson Mountain Trail** (FT 107). The latter leads from Cow Camp for a little more than 2½ miles to Forest Service Road (FSR) 40823.

You can hike a loop trail by starting out at the Bald River trailhead by the gorge, turn onto Cow Camp, and then onto Henderson and go to FSR 40823. Turn left onto 40823 and go for two miles to FSR 126. Make a right and proceed along 126 for five miles to the Cantrell Parking Area. A right will put you back onto the Bald River Trail, which you can follow back to the falls. It's a hike of about 16 miles.

Bushey Ridge Area

McNABB CREEK TRAIL: McNabb is a fairly easy hike for most of its four miles, but becomes somewhat strenuous towards the end, when it rises steeply to finish some 1,500 feet higher at Grassy Gap. Along the way, the trail follows McNabb Creek, a beautiful mountain stream that flows through pine forest and rhododendron beds. It's a scenic trail, ideal for photography and bird watching.

From Highway 411 in Madisonville, take Highway 68 to Tellico Plains and Highway 165. Turn left onto 165 and drive for a little more than a half-mile to the junction with Highway 360. Stay on 165, drive four more miles to the Tellico River Road and turn right. Continue on along Tellico River Road, past Bald River Falls, to the junction with North River Road (FT 217). You'll find the trailhead for McNabb about two miles farther on.

LAUREL BRANCH TRAIL: Laurel Branch is quite an easy hike for the first two thirds of its length. From there it rises quite quickly to finish more than 1,800 feet above its trailhead. It's a quiet, scenic trail with lots of wildflowers and other blooming plants.

The trailhead for Laurel Branch is on FT 217, some three miles farther on from the McNabb trailhead. Follow the directions from Madisonville as described for the McNabb Trail above.

HEMLOCK CREEK: Hemlock Creek is an easy trail early on, and very picturesque. But it becomes quite difficult as it rises 2,000 feet to Hemlock Knob, where the trail ends. The 3½-mile hike is, in places, somewhat tangled and overgrown, but very rewarding. There is no water available over the last half of the trail, so take along plenty to drink.

The trailhead for Hemlock Creek is on FT 217, just before the one for the McNabb Creek Trail. Follow the directions from Madisonville as described for McNabb, but drive only 1½ miles on FT 217 from its junction with Tellico River Road.

Citico Creek Area

PINE RIDGE TRAIL: There are more than a dozen trails in the Citico Creek Area. Of those, the Pine Ridge Trail is the most scenic. It's a fairly stiff hike of about 3½ miles that rises more than 2,000 feet to its highest point at the trail end, where it joins with the Fodderstack Trail. Along the way you enjoy some wonderful scenery, many species of wildflowers, and a very pretty mountain stream on the early section. Great for photography.

From Highway 411 in Madisonville, take Highway 68 to Tellico Plains and Highway 165. Turn left onto 165 and drive 1.7 miles to the junction with Highway 360; stay on 165 to its junction with Tellico River Road, about four miles. At that point the road forks right and left. The right fork leads on to Bald River Falls, the left fork, the one you want, continues on as Highway 165. Bear left and drive nine miles until you reach FT 345. This road takes you to Indian Boundary Lake and Recreation Area and Citico Creek Road, which leads to the Warden Station Area. Go to Citico Creek Road and drive until you come to a hairpin bend in the road. Turn off there and cross the low-water bridge to the parking area. The trail starts about one-tenth of a mile up the dirt road from the bridge; there's a horse trail sign on the right and a hiker's sign a little farther on.

CHEROKEE NATIONAL FOREST: HIWASSEE RANGER DISTRICT

CONASAUGA FALLS TRAIL: A moderately difficult one-mile trail that offers hikers an opportunity to view two distinct types of forest. You'll hike along a pine forest ridge where fires have altered the vegetation and habitat. From there you'll pass through a hollow where hemlocks grow. Conasauga Falls, a 30-foot cascade at the end of the trail, offers excellent photographic opportunities.

From Etowah, drive east on Highway 310 to its junction with Highway 68 in Tellico Plains. Turn right. Go for three miles, then turn right onto Old Highway 68 and go one mile to FR 341. Follow 341 for 1.3 miles to FR 341A and go for about a half-mile more on that. The trailhead is on your left.

UNICOI MOUNTAIN TRAIL: From the trailhead at the John Muir Trail to its end, Unicoi is an easy six-mile hike through hollows and pine woods, over ridges and alongside babbling streams. It connects to the John Muir Trail, which itself connects, just a short distance away, to the Coker Creek Falls Trail.

From Etowah, drive east on Highway 310 to its junction of Highway 68 in Tellico Plains and turn right. Go 16.8 miles to its junction with Forest Road (FDR) 2135 and FDR 2135A. The trailhead is at the top of the hill and is not easy to see from the road.

COKER CREEK: An easy hike of three miles, the route takes you through the Coker Creek Scenic Corridor. The trail is well marked, open, and provides lots of views of the cascades. There are picnic tables at the trailhead and the path offers many excellent opportunities for nature and wildlife photographers.

From Etowah, drive east on Highway 310 to its junction with Highway 68 in Tellico Plains and turn right. Go 13.3 miles to an intersection just beyond the Ironsburg Methodist Church and turn right. From there, drive .8 miles, turn left at the cemetery and continue .6 miles to the intersection of the paved and gravel roads. Bear right on the paved road for 3.9 miles – it becomes a gravel road – to the intersection of Ducket Ridge Road and Lost Creek Road. Bear left for 1.6 miles to the parking area and the trailhead.

JOHN MUIR NATIONAL RECREATION TRAIL: This trail was built in 1972 and named for the founder of the Sierra Club, who supposedly traveled this section of the Hiwassee River while walking from Kentucky to Florida. The John Muir Trail takes in some 18 miles of the north bank of the Hiwassee River from a trailhead at Childer's Creek to Forest Service Road (FSR) 311. It's a hike of varying grades, but the first three miles from the Childer's Creek trailhead has been designed for use by senior citizens and is a very easy, scenic walk. Beyond that, you'll pass the Appalachia Power Plant, go under the suspension bridge and on along the river bank, past Coker Creek to Highway 68 at the trail's end.

From Cleveland, drive east on Highway 64 to the junction with Highway 411. Turn north and go to Highway 30, where you'll turn right for almost six miles to the river bridge at Reliance – it's next to Webb's Country Store. Turn left over the bridge, take the first road to the right (FS 108, a paved road that becomes a gravel road) and go a half-mile. The parking lot and trailhead at Childer's Creek are on the right. If you wish, you can drive on along 108 for six miles to the Appalachia Power Plant and begin your hike there.

TURTLETOWN CREEK TRAIL: An easy-to-moderate loop trail that follows Turtletown Creek for almost four miles, returning eventually to Shinbone Ridge. Along the way you'll enjoy scenic views of the Hiwassee River and overlooks of two major waterfalls. You can take a spur trail that leads to Forest Service Road 1166 for an extended hike back to the parking lot.

From the junction of Highways 64 and 68 at Copper Hill, take 68 and go north 15 miles to Farner. Alternately, you can travel south on 68 from Tellico Plains to Farner. From the post office in Farner, take 68 south .2 miles and turn right. Cross the railroad tracks and bear left on each of the paved roads as you come to them – it's a drive of about one mile – to a junction with FDR 1166 where you'll see a sign for the Turtletown Scenic Area. Turn right onto FDR 1166 and go for another mile to its junction with 11651 – the only left turn. Make this turn and travel a half-mile to the parking lot and trailhead.

FISHERMAN'S TRAIL: With a total length of 1½ miles, Fisherman's Trail provides an extremely easy walk. The trail begins at Quinn Springs Pavilion in the Fisherman's Parking Area on Highway 30. From there, it follows the Hiwassee River to the Hiwassee River Picnic Area. Along the way you'll see many species of plants and small animal life. And, if you like to fish, you can do that too.

The riverbank provides easy access to the water. The trail ends at the roadside. There's no parking area at the end, but the Hiwassee River Picnic Area, which has plenty of parking, is just a couple of hundred yards away.

From Etowah, drive south on Highway 411 for 7½ miles and turn left onto Highway 30 east – the Hiwassee Market will be on your right. From there, drive 1.6 miles to the trailhead at the Hiwassee Scenic Parking Area on your left.

From Cleveland, take Highway 64 east to its junction with Highway 411, turn left and go north for 13 miles to the junction with Highway 30. Turn right and proceed as before.

OSWALD DOME TRAIL: This is a more difficult trail that also begins at the Quinn Springs Pavilion. From the pavilion, it threads through the woods and upward for almost four miles to the Oswold Dome Fire Lookout Tower on Bean Mountain. Here, you can access FSR 77 and walk all the way to Lake McCamy and the Chilhowee Mountain Recreation Area. You'll have to double-back on yourself to return, making a total walk of eight miles.

See directions for the Fisherman's Trail, above, to reach the pavilion.

Gee Creek Wilderness Area

CHESTNUT MOUNTAIN TRAIL: Once an old jeep trail, Chestnut Mountain is now pretty much off-limits to motor vehicles. It winds its way up the mountain for about 5½ miles to end at Iron Gap, with an elevation of 2,000 feet. The first three miles are the most strenuous, but beyond that the going gets slightly easier. The trail is a lonely one, often overgrown, but generally passable if you don't mind roughing it a bit. The trail end is a long drive from its head, so plan to hike both ways. From the higher elevations along the way you'll enjoy splendid views over the entire length of the Gee Creek Gorge.

From Etowah, drive south on Highway 411 for six miles to a point just four-tenths of a mile north of the Hiwassee River Bridge. Turn left. You should see a sign for the Gee Creek Campground. Go .7 miles and take the second dirt road to the left, across the railroad tracks to a large dirt parking area. The trailhead is beyond the gate at the back right-hand corner of the lot.

From Cleveland, take Highway 64 east to Highway 411. Turn left and go north. After 13 miles you'll cross the Hiwassee River Bridge. From the bridge, drive another .4 miles. Turn right and proceed as indicated above.

GEE CREEK TRAIL: This is an old fisherman's trail that follows the creek through the woods for about two miles. It's a moderately difficult hike that dead ends, so be prepared to walk it both ways. En route you'll pass two magnificent waterfalls. The trail provides many excellent opportunities for nature and wildlife photographers.

From Etowah, drive south on Highway 411 for five miles and turn left through the village of Wetmore. Follow the road that runs alongside the railroad tracks for a little more than two miles where you'll find the trailhead (by this time the paved road will have turned into a gravel one).

From Cleveland, take Highway 64 east to Highway 411, turn left and go north for 15 miles. You'll cross the Hiwassee River Bridge about 1½ miles before you turn right into Wetmore. From there, proceed as indicated above.

STARR MOUNTAIN TRAIL: This trail begins at Gee Creek and meanders upward for five miles to end at FT 297 on top of Starr Mountain. It's a fairly strenuous hike for most of the way, ending at an elevation of about 2,350 feet above sea level. It's a secluded trail, ideal for taking your time and enjoying nature at its unspoiled best.

In places the trail can become a bit tangled, so it's a good idea to take a long-sleeved jacket to protect your arms.

A spur halfway along the trail leads off to the south. The trail's end is a long drive from the trailhead, so plan to hike both ways; the return journey is much easier. Be sure to take plenty to drink; there is nothing available on the trail.

The trailhead is just 30 yards from the Gee Creek trailhead on the right. Just follow the directions for the Gee Creek Trail, above.

CHEROKEE NATIONAL FOREST: OCOEE RANGER DISTRICT

LAKE McCAMY & BENTON FALLS: The trailhead for your hike to Benton Falls is located in the Chilhowee Recreation Area on the top of Chilhowee Mountain high above Parksville Lake. It is set off Highway 64, east of Cleveland. This is a very easy two-mile hike through the woods to one of the most scenic waterfalls in the southern section of the Cherokee National Forest.

From Cleveland, take Highway 64 and drive east toward Copper Hill and North Carolina. Continue past Parksville Lake and the Ocoee Inn for a mile to 64's junction with Forest Route 77. Turn left onto 77 and follow it through the forest and upward some 3,000 feet to the top of Chilhowee Mountain and Lake McCamy. Forest Route 77 is one of many paths created during the 1930s by the Civilian Conservation Corps to open up the wilderness areas. Chilhowee Lake is a creation of the TVA.

The drive up the mountain is, in itself, something of an adventure. For about six miles the road twists and turns through the forest, but it seems much farther. Along the way you find a number of scenic overlooks, each providing a unique and spectacular view of the surrounding countryside. When you reach the top of the mountain you'll be able to see the Ocoee Inn and Ocoee Dam Number One, like dots on a map, and Parksville Lake reveals itself for what it is, a very wide section of the Ocoee River.

Lake McCamy is a mile farther on to the right, a small expanse of still water at the top of the mountain. You'll find a large parking area (put the designated fee into the box) and a small pathway that leads down to the lakeshore, passing a small amphitheater, a picnic area and public restrooms. At the lake shore you'll find a small, sandy beach for relaxing and swimming, and a signpost that points the way along a two-mile trail to Benton Falls. The trail is easy and well marked.

Benton Falls is a picturesque waterfall on the Chilhowee River, deep in the woods and far from civilization. In spring and fall the wildflowers grow in profusion; in winter the whole area turns into fairyland of ice and snow.

Southeastern Tennessee

Be careful at the head of the falls and while climbing down to the river; the rocks are wet and often slippery.

DRY POND LEAD TRAIL: This trail leads upward through the forest for 4½ miles and about 1,500 feet to Kimsey Highway where it ends. Along the way you'll go through some of the most beautiful woodland in the Ocoee area. It's a fairly strenuous, uphill hike, but well worth the effort.

From Cleveland, take Highway 64 east to its junction with Highway 411. From there, continue east along 64 for 18½ miles to Powerhouse Number Three, about a half-mile from Ocoee Dam Number Two. The trailhead marker is directly opposite the Powerhouse.

ROCK CREEK TRAIL: This trail meanders through the center of the Little Frog Mountain Wilderness for 5½ miles. It's a fairly level hike – sometimes difficult, sometimes easy – rising only 400 feet over its entire length. The trail leads to a pleasant little valley where Rock Creek flows swiftly through its center, passing wildflowers: rhododendron, dogwood, hemlock, mountain fire and holly. The trail ends at its intersection with the Dry Pond Lead Trail. There, you turn left onto Dry Pond and follow it back to Highway 64, where you'll turn left again and follow 64 back to the Rock Creek trailhead.

From Cleveland, take Highway 64 east to Highway 411. Continue east along 64 for 21 miles to a parking area on the left alongside an old paved road. The trailhead is 20 yards away to the right.

ROGERS BRANCH TRAIL: Rogers Branch is a hike of a little more than two miles up a creek valley to the foot of Brock Mountain. It's a fairly easy, very pleasant walk, often very busy during the summer months, that dead-ends at a small grove of hemlock trees. You'll cross and re-cross the creek several times – be careful of the slippery rocks – pass through stands of pine and hardwood forest, and enjoy a variety of wildflowers and shrubs.

From Cleveland, take Highway 64 east to Highway 411. Continue east on 64 for 18 miles to Ocoee Dam Number Two; the well-marked trailhead is on the north side of the parking area.

■ Whitewater Sports

OCOEE RIVER

 The Ocoee River, east of Parksville Lake, was the site of the 1996 Olympic whitewater kayaking events. Visitors and kayakers from around the world descended upon the Ocoee for two weeks in July to enjoy the spectacle. What once had been an adventure spot of only local reputation suddenly became the whitewater capital of the world.

Prior to the Olympics, the Ocoee had always been a popular rafting spot. By 1996, a large number of companies describing themselves as "high adventure" sports providers had sprung up along the riverbanks and Highway 64 all the way from Cleveland to Parksville Lake. Today, the number of such companies has increased to a point where, as you drive along the road, you can't miss them.

The river itself, extremely wild and fast-moving (when the TVA opens the weir gates, that is), was somewhat changed for the Olympic Games. The river bed was dredged, new rocks added – some made of concrete – and the course of the water changed and controlled to provide a truly challenging run. This, of course, improved things for rafters too. The ride down the river is exciting, though rarely dangerous, and an outing can last for more than four hours, much of which is taken up traveling from the outfitter to the access point, and then waiting in line at the water's edge. Once in the water you ride a large rubber raft in the company of an "experienced" guide and a half-dozen other adventurers. The five-mile ride downriver usually takes at least two hours.

Unfortunately, at the height of the summer rafting season the river becomes something of a circus. Highway 64, narrow, winding and a trial even at the best of times, turns into a log-jam of cars, trailers and sightseers. The river itself turns black as hundreds of rubber rafts, so close they often touch one another, bob and dip from the access point below Ocoee Dam Number Two all the way to the exit point some five miles downstream.

The Ocoee is easily accessible from Chattanooga and Cleveland, and that makes it appealing, but there are less-crowded places to go whitewater rafting, some offering better value. A two-hour ride down the Ocoee will cost at least $50 and probably more as the de-

Southeastern Tennessee

mand continues to far exceed the supply. Still, if you don't mind the crowds, the Ocoee offers an exciting and safe whitewater adventure.

Take Highway 64 east from Cleveland. Watch out for the signs advertising the rafting companies along the way. Don't turn in at the first one you see – take your time and shop around.

> *Competition means competitive pricing, and you might as well take advantage of it. After all, one rafting company is very much like another; all are licensed, all employ guides, and all observe certain safety standards. See page 331 for a listing.*

Shopping

Southeastern Tennessee offers a number of shopping options, most of them in the Chattanooga/Cleveland area. Chattanooga has four major shopping malls, as well as a burgeoning, revitalized downtown area. The largest mall, Hamilton Place, is just off I-75 on the north side of the city; Eastgate is a little further south off Brainard Road; Northgate is off Highway 153; and Warehouse Row, a converted commercial district now an outlet mall, is on Market Street just outside the downtown area. Chattanooga's downtown district has been pulled back from decay and is now a busy, thriving area where you can walk the streets, at least a couple of blocks or so, in relative safety.

■ Chattanooga

Hamilton Place Mall claims to be the largest mall in Tennessee. Inside you'll find such retail giants as Parisian, Sears, J.C. Penney and Proffitts, as well as a hundred or so smaller national chain outlets. Beyond and around the mall itself, **Hamilton Crossing** is a sprawling shopping district covering several hundred acres with numerous restaurants and fast-food outlets dotted around.

Eastgate and **Northgate** are smaller but no less popular versions of Hamilton Place. **Warehouse Row**, however, is unique. It has a sophisticated air about it. It is very clean and smells of expensive leather. The shops there are, for the most part, upscale factory outlets.

■ Cleveland

The City of Cleveland, too, just a few miles north up I-75, has a brand new mall. **Bradley Square** is on the north side of the city; take Exit 27 off the interstate and follow the road east until it becomes Paul Huff Parkway. You'll see the mall on your left.

Southeastern Tennessee

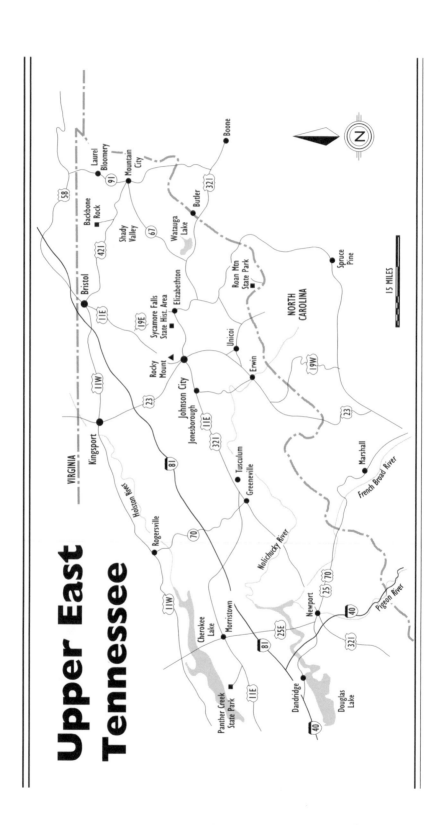

Upper East Tennessee

N

15 MILES

VIRGINIA

NORTH CAROLINA

Kingsport
Bristol
Rogersville
Johnson City
Jonesborough
Rocky Mount
Elizabethton
Sycamore Falls State Hist. Area
Unicoi
Erwin
Roan Mtn State Park
Shady Valley
Backbone Rock
Laurel Bloomery
Mountain City
Boone
Butler
Watauga Lake
Spruce Pine
Tusculum
Greeneville
Marshall
Cherokee Lake
Morristown
Panther Creek State Park
Dandridge
Newport
Douglas Lake

French Broad River
Pigeon River
Nolichucky River
Holston River

58
421
91
321
67
19E
11E
19W
23
321
11E
321
70
81
11W
25E
25
70
40
40
11E

Upper East Tennessee

Getting Around

Getting around in upper east Tennessee is quite easy. The area is well served by I-40 and I-81, and by such major highways as US 223, 34, 11 and 25. When in the mountains around Gatlinburg and Great Smoky Mountains National Park, however, remember that many of the roads are narrow, often twisting and turning without warning. When these become covered with ice and snow, as they almost always are in the early morning during the winter, they are extremely hazardous.

Sightseeing

■ Cherokee National Forest

This section of the forest has much to offer outdoor enthusiasts. The recreational facilities that follow are available for day and overnight use.

NOLICHUCKY RANGER DISTRICT

Camping is available at five locations: **Horse Creek, Houston Valley, Old Forge, Paint Creek** and **Round Recreation Areas**. For more details, see the *Camping Directory*, page 275.

Hiking is very popular in all sections of the forest and a large number of trails are described in detail in the *Adventures* section of this chapter.

There are extensive **boating** opportunities available throughout upper east Tennessee. Many of them are described in the *Adventures* section of this chapter.

Horseback riding can be done on seven designated horse trails totaling more than 25 miles. Horses may also be ridden on many of the region's roads, both open and closed.

Good **driving excursions** can be enjoyed along **Big Clifty Road** (Forest Service Road 404), which leads to the Meadow Creek Fire Tower; **Brush Creek Road** (FSR 209), which follows the French Broad River through White Oak Flats; **Hall Top Road** (FSR 207), which leads to the Hall Top Fire Tower; **Paint Creek Road** (FSR 41), and **Hurricane Gap Road** (FSR 31). These are the most popular scenic roads in the Nolichucky District, although all of them are gravel and subject to quite a lot of traffic during spring and fall.

Off-road vehicles may be driven at several spots within the district. Currently, the **Horse Creek ORV Road** (five miles) and **Round Knob ORV Road** (just over a mile) are open to the sport. In addition, the **Bullen Hollow Motorcycle Road** is open to ATVs and motorcycles (see *Adventures* section later in this chapter). For information, contact the District Office at ☎ 423-638-4108.

Canoeing, kayaking and tubing are all popular in this section of the forest. Both the **Nolichucky** and **French Broad Rivers** provide whitewater opportunities (see *Adventures* section, pages 117-118). Outfitters for the Nolichucky are based in Erwin, Tennessee; for the French Broad, you'll find several operators in Hot Springs, North Carolina (see page 331).

There are lots of great fishing opportunities on a variety of waters (see *Fishing* section, page 123).

UNAKA RANGER DISTRICT

Camping is offered at three locations: **Rock Creek, Limestone Cove** and **Dennis Cove**. See *Camping Directory* listings, starting on page 275, under Cherokee National Forest.

The Unaka Ranger District of the forest has more developed **hiking** trails than any of the other five districts. These range from the fairly easy to the downright difficult. Check *Hiking,* page 126 in the *Adventures* section, for full details.

Boating, canoeing, whitewater sports and fishing are all covered under *Adventures*, below.

WATAUGA RANGER DISTRICT

Camping is at five locations in Watauga: **Carden's Bluff, Backbone Rock, Jacob's Creek, Low Gap** and **Little Oak**. Check the *Camping Directory* listings under Cherokee National Forest.

This district offers more than 100 miles of developed **hiking** trails through some of the most beautiful country in the entire Smoky Mountain region. Check the *Hiking* section under *Adventures* for details.

More than 15,000 acres of water provide a variety of water-based recreational activities. For further details and descriptions, check under *Boating* in the *Adventures* section.

Horseback riding is offered on 25 miles of wilderness trails set aside for use by equestrians.

Off-road vehicles have access to nine miles of motorcycle and ATV trails, as well as more than 220 miles of Forest Service Roads.

■ Elizabethton

CARTER MANSION

Now the Carter County Courthouse, this old mansion marks the spot where the early pioneers formed the Watauga Association in 1772. Their constitution was the first to be adopted by independent Americans, and it united the people of eastern Tennessee during the War of Independence.

The house, once the home of John Carter, is more than 200 years old and retains the atmosphere of the times that made it famous. It has been preserved by its owners in almost pristine original condition and there is little evidence of restoration. The rooms are decorated with original wall coverings, the paneling, fireplaces and original paintings are all intact. The Carter Mansion, open weekdays from 9 am until 5 pm, is three miles north of Sycamore Shoals State Historic Area. ☎ 423-547-3850.

DOE RIVER COVERED BRIDGE

This bridge, set on the banks of the Doe River, was built in 1882. It's the oldest covered bridge still in use in the state, and is included in the National Registry of Historic Places. The very photo-

Upper East Tennessee

genic structure is in the small Riverside Park on Riverside Avenue in Elizabethton.

SYCAMORE SHOALS STATE HISTORIC AREA

Sycamore Shoals, a 47-acre park on the outskirts of Elizabethton, is famous for the historic events that took place in the area during the American War of Independence.

The park museum is filled with exhibits and artifacts that interpret the history of Elizabethton and eastern Tennessee. The reconstruction of the frontier Fort Watauga provides visitors with a unique day out that's just as interesting for adults as it is for kids. The fort has been reconstructed to faithfully portray the one that stood on the same spot in the early 18th century when the area was a part of the now defunct state of Franklin.

 It was at Fort Watauga that the mountain men of east Tennessee gathered in September, 1780, before heading out to fight the English at the battle of King's Mountain.

Facilities at the park are limited to day-use only, but there is a visitors center, along with the museum and a gift shop. There's also a boat ramp and river access for canoes to the Watauga River, a hiking trail, and a picnic area.

The park is on the city's west side on Highway 321. ☎ 423-543-5808.

■ Erwin

This little town, nestled in the heart of the Unaka Mountains, should have been named Ervin after a local doctor of that name, but a clerk in the US Postal Service misspelled the name and so Erwin it became.

NATIONAL FISH HATCHERY

Personnel at the hatchery extract some 18 million rainbow trout eggs each year for distribution to other hatcheries around the country. It's an interesting stop. The long tanks are filled with trout; the grounds are beautiful and include a picnic area; and the Erwin City Park, with a swimming pool, ball parks, tennis courts and nature trail, is just next door.

The hatchery, on Highway 23 in Erwin, is open daily throughout the year from 7:30 am until 4 pm.

UNICOI COUNTY HERITAGE MUSEUM

This neat museum is situated in what once was the home of the superintendent of the National Fish Hatchery. The house was built in 1903, but was abandoned when rising costs made living in it prohibitive. Today, the fine old house has been rescued and turned into a museum filled with artifacts and exhibits that interpret local history from Indian times through the Civil War, and on through the turn of the 20th century. A large exhibit called "Main Street" has made a row of small rooms into a tiny, turn-of-the-century street complete with apothecary, general store, post office, and a bank. The museum is on the grounds of the National Fish Hatchery on Highway 23 in Erwin. It's open daily from 1 until 5 pm, May through October. ☎ 423-743-9449.

■ Gatlinburg

No trip to the mountains would be complete without a visit to Gatlinburg, eastern Tennessee's answer to the mountain resorts of Europe. And resort it is. There's never a time when the streets aren't filled with people, sightseeing and shopping, or just wandering around enjoying the scenery and cool mountain air.

It's a pretty little town nestled in the heart of the mountains just to the south of Sevierville on Highway 71. Like all resorts, however, the emphasis in Gatlinburg is on making money. In places, the city is, or seems to be, a great city-within-a-city of time-share condominiums; in others, one catch-penny operation after another lines both sides of the streets. Set aside the glitz, however, and Gatlinburg becomes exactly what its founders intended it to be, a neat little mountain town full of interesting shops reminiscent of those found high in the alps of northern Germany.

True, it's jammed with traffic most of the time, and it's one of the most popular honeymoon spots in the nation, but it's also a good base from which to plan and set out upon your excursions into the mountains. Hotel rates, considering the area, aren't too bad, and there are many fine restaurants offering all sorts of cuisine, including German, Thai, French and Greek.

Fall and spring are the two seasons when people flock into the area to see the color. Other than that, you'll have to take your chances; there's never a quiet time in Gatlinburg.

CHRISTUS GARDENS

As wax museums go, Christus Gardens really is one of a kind. The exhibits are all religiously oriented and attract the devout in large numbers. They depict the Last Supper, the Good Samaritan, and many other biblical epics, including nine of Jesus' parables. The gardens, on River Road, are open daily from 8 am until 9 pm during the summer, and from 9 am until 5 pm, November through March. You'll pay a small entrance fee, but parking is free. ☎ 865-436-5155.

OBER GATLINBURG SKI RESORT & AMUSEMENT PARK

Snow is very much a winter item in the Smokies and, in order to extend a short season into a year-round attraction, the management at Ober Gatlinburg decided to build a resort that would attract not only the ski fraternity, but the general public as well. Today, this is a high-class fairground with all sorts of rides and amusements to keep you occupied and on-site for most of the day. You can get here either by driving to the top of Mount Harrison, or by taking the Aerial Tramway from the town center and riding high over the hills and valleys for more than 2½ miles to the mountaintop. Once there, you can spend the day skiing and enjoying the amusements.

From December through March you can ski on seven slopes and take skiing lessons at the Ski School. You can go ice skating in the arena, bungee jumping, or ride the Blue Cyclone Rapids in a boat. You can try your hand at motor racing around the go-kart track, or steer your little ones around the wonders of Kiddie-Land – a neat place where all the rides, ladders, chutes and slides are scaled down for the kids to enjoy. It even has a carousel, snowmobiles and a train.

Other than the obvious amusement-style attractions, there's plenty more for you to see and do, including dancing, a crafts market, and several restaurants.

The resort can be very busy. The best time to visit is on a weekday when most kids are in school.

The ski resort is open December through March; the amusement park is open year-round. Tram cars leave Gatlinburg every 20 minutes. ☎ 865-436-5423.

■ Great Smoky Mountains National Park

This, the busiest national park in the nation, draws almost 10 million visitors a year from all over the world. In the spring it's a vast expanse of meadow and forest where wildflowers bloom in profusion and fill the air with sweet smells. In summer, the mountain air is cooler and sweeter than it is in the valleys and on the plains. Fall turns the mountains into a spectacular show of color and brings more visitors to the park during a single two-week period than at any other time of the year. In winter, things tend to slow down a little as the roads become icy and often impassable, and the woodland turns into a stark, but beautiful, snowy wonderland of snow-bound trees, frozen lakes and deep drifts of white powder.

There are many ways to see the park: you can hike, ride a bicycle, take a guided tour, or you can do it the most popular way – drive around on your own.

ENTRY POINTS

There are three main entry points into the park: the North Carolina town of Cherokee, Gatlinburg, and the small mountain city of Townsend.

Cherokee

Cherokee is the capital of the Cherokee Nation in the east. A small city-cum-theme-park on the edge of the national park, it is one of the most important stops on any tour of the Great Smoky Mountains. The park entrance in Cherokee is well signposted, and most visitors arriving from eastern North Carolina enter here. Stop at the Oconoluftee Visitor Center for maps and brochures and then make your way to the Pioneer Farmstead, Mingus Mill and the

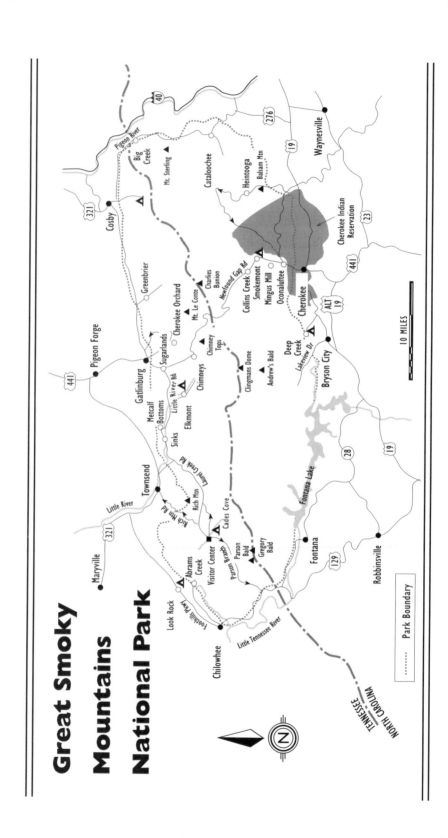

Great Smoky Mountains National Park

Maryville

Pigeon Forge

Cosby

Gatlinburg

Townsend

Chilowhee

Look Rock

Foothills Pkwy

Abrams Creek

Visitor Center

Cades Cove

Parson Branch

Parson Bald

Gregory Bald

Rich Mtn

Rich Mtn Rd

Little River

Laurel Creek Rd

Sinks

Metcalf Bottoms

Elkmont

Little River Rd

Chimneys

Sugarlands

Cherokee Orchard

Chimney Tops

Clingmans Dome

Andrew's Bald

Greenbrier

Mt. Le Conte

Charlies Bunion

Collins Creek

Newfound Gap Rd

Smokemont

Mingus Mill

Oconaluftee

Cherokee

Deep Creek

Lakeview Dr.

Bryson City

Fontana

Fontana Lake

Little Tennessee River

Robbinsville

Pigeon River

Big Creek

Mt. Sterling

Cataloochee

Heintooga

Balsam Mtn

Cherokee Indian Reservation

Waynesville

TENNESSEE

NORTH CAROLINA

N

10 MILES

321

441

321

441

40

276

19

23

441

ALT 19

28

19

129

········· Park Boundary

Smokemont Area. From there it's on to Clingmans Dome, 10 miles away.

Gatlinburg

This is where most people enter the park. In fact, more than five million people travel through Gatlinburg to the Sugarlands Visitor Center each year.

Sugarlands is, without doubt, the best place to start your visit to the park. The center can supply you with maps and brochures, and there are a number of interpretive exhibits to help you make the best of your tour.

From Sugarlands, you can either take Newfound Gap Road up the mountain, or turn right along Little River Road to Cades Cove, the most popular spot on the Smoky Mountain National Park Map. Either way, the ride is interesting, scenic, and, except for the traffic, delightful.

Townsend

This is the quietest entrance to the park. From Townsend the entry road leads to an intersection with Little River Road, and from there you can turn left to the Sugarland Visitor Center with Gatlinburg beyond, or turn right onto Laurel Creek Road and drive four miles to Cades Cove. The park entrance is well signposted and easy to find.

SCENIC DRIVES

Blue Ridge Parkway

When it reaches the vicinity of the Great Smoky National Park in Cherokee, North Carolina, this parkway is nearing its end. No matter, if you like scenic drives, there's no better one than this.

Cades Cove Road

Cades Cove, dealt with in some detail a little later in this section, page 98, is a large historic area of the greater park with a series of scenic roads winding through it. Of those, two stand out as worthy of mention here.

Parson Branch Road is an eight-mile drive that takes you out of the cove just beyond the Cable Mill Parking Area. It's one of the most scenic roads in Cades Cove, winding through stands of mountain laurel, pine and hardwood, to cross and re-cross the creek by way of several shallow fords. In the spring and fall, the road is a photographer's paradise. Unfortunately, it's closed to cars in winter, but there's no reason why you can't walk it, at least for a short distance.

Rich Mountain Road is the route taken by the residents of the cove when they moved from the park northwest to Maryville. It's a narrow, winding seven-mile ride that leads to Rich Mountain and the park boundary. Along the way you'll enjoy nice views of the old farmsteads. Lots to see and photograph here. This road is also closed in winter.

Cherokee to Fontana

This road is outside the park, but is worthy of mention here because its a very pretty route that takes you through the mountains of the Nantahala National Forest. The scenery is spectacular, and often wild.

Take Highway 19 through Bryson City to the junction with Highway 28. Follow 28 all the way to Fontana.

Warning: Highway 28 is an extremely winding road, probably not suitable for large RVs or those prone to car sickness.

Cherokee Orchard Road

A nice quiet drive of about four miles that takes you out of Gatlinburg into the country, through an old orchard, past old log buildings, and through new-growth forest. Great for photography. Take the Airport Road from Gatlinburg to Cherokee Orchard Road.

Clingmans Dome Road

This one is a must. The seven-mile drive takes you to a parking lot near the top of Clingmans Dome, where a paved, half-mile walking trail goes to the summit. There, you'll find an observation platform that offers spectacular views over the surrounding countryside. If you're a photographer, you won't want to miss this unique opportunity to capture on film the mountains as they are seen on postcards. The road, although closed in the winter, can be very busy, even jammed, on weekends during the spring, summer, and especially fall.

Foothills Parkway

There are two sections of this one road. The first, a scenic 17-mile drive takes you on a jaunt along the park perimeter between Townsend and Maryville, is highly recommended. The other, a drive of just six miles, connects I-40 to Highway 32.

To drive the scenic route, begin in Cades Cove by taking Parson Branch Road to Highway 129, then turn right onto the parkway. From there you'll drive to Look Rock, where you can take time out to enjoy the view over the mountains. Continue along the parkway to Highway 321, where it ends. From Look Rock to 321, the views are wonderful. The road could be closed during winter snows.

Little River Road

This is one of the two main routes through the park. It begins at the Sugarlands Visitor Center, takes you over Sugarlands Mountain and down to the Little River itself. From there, the road follows the river to Cades Cove. It's an 18-mile drive and the river, always beautiful and often spectacular, increases in volume as the road continues. Along the way you'll see a waterfall, rushing whitewater, and lots of beautiful backcountry views of the park.

Newfound Gap Road

This is actually US 441 and is the only road that will take you over the mountains from Gatlinburg to Cherokee, North Carolina. The drive is long, slow and winding. It is often extremely busy, especially during weekends in the fall when it might even stop moving altogether. If you can drive it one day during the week, however, you won't be disappointed. The views are spectacular and the mountain air sweet and heady.

You'll begin your drive at the Sugarlands Visitor Center and head east. Drive for five miles to the Chimneys Picnic Area, where you might like to stop for a snack or a short walk. At this point the road begins to climb very quickly.

Upper East Tennessee

The climb is so steep here that the engineers who built it had to employ a special technique called a "loopover" to make it passable. And loop over it does, for the road makes a great circle and loops over itself.

Once at the top, you'll find yourself at Newfound Gap, where President Franklin D. Roosevelt dedicated the park in 1940. The view from the top is magnificent. The mountains stretch off into the distance in all directions. This is a good time to stop for photographs, to relax and breathe in the cool mountain air before moving on into North Carolina.

You can turn around and head back down the road to the park, or you can continue on to Cherokee. Either way, it's all downhill from Newfound Gap. It's a mountain road – curvy, narrow, and extremely hazardous during the winter. Be careful.

Roaring Fork Motor Nature Road

This road is a photographer's paradise. Five miles of delightful driving take you from just outside Gatlinburg to Grotto Falls and back again. It follows the rushing waters of the creek – there are plenty of places to stop – through some of the prettiest woodland in the Smokies. Campers and motor homes are not permitted on this road. Unfortunately, this is another of those roads that can be extremely busy, especially in the fall.

Try to make the drive on a weekday. The road is closed during winter.

CADES COVE

Cades Cove, thought to have been named for Kate, the wife of a Cherokee Indian chief, is arguably the most popular section of the Great Smoky Mountains National Park; it's certainly the busiest.

Cades Cove is the historic section of the park and old buildings and farms are all situated on an 11-mile loop road. If you feel energetic, you might want to park the car, rent a bicycle, and pedal your way around (you can rent them at the campground store: see *Camping Directory*, page 275).

The white man came to Cades Cove in 1821. By 1851, the population had reached almost 700. It was a community encompassing more than 15,000 acres, several churches and a mill. Unfortunately, the numbers were too big and the land was unable to support them. Slowly, people began to drift away until, during the early part of this century, only a few were left. When the land became a National Park in 1936, the few remaining families were moved out of the area to the Tennessee city of Maryville. Today, the old farmhouses and buildings, empty and a little depressing, offer a look back across the years to the days when Cades Cove was a bustling rural community.

Always busy, Cades Cove is best visited early in the morning or late in the afternoon.

Try to avoid visiting over a weekend, especially during the fall when traffic is often nose to tail.

CATALOOCHEE

Located on the extreme eastern edge of the park in North Carolina, this is another old community, somewhat reminiscent of Cades Cove, but a little larger. At its peak, more than 1,200 souls lived, worked and died in Cataloochee. Today, all that's left is an old schoolhouse, a couple of barns and one or two houses. Cades Cove is a better stop on your tour but, if you happen to be in the area, Cataloochee is worth a visit.

MINGUS MILL

Also on the North Carolina side of the park is Mingus Mill, a fine example of a "tub mill." Rather than the large wheel-type operation we are all familiar with, this mill works by the action of a sort of turbine. It's quite sophisticated, and still in operation from May through October. You'll find it just off Newfound Gap Road near the park entrance.

OCONOLUFTEE PIONEER-FARMSTEAD

Also near the entrance to the park on the North Carolina side, not far from Mingus Mill on Newfound Gap Road, is this farmstead. Just as Cades Cove is the historic area in the Tennessee section of the park, so Oconoluftee serves as its counterpart in North Carolina. You'll find it interesting enough to warrant a visit, especially if you're making the scenic drive to the gap. The park staff puts on a series of interpretive demonstrations and exhibits from May through October.

ANIMALS IN THE PARK
Bears

You're quite likely to see bears wandering around the park during most of the tourist season. And, though they may seem tame, they aren't. Bears are extremely quick on their feet and can easily outrun a horse over a short distance. They have been known to attack interfering visitors. Bears are best seen at a distance, through binoculars, a long camera lens, or up close from the inside of a motor vehicle. Do not feed them. It makes them them lazy, but aggressive, and they lose their natural fear of humans. Plus, our food is not good for them.

Hikers often encounter bears and the bears have learned that the brightly colored packs contain tasty things to eat. If you do come across a hungry or inquisitive bear, it's best that you abandon your pack, returning to recover it only when the bear has finished dining.

On the whole, most bear encounters are pleasant. Attacks occur most often when cubs are involved and, unfortunately, the friendly little critters often wander off looking for fun. But where there's a bear cub, there's a mama bear nearby, and she will come roaring out of the undergrowth like a runaway train if you play with her babies.

Wild Hogs

These nasty but fascinating creatures were imported from Europe to stock hunting preserves in North Carolina. Unfortunately, the hogs got out of hand. Now they are prevalent in large numbers throughout the four national forests covered in this book, and are often seen in the park.

A wild hog can reach a staggering 400 lbs, has razor-sharp tusks, is extremely aggressive when cornered, and can easily kill large dogs and other animals. Fortunately, it's a nocturnal creature; it also has a keen sense of smell. A wild hog will always be aware of you before you are aware of it, and thus will stay well out of your way.

ACTIVITIES IN THE PARK

Bicycling

The Great Smoky Mountains National Park is not the place for bicycling. Bikes are not allowed on any of the woodland trails; and the traffic is so heavy on the roads, where bicycles are allowed, that riding can be hazardous.

Camping

Camping is very popular here. There are 10 campgrounds within the park boundaries. Seven of them are considered to be "developed" and have at least some facilities: fresh water, flush toilets, tables and picnic grills. Unfortunately, there are no showers or utility hookups. Three of the campgrounds are considered "primitive," offering only the basics: fresh water and pit toilets. The fee for a night camping at one of the developed campgrounds is $8 and your stay will be limited to seven days. For more details and a complete listing of Great Smoky Mountains National Park campgrounds, check the *Camping Directory* at the back of the book.

Backcountry camping is very much an outdoor experience. Many died-in-the-wool enthusiasts say it is second to none. There are more than 100 sites within the park's bounds, although locations are often changed to minimize damage to the environment. Most sites can accommodate up to eight people. Stays are limited to three days at each site and you'll need to make a reservation (see *Camping Directory*).

Commercial Campgrounds: There are many privately owned campgrounds close to the park. Some are small and offer little more than the basic hookups; others seem like resorts and offer everything from Olympic-size swimming pools to fine dining. You'll find some of them listed in the *Camping Directory*.

Fishing

Fishing is a another major pastime, not just in the park, but throughout most of eastern Tennessee and western North Carolina. There are more than 7,600 miles of creeks and streams in the park alone, and four major lakes border the park.

Upper East Tennessee

You can expect to find smallmouth and largemouth bass in the lakes, along with bluegill, crappie, sauger, walleye and catfish. In the mountain streams within the park you may find rock bass, along with a variety of trout, including brook, rainbow and brown. You cannot keep brook trout.

BAG LIMITS: The daily limit for fish caught in the park, in any combination, is five. Trout must be at least seven inches long.

LICENSES: If you are over 16, you will need a valid license for the state in which you intend to fish, either Tennessee or North Carolina. If you fish on the Cherokee Indian Reservation in North Carolina, you'll need a license issued there too. Licenses can be purchased at many country stores and bait shops in both states, or at any local tax office, but not in the park.

Local Fishing Rules

- Natural bait is not allowed in the park.
- One hand-held rod is allowed per person.
- Fishing is permitted year-round from dawn to dusk.
- A trout stamp is not required for fishing in the park.

Hiking

Most major hiking trails and popular hiking destinations are covered in some detail in the *Hiking* section under *Adventures* below (page 131). Be aware that it's possible to get well and truly lost, even within the park. Take all the usual precautions. Buy a good topographical map, and obtain a trail guide from the National Park Service.

DAY HIKING: Even if you have only a short time to spend, hiking is the only way to experience the park properly. There are many short hikes and walks that are well worth the effort. They, too, are listed in the *Hiking* section.

Horseback Riding

Horseback riding is always popular with visitors to the Great Smoky Mountains, although it is somewhat limited. There are a number of equestrian trails, but the Park Service contends that horses do a great deal of damage to the trails, so certain rules must be followed.

You can bring your own horse, but there are no lodging facilities inside the park.

Renting is encouraged by the Park Service. They require that qualified guides are present with each party to ensure the rules are followed. Several companies provide service to visitors. You'll find them listed under *Horseback Riding* in the *Great Smoky Mountains National Park* section of the *Information Directory* at the back of the book (page 328).

Picnicking

You can picnic anywhere, provided you don't cause an obstruction, but there are nine popular picnic areas within the park boundaries – **Cades Cove, Collins Creek, Cosby, The Chimneys, Deep Creek, Greenbrier, Heintooga, Look Rock**, and **Metcalf Bottoms**. All have picnic tables and grills, as well as restrooms.

The Chimneys, five miles from Sugarlands Visitor Center, is open all year. The other are closed from December through March.

■ Greeneville

The heart of Tennessee's tobacco industry, Greeneville is a neat little town on the western edge of the Great Smoky Mountains. It's a typical small Tennessee country town with a shopping center, hospital, a couple of hotels and several nice restaurants. It offers some special attractions worthy of a mention and a visit.

ANDREW JOHNSON NATIONAL HISTORIC SITE

You can tour the tailor shop where Andrew Johnson worked during the years when he wasn't in politics. Inside, you'll see the tools he used, his work table and a number of personal artifacts and other memorabilia.

Two of the houses where Johnson lived are also a part of the site. The first is not open to the public – you can peek in through the windows, though. It is just across the street from the Greeneville Visitor Center. The second, where Johnson lived from 1851 until his death, is just down the street and is open to the public. The house has been restored to its original condition and offers a look at what life must have been like for an aging and disgraced ex-president of the United States.

Andrew Johnson

Andrew Johnson became a public figure during the Civil War. As senator from Tennessee, he refused to resign his seat when the state seceded from the Union; instead he worked to preserve the Union. Johnson was Lincoln's running mate in the 1864 presidential election, which Lincoln, of course, won. Johnson's time came when he succeeded Abraham Lincoln as president upon Lincoln's assassination. Charges of impeachment were brought against Johnson by the House of Representatives because his Reconstruction policies were bitterly opposed. The impeachment was defeated by a vote in the Senate of 35 for and 16 against – 36 votes were needed to uphold it.

The cemetery and the Johnson gravesite is one block south of West Main Street.

The site is open daily from 9 am until 5 pm. ☎ 423-638-3503.

DAVY CROCKETT BIRTHPLACE STATE PARK

Beyond the coonskin hat, Old Betsy (his musket), and his ignominious end at the Alamo, Davy Crockett was also a three-term congressman and an author. He made a great contribution to his native state of Tennessee, and to the expansion of the American frontier. The original cabin where his family lived and where he was born is long gone, but an authentic replica is found on the banks of the Nolichucky River in Greene County. It is located in a state park dedicated to his memory.

Davy Crockett was born on the banks of the river near the mouth of Limestone Creek in 1786. In the mid-1950's, spurred on by the enthusiasm generated for the famous backwoodsman by the TV series *King of the Wild Frontier*, the Davy Crockett Birthplace Association built and furnished this replica of the log cabin in which Crockett was supposedly born. Then they developed the three-acre site into a park, which they presented to the state in 1973. Historical inaccuracies, among other things, however, caused the Department of Conservation to dismantle the cabin and rebuild it. The new construction is a more accurate reflection of the original.

In 1976 more land was added to the already popular park and, today, the facilities have been extended to include a visitor center, a modern, well-developed campground (see *Camping Directory*), three picnic pavilions, many scenic picnic areas with tables and grills conveniently located around the park, boat access to the river, a hiking trail and a swimming pool.

The park and Davy Crockett Cabin are open daily from 8 am to 10 pm. Davy Crocket Birthplace, Route 3, Box 103A, Limestone, TN 37681. ☎ 423-257-2167.

The park is 3½ miles off US 11E near Limestone, Tennessee.

■ Jonesborough

This little town just off Highway 11E, close to I-81 in northeast Tennessee, is the state's oldest community, founded in 1779. It's only been during the last few years, however, that local residents have acknowledged that fact. For centuries it was a sleepy backcountry town where nothing much ever happened. Now, after a flurry of activity, Jonesborough is coming to life. The old buildings have been restored. Businesses have become tourist-oriented. And the little city now welcomes visitors with open arms.

Today, you'll find a modern and efficient visitor center where you can obtain brochures and maps, most of them free, and a large staff ready and willing to help. The many old buildings and attractions in and around the downtown area can easily be seen in a couple of hours; you'll even have time to stop for some breakfast or lunch. Most of the interesting sites are centered along the main street, but you'll also find a number of unique shops and craft stores on the tiny side streets. For more information, contact the Jonesborough Visitor Center, PO Box 375, Jonesborough, TN 37659. ☎ 423-753-5961.

■ Knoxville

Although Knoxville is a little farther west than is commonly associated with the Great Smoky Mountains, there are a couple of attractions worth mentioning, as well as two of the finest shopping malls in eastern Tennessee.

BIG RIDGE STATE PARK

This is one of Tennessee's finest parks, offering a wide range of recreational activities and more than 3,600 acres of scenic and heavily forested parkland. It's easy to escape here, if only for an hour or two, into the natural refuge of the great outdoors without ever leaving civilization too far behind.

The park was one of five joint ventures between the Tennessee Valley Authority, the National Park Service, and the Civilian Conservation Corps that were developed for public recreation on the shores of several TVA lakes. Big Ridge State Park lies on the southern shore of TVA's Norris Lake.

Picnicking facilities are provided at three separate sites, all with tables, grills and playgrounds for the children. There are three pavilions, also with tables and grills, available for large groups. The pavilions may be reserved through the park office.

The park features some 15 miles of backpacking, hiking and nature trails that meander through the park and surrounding woodlands. They offer an opportunity to observe many species of wild birds, native plants, wildflowers, and animals.

Popular activities include nature study, bird watching and photography. And, for the visitor who might need a little help and instruction, the Park Service offers a variety of planned daily activities for all the family in summer, including guided hikes, arts and crafts, nature programs, field sports, and campfire programs.

Camping is also a major part of what Big Ridge has to offer, as are fishing and boating on Norris Lake. Canoes, paddleboats, and flat-bottomed rowboats are available for rent, and visitors may use their own electric trolling motors. Gasoline-powered outboards are not permitted. There's a large sandy beach for swimming and sunbathing open from Memorial Day through Labor Day, and there's a concrete-bottomed, shallow area for the children. There's also a diving area with two diving stands: one at nine feet high, the other at three feet. Lifeguards are on duty during swimming hours (10-5:30).

Big Ridge State Park, Maynardville, TN 37807. ☎ 865-992-5523.

The park is approximately 25 miles north of Knoxville, on State Highway 61, 12 miles east of I-75.

KNOXVILLE ZOO

As the premier zoo in eastern Tennessee, this one competes with the very best. Hundreds of wild and exotic animals live in well-kept surroundings that are as natural as they can be within the confines of a major metropolitan city. The list of species is far too extensive to include, but those that warrant special mention include snow leopards, Bengal tigers, lions, white rhinoceros, hippos, yak, elephants, red pandas, and polar bears. There are also a number of wily primates, including long-tailed macaques, mandrills and, of course, the chimps. There's also a petting zoo, where the kids can get up close with the animals. If you have to go out of your way to visit the Knoxville Zoo, you should do it. You won't be disappointed.

The zoo is open all year except Christmas Day. Admission is $9.95 for adults, or $5.95 for senior citizens and children aged three to 12.

From downtown Knoxville, take I-40 east toward Asheville and follow the signs.

■ Morristown

PANTHER CREEK STATE PARK

Panther Creek, 1,440 acres of lush park land six miles west of the city of Morristown, is named for the nearby Panther Creek Springs, a landmark of pioneer times. The signature feature of the park is a 1,460-foot-long ridge that provides a spectacular panoramic view of the East Tennessee Ridge and Valley region. The park is a hotspot for naturalists and bird watchers, who come to admire the birds of prey and migrating waterfowl.

Other popular activities include fishing, swimming, and boating on the lake, hiking the many miles of backcountry trails, camping (see *Camping Directory*) and picnicking. The park is open during the summer months from 8 am until 10 pm; until sundown during the winter.

Panther Creek State Park, 2010 Panther Creek Road, Morristown, TN 37814. ☎ 423-723-5073.

Panther Creek is west of I-81, off Highway 11E.

PIGEON FORGE

Pigeon Forge discovered tourism quite a few years ago but, for a while at least, it remained very much as it had been for several centuries, a small country town in the foothills of the Great Smoky Mountains and poor sister to nearby Gatlinburg. It wasn't until

Upper East Tennessee

the 1970s that local entrepreneurs suddenly realized that anyone visiting Gatlinburg and the Great Smoky Mountains National Park had to go through Pigeon Forge to get there. The major portion of the 10 million visitors who came to the mountains each year were regarded as a self-renewing resource that couldn't be ignored; it was a gold rush of major proportions.

At first, the attractions built to waylay visitors were garish and audacious, but they did stop traffic. In recent years, however, Pigeon Forge has toned down its image and become a little more sophisticated in its approach, although no less commercial. And it does have a lot to offer.

The Old Mill

Built in 1830 to process grain from around the area, the mill is a picture-postcard example of its type, and one of the most photographed attractions in the entire Smoky Mountain region. It stands just off the road by the water's edge, its great wheel still turning, and its ancient machinery still grinding out more than a dozen types of meal and flour. Inside, you can visit the shop to purchase flour and souvenirs, and see the old machinery in action. The mill, open daily March through November, is just off the main street toward the south end of town. ☎ 423-453-4628.

Pigeon Forge Pottery

Here you can see local potters at work and buy their products in the shop. The pottery is near the Old Mill just off Highway 441. Open daily from 8 am until 6 pm. ☎ 423-453-3883.

Dollywood

The shining star in Pigeon Forge's firmament, Dollywood is a theme park of major proportions. Obviously, carrying the famous name of Dolly Parton that it does, the park has a strong country music theme. But that's not all there is. You'll find carnival rides, sideshows and games, and a variety of craftspeople making and selling their goods, along with live shows of country and bluegrass music and several seasonal festivals.

Dollywood is just off Highway 441 at the southern end of the town. ☎ 423-428-9488.

■ Rugby

This historic site is all that's left of a dream, and one of the last American colonies. It came about as a result of one man's abhorrence of the old, upper-class British tradition that required a gentleman's entire estate to be inherited by the eldest son. Nothing at all was left to younger sons, who were expected to take up a "gentlemanly" profession, such as the law or church, or they were meant to exist on handouts from the inheriting elder brother. Manual labor for the sons of gentlemen was deeply frowned upon and would bring disgrace to the rest of the family.

Thomas Hughes, the English author of Tom Brown's School Days, felt that the system was deplorable, and he determined to do something about it; the result was Rugby. Hughes founded the town in 1880 as a refuge for aristocrats far away from the disapproving eyes of Victorian, upper-class society.

But these were no men for the rugged life on what was, even in those late days, still a frontier. The colony failed. Today, 17 of the old buildings have been restored for you to explore. Some are private homes that open only during the annual Rugby pilgrimage, a festival when many private homes in the historic district are open to the public, held during the first weekend in August; the other buildings are open to the public year-round. ☎ 423-628-2441.

■ Sevierville

This small town is on Highway 441 just northwest of Pigeon Forge and Gatlinburg. It serves as the gateway to the commercial side of the Great Smoky Mountains. There's not much to see; it's just a little too far away from the action, but its magnificent county courthouse is worthy of mention. The old building features an unusual design and a clock tower that dominates the town. The courthouse is open Monday through Friday during normal business hours.

THE FORBIDDEN CAVERNS

These are Sevierville's other claim to fame. Typical of commercial caverns and caves, they have been worked to accommodate large numbers of visitors. Unlike some, however, man's intrusion has been kept to a minimum. Once used by local Indians and moonshiners, the caves have some unusual rock formations, including a large section of onyx on one of the walls. Lighting is tasteful and subdued, and the experience is one you'll enjoy. Open daily from April through November, the caverns are just a few miles outside Sevierville going east on Tennessee Highway 8.

■ Townsend

This quaint little country town is one of the three gateways into the Great Smoky Mountains National Park and, even though it sees more than its fair share of tourists, it remains very much unspoiled. Although the influence of so many visitors can be seen and felt almost everywhere, tourism has been kept as low-key as possible. Neat shops and good country cooking, with one or two special attractions on the side, are what Townsend is all about.

TUCKALEECHEE CAVERNS

Tuckaleechee has been maintained very much in its natural state. The formations are only slightly illuminated with natural color. The cave, estimated to be between 20 and 30 million years old, is reached by way of a 200-foot winding stairway from the visitor center.

It took 10 men more than four years to build the concrete steps and walk-ways. Vast amounts of raw materials were carried down the stairs and then mixed by hand with water carried from the underground river, also by hand.

The tour is taken in two sections. The first half takes you from the foot of the stairs along a narrow concrete walk-way to what the owners call the "Big Room," an understatement if ever there was one.

The Big Room is more than 400 feet long, 300 feet wide, and 150 feet from floor to ceiling (Mammoth Cave in Kentucky is only 120 feet high). It is one of the largest, single cave rooms in the eastern United States. The great cavern contains some of the finest examples of stalactite, stalagmite, drapery, helictite, calcite, and palette formations in the world. Two stalagmites alone stand more than 24 feet tall.

From the Big Room, you return the way you came to the foot of the spiral staircase, and from there you continue on along the concrete walkways to Silver Falls. Although you can't see the full extent of the falls, they cascade down through the mountain some 200 feet into a crystal-clear river – yes, you can drink it – that teems with rainbow trout.

The attraction can become very crowded during the summer season, especially on weekends and holidays, and tour groups often fill the place. Try to visit during the week if you can. The tour lasts about an hour and costs $6.95 for adults and $3.95 for children. Be sure to take your camera and flash unit.

Tuckaleechee Caverns are just outside Townsend on the edge of the Great Smoky Mountains National Park. Take I-75 south from Knoxville for 15 miles, then take Exit 73, go east through Maryville to Townsend and follow the signs.

■ Tri-Cities

The Tri-Cities area of upper eastern Tennessee comprises the three sister towns of Bristol, Kingsport and Johnson City. They make up the fifth largest metropolitan area in the state and, as such, have quite a lot to offer in the way of attractions and shopping.

BRISTOL

Bristol straddles the Virginia-Tennessee state line in an elevated region just off the Blue Ridge. It's a scenic city, old and historic, where the people are friendly and the surrounding countryside spectacular.

Although it's essentially a single city located in two states, Bristol has all the signs of being two cities. In 1881, both sides of the town agreed to accept the center of the city's main street, known today as State Street, as the Tennessee-Virginia state line, and brass markers down the center of the street clearly indicate the division.

The Birthplace of Country Music

Bristol is widely recognized as the birthplace of country music. In 1927, Ralph Peer of the Victory Talking Machine Company established a recording studio in Bristol. That studio launched the careers of Jimmy Rogers, The Stonemans and the Carter family. What was then known as Appalachian folk music soon became the country music we know today.

Bristol Caverns

These caverns were carved from the virgin rock by a mighty underground river more than 200 million years ago. The river, its great force spent, remains a shallow, tinkling, underground creek that teams with tiny fish and meanders quietly through the darkness where once it roared like a great tornado. Evidence of its cataclysmic force can still be seen in the scars and gouges scoured into the rock face.

The cave has been maintained in its natural state. Entrance is made through a natural opening in the mountain, and from there the trail leads downward and inward. The way is illuminated, but barely; no colored lights have been used.

The formations here are unique. The cave contains several rare examples of palette, stalactite, stalagmite, and flowstone rocks. True to commercial form, these have been given fancy names: Bridal Veil Falls is a giant palette that stretches almost from floor to ceiling; the Zoo is a flowstone formation that seems to feature dozens of different animals, gathered together two-by-two, reduced, and then frozen in stone.

Bristol Caverns are open daily from 9 am until 6 pm through the summer, and from 11 am until 4 pm, November through March 14.

From Bristol, go northeast on I-81 to Virginia Exit 2. Take Highway 421 east, drive for about six miles, then follow the signs.

Bristol City International Raceway

The raceway is a member of the National Association for Stock Car Auto Racing Tracks, and lays claim to the world's fastest half-mile. Each year the management presents a number of race meetings, including legs of the Winston Cup Championship. The raceway is eight miles south of Bristol on Highway 11E. ☎ 615-764-1161 for information and racing schedules.

JOHNSON CITY

In 1854, David Johnson arrived in what is now the Tri-Cities area and set about building the town he named for himself. Johnson was the first postmaster, depot agent, merchant, hotel keeper and magistrate, all at the same time. In 1869 when the city received its charter, Johnson also became the first mayor.

East Tennessee State University

ETSU, as it's known locally, is perhaps the centerpiece of Johnson City. Its main claim to fame, other than the excellent quality of its education, is the Memorial Center, an indoor football stadium capable of seating more than 12,000 people. ☎ 423-929-4352.

Carroll Reece Museum

Located on the campus of ETSU, this museum has a number of permanent art exhibits, Appalachian crafts and historical artifacts. ☎ 423-929-4392.

Tipton-Haynes Living History Farm

This state-owned historical site and working farm offers a peek into the lives of the two families that once lived there. For more than 200 years they worked the land, through one war after another. The farm buildings, now restored to their pre-Civil War appearance, are open to the public.

The farm is just off Highway 23 south of the city. It is open on weekdays from 10 am until 6 pm, and from 2 until 6 pm on weekends.

Upper East Tennessee

KINGSPORT

Hanging an Elephant

Kingsport has a somewhat dubious claim to fame. It was in 1916 that an elephant by the name of Mary, part of a visiting circus, killed two people. And the people of the city demanded justice. The poor elephant was put on trial forthwith and, and after due process, was found guilty as charged. The beast was then sentenced to death for its crimes. But that was not the end of the story. Elephants are tough creatures, and five pistol shots had little effect on the animal. A great debate ensued, and it was decided to transport the unfortunate beast to the nearby town of Erwin where, in the railway yards, it would be hung to death from a large crane. Large numbers of people turned out to see the execution. Mary was duly dispatched. Erwin and Kingsport have yet to live down their ignominious reputations.

Kingsport is an industrial city and home to such commercial giants as Eastman Kodak and Mead Paper. The commercial center of the Tri-Cities, it's a busy little place where the advantages brought by the advent of big business and big money have not come without cost: dirt, pollution and a new shopping mall led to the demise of the downtown shopping district. With one small exception, the downtown district is still something of a wasteland. Efforts are being made to revitalize it, but there is still a long way to go before it becomes the pleasant shopping area that is the vision of many local residents and business owners.

Kingsport also has several nearby attractions.

Bays Mountain Park

This 3,000-acre facility is perhaps one of the finest city parks in Tennessee. It is a nature preserve and outdoor education center where the environment and local ecology is top priority. It's not a recreational area in the true sense of the word, although it is a great place to go for a few hours of quiet walking on the park's many miles of hiking and nature trails.

You'll find no boat ramps or swimming beaches on the lakeshore, nor will you see concession stands or soft drink machines. What you will find is a planetarium, a museum, and thousands of acres of beautiful countryside set aside against the overflow of urban expansion and industrial exploitation that was in full swing in the Tri-City area only a few years ago.

The park is on Highway 23. Just go south from Kingsport and follow the signs. ☎ 423-245-4195.

Warrior's Path State Park

Warrior's Path, on the shores of Fort Patrick Henry Lake, is one of the most scenic recreational areas in Tennessee's state park system. The park is named for the ancient war paths and trading trails used by the Cherokee Indians in pioneer times. Today, activities here are largely water-related, but more than nine miles of hiking trails wind their way through the scenic woodland glades and up Holston Bluffs to Devils Backbone for breathtaking views of the surrounding countryside. The neighboring forests and the rolling hills and valleys provide habitats for a good number of woodland creatures, wild birds, and plant life.

Facilities at the park include a campground (see *Camping Directory*), an 18-hole golf course, a marina, several picnic areas, and overnight facilities for horses. Outdoor recreational activities include fishing, hiking, tennis, bicycling and horseback riding.

The fishing at Warrior's Path is claimed to the best in upper east Tennessee, and many fine catches of largemouth, smallmouth, and white bass, rainbow trout, crappie, bluegill, catfish, muskie, and walleye have been recorded at Fort Patrick Henry Lake.

The park is open from 8 am until 10 pm. Warrior's Path State Park, PO Box 5026, Kingsport, TN 37663. ☎ 423-239-8531.

The park is on State Route 36. From I-81 take Exit 59.

The Netherland Inn

Once an important overnight stop for travelers in the 19th century, the Netherland is now something of a museum and interpretive exhibit in its own right. You can tour the old inn, take in its restored living quarters and one-time guest rooms, or visit the old stables and slave quarters. At the wharf you'll see an example of a

Upper East Tennessee

flatboat like the ones used on the river when Kingsport was, in fact, the King's Port.

The inn is on Netherland Inn Road, and is open in the afternoons, Wednesday through Sunday, from May through October. ☎ 423-246-2662 or 423-247-3211.

■ Roan Mountain

At an elevation of more than 6,200 feet, Roan Mountain is one of the highest peaks in the eastern United States. The park is surrounded by Cherokee National Forest, more than 700,000 acres of dense, unspoiled woodland in eastern Tennessee.

Roan Mountain's signature attraction is its 700-acre rhododendron park high atop the mountain. During early summer the garden sets the entire mountaintop ablaze with color. It's a natural spectacle of unbelievable beauty that must be seen to be believed.

Roan Mountain Park restaurant can seat up to 50 persons and is open for breakfast, lunch, and dinner. There are camping facilities, a visitors center and museum, a gift shop, tennis courts, several picnic areas with tables and grills, and a playground. More than four miles of hiking trails meander around the park. Some lead upward to the peak of Roan Mountain, others follow the mountain streams or the banks of the Doe River.

Activities here include hiking, nature study and bird watching, picnicking, camping and, especially during the rhododendron flowering season, photography. Cross-country skiing is a popular sport during the winter. There are three well-developed ski trails to suit all skill levels. During the summer months a qualified park naturalist offers guided tours, campfire programs, slide shows, and demonstrations.

Annual special events at the park include the Carter County Wildflowers Tours and Bird Walks in May, the Rhododendron Festival in June, and the Roan Mountain Naturalist Rally in September.

Roan Mountain State Park, Route 1, Box 236, Roan Mountain, TN 37687. ☎ 423-772-3303. The park is open all year from 8 am until 10 pm daily. It is on the Tennessee-North Carolina border, off Highway 19E on State Highway 143.

Adventures

■ Antiquing

This region of Tennessee, the oldest inhabited area, offers a great many opportunities for antique hunting. The villages nestled amid the mountains abound with all sorts of stores full of bric-a-brac, antique furniture, jewelry and decorative art. There's something new around every corner and at the end of every side street. In the country, almost every side road sports a small, hand-lettered sign pointing the way to an old, converted house or barn full of dusty treasures.

Gatlinburg, of course, offers the greatest selection – Main Street has dozens of antique stores – but Bristol, Johnson City, Townsend and Greeneville also have a lot to offer.

■ Boating & Canoeing

As in southeastern Tennessee, this upper eastern section of the state offers a great many opportunities for those who like to spend time on the water.

FRENCH BROAD RIVER

From Douglas Lake for more than 35 miles to the North Carolina border, French Broad River is one long stretch of recreational water. It has more public boat ramps than you'd care to count; Douglas Lake alone, a vast expanse that interrupts the flow of the river from Knoxville, has more than 20.

The river has been designated a canoe trail, with difficulty ratings from Class I to III, beginning at the Highway 70 bridge near Hot Springs in North Carolina and then heading out through miles of pastoral and woodland scenery to Douglas Lake. The take-out is at Rankin Bridge on Douglas Lake, or at other sites along the way.

HOLSTON RIVER

The Holston is over two miles wide in places, more lake than river, in the 40-mile stretch between Jefferson City and Rogersville. Over 40 public ramps provide access to the great river and its tiny, wooded islands, grassy banks and riverside meadows. Popular

Upper East Tennessee

though it often is, the Holston has room enough for everyone, and you will sometimes go for miles with only an occasional glimpse of other boaters in the distance.

LITTLE RIVER

From a put-in at the Webb Road bridge to a take-out point more than 16 miles away at the Highway 411 bridge, the Little River is a designated canoe trail of outstanding natural beauty. You'll have to take your canoe out of the water to bypass a couple of dams, but the overall experience is well worth the extra effort. Scenery along this route is often breathtaking.

NOLICHUCKY RIVER

Public access to the Nolichucky is not as readily available as it is on the French Broad and Holston rivers, but you will find a couple of ramps at the Davy Crockett Birthplace State Park, and there are several more on Davy Crockett Lake some 15 miles southwest of the park and eight miles south of Greeneville on Highway 70. The 15 miles of river from the park to Davy Crockett Lake have been designated a canoe trail. The put-in is at the park, the take-out at the Nolichucky Dam. You can, however, continue to the confluence with the French Broad River at Douglas Lake.

PIGEON RIVER

This is a canoeist's dream. For more than 22 miles, from the Walters Powerhouse, at Hartford on I-40 south of Newport, all the way to Douglas Lake on the French Broad River, the Pigeon surges along through Class III to Class V waters (see page 43 for chart). It often takes the form of whitewater and roaring rapids, flowing through the mountains and under rocky cliffs. This is not a river for the faint-hearted; only experienced canoeists should attempt it.

SOUTH FORK OF THE HOLSTON & BOONE LAKE

More a lake than a river, the South Fork is accessed by Highway 421 from Bristol. There are more than a dozen public access ramps within a two-mile radius of the Highway 421 bridge, and there are a number of marinas offering all sorts of services, as well as fishing and boating supplies.

At the western end of the South Fork is Boone Lake, one of the most picturesque bodies of water in Tennessee, especially in the fall. Boone, on the South Fork north of its confluence with the Watauga River, is one of the most popular boating locations in the area.

On weekends, you'll find the number of craft on the water a little disconcerting but, if you persevere and head up the river, the traffic lessens.

Boone Lake is accessed most easily from I-81 and Warrior's Path State Park. There are also more than 20 public access ramps at various spots off Highways 36, 11E and 75.

For the canoeist, a 26-mile section of the South Fork has been designated a Class I canoe trail. The put-in is at South Holston Dam at Emmett, just off Highway 421 west of the South Fork; take-out is just off Hamilton Road in Holston.

WATAUGA RIVER & LAKE

For more than 40 miles the Watauga winds its way through the countryside from Boone Lake in the north to Watauga Lake in the southeast. Along the way there are a number of public access ramps, most on the two lakes themselves, but there are a few at Flourville just off Highway 36, and at Austin Springs off 11E.

For canoeists, 19 miles of the river offer Class I and II paddling for most of the way. Put in just below the Wilber Dam at Siam and take out at the end of Carroll Creek in Austin Springs on Highway 11E. As you go, you'll enjoy some great scenery, especially in October when the fall colors are at their best. The route will take you through woodlands of varying density, farmland, meadowland, and Sycamore Shoals State Park.

■ Camping

There are a great many campgrounds in this region, especially in the Gatlinburg and Great Smoky Mountains National Park areas. Most of them are commercial, some are at state parks, and still more are located in the national park itself. For a full listing and individual descriptions, check the *Camping Directory* at the back of the book.

■ Craft Hunting

 Upper east Tennessee is the home of country crafting. Wherever you go you'll find craft shops, roadside stalls, craft malls and even a number of private homes where you can purchase homemade crafts of every description from dolls to furniture, and from jewelry to musical instruments. If that's not enough, there seems to be a craft festival or fair going on somewhere every week of the year.

GATLINBURG

Arrowmont School For Arts & Crafts draws its students from all over the country. Their products, as well as those of more than 150 full-time crafts people, are sold through the Arrowcraft Shop. The shop is on the parkway. ☎ 423-436-4604.

Dave's Dulcimer Shop is a unique outlet where you can watch dulcimers being made and listen to dulcimer music as it can be played only in the Great Smoky Mountains. It's on Highway 73 just two miles east of Gatlinburg. ☎ 423-436-7461.

Great Smoky Mountain Arts & Crafts Community is a colony of artists and crafts people, more than 40 of them, who live along Glade Springs Road to the north of Gatlinburg and work from their homes. It's a remarkable little community where you can find all sorts of interesting and unusual items; the prices aren't bad either.

Craft Fairs In Gatlinburg

Annual Easter Craft Show: Easter weekend at Gatlinburg Convention Center. Free admission. ☎ 423-671-3600.

Summer Fair: July in Gatlinburg Convention Center. Free admission. ☎ 423-436-7479.

Fall Fair: October at the Gatlinburg Convention Center. Free admission. ☎ 423-436-7479.

Annual Christmas Craft Show: Thanksgiving weekend in Gatlinburg Convention Center. ☎ 423-671-3600.

Annual 12 Days Of Christmas Craft Show: First two weeks in November at the Gatlinburg Convention Center. ☎ 423-671-3600.

Craft fairs are also held in July and August. Call the Chamber of Commerce for full information at ☎ 423-436-4178.

■ Fishing

CHEROKEE LAKE

 The lake is actually a large section of the Holston River that runs almost 30 miles from Jefferson City to Rogersville. The Holston is covered in detail on page 123.

BOONE LAKE

Boone Lake is really a section of the Watauga and South Fork of the Holston rivers just north of Johnson City. It's a popular haunt of the boating community and can become very busy at times, especially on summer weekends.

The fishing is said to be very good to excellent, with a wide variety of fish, including four species of bass, bluegill, crappie, walleye and catfish. There are at least 20 public access ramps into the waters of Watauga, and they are easily found from Highway 36 going north from Johnson City; Highway 11E, also going north from Johnson City, and from Highways 357 and 75 that connect I-81 to the northern side of the lake.

CLINCH RIVER

The Clinch is the northernmost river covered in this book. In places it more resembles a lake than it does a river. At its widest point, south of Tazwell, Tennessee, it's more than a mile wide. The fishing is good to very good, and you can expect to catch smallmouth, largemouth, spotted and white bass, bluegill, crappie and catfish. There are a dozen or so public boat ramps, all centered on and around the bridge on Highway 33. This is a much quieter river than are those farther to the south. From Knoxville, take Highway 33 north.

Upper East Tennessee

DOUGLAS LAKE

Douglas Lake is a vast expanse of water on the French Broad River east of Knoxville and west of Newport. The lake, very popular with the boating crowd, can become busy during the summer months, but it's large enough to accommodate everyone. The fishing is considered excellent, and anglers can expect to catch largemouth, smallmouth and white bass, crappie, bluegill, catfish, and sauger.

Douglas is easily reached from all directions, but it's best if you approach from the north as there are more access points in the northern section. There are more than 20 public boat ramps around the perimeter of the lake, 17 of them on the north shore alone.

From Knoxville, take I-40 east and follow it to French Broad River; you will find boat ramps to the north at Oak Grove, and to the south side just at the foot of the river bridge.

From Virginia and the Tri-Cities area of upper eastern Tennessee, follow I-81 to its junction with I-40. Travel south toward Asheville on 40 until you come to the French Broad River bridge and the boat ramps scattered thereabouts.

From Newport in the north and Sevierville and Gatlinburg in the south, you can take Highway 411 to its junction with Highway 92. Turn north on 92 and follow it to the river where you'll find several side roads with access ramps into the river and Douglas Lake.

FRENCH BROAD RIVER

The French Broad River runs east-west through the Great Smoky Mountains from Knoxville, through Douglas Lake, north of Newport, through Bald Mountain, and into North Carolina. Along the way there are literally dozens of places where you can park the car and access the river.

The fishing is considered good, with catches of smallmouth, largemouth, spotted and white bass, as well as bluegill, crappie, catfish and sauger.

East of Douglas Lake, Highways 25 and 70 follow the northern river bank all the way into North Carolina.

From Knoxville east to Douglas Lake, the river must be approached via I-40 and any one of a number of narrow, winding secondary roads.

FORT PATRICK HENRY LAKE

Patrick Henry is a section of the Holston River just southeast of Kingsport, adjacent to Warrior's Path State Park, and just to the north of Boone Lake and the Watauga River. Sometimes extremely busy, the lake is best fished during the week, when crowds are small. The lake is well stocked with a variety of fish, including rainbow trout and three species of bass.

The lake can best be approached from I-81, and there are public access ramps located in Warrior's Path State Park north of the interstate, and a little farther south off Highway 36.

HOLSTON RIVER

The Holston is a vast tract of water that, in places, is more than two miles wide. The main body of water, and the most popular fishing area, is a 30-mile stretch of lakeland known as Cherokee Lake that begins in the vicinity of Jefferson City, bypasses Morristown to the south, and ends almost in Rogersville. That stretch of water alone has more than 50 public boat ramps. Fishing on the Holston is about as good as it gets, with four varieties of bass, plus bluegill and catfish.

Unfortunately for anglers, the river is often used by the boating community, but things are not unbearably crowded.

The river is best approached from the south via Highway 11E either from Jefferson City or Morristown, but you can also access it from side roads leading north from 11E.

From the north, you'll come via Highway 11W and its two major connector roads, Highways 92 and 32.

NOLICHUCKY RIVER

From White Pine south of Morristown, the Nolichucky winds its way back and forth for more than 50 miles through some of the prettiest country in eastern Tennessee, all the way across the Great Smoky Mountains and on into North Carolina. It offers anglers opportunities to get away from the hustle and bustle of the busy lakes to enjoy their sport without interruption from the boating set. The fishing is excellent. White bass, as well as smallmouth and largemouth bass, rainbow trout, bluegill, muskie (the Nolichucky is one of the few areas in eastern Tennessee where muskellunge are found), and the inevitable catfish.

Upper East Tennessee

There are not quite as many public access ramps on this river as there are on the French Broad and the Holston, but there are a number of marinas along the way. Public access ramps can be found at Davy Crockett Lake just off Highway 70 south of Greeneville, at the Davy Crockett Birthplace State Park off Highway 11E about 12 miles east of Greeneville, and off Highway 81 near Banner Hill and Erwin. There's also a ramp at Unaka Springs southeast of Banner Hill off Highway 23.

SOUTH HOLSTON LAKE

South Holston is east of Bristol and crosses the Tennessee-Virginia border into Washington County, Virginia. Best approached from Highway 421 going east toward Mountain City, the lake is well known for its excellent fishing and large stocks of largemouth and smallmouth bass. It is also well stocked with brown and rainbow trout. If you enjoy fishing for crappie, you'll find plenty of those, too, along with bluegill, walleye and catfish. South Holston is well-blessed with public boat ramps. There at least a dozen in the vicinity of the Highway 421 bridge and the small community of Emmett. A few more can be found off Highway 421.

WATAUGA LAKE

This large body of water southeast of Elizabethton is one of the finest fishing lakes in upper east Tennessee. Anglers will find the lake quite busy on weekends when the boating crowd descends in large numbers, but weekdays offer long lazy afternoons and catches to tell stories about. Experienced bass anglers know about the lake's population of largemouth, smallmouth, striped, spotted and white bass, but there's much more. The crappie is present in large numbers, as are bluegill, catfish and sauger.

There are a large number of public access ramps to Watauga, most of them in the vicinity of Highway 321 and the Big Laurel Branch Wilderness, and there are more near the Highway 67 bridge. The lake is best reached from the south via Highway 321 from Elizabethton, or from the north via Highway 67 from Mountain City.

■ Hiking

CHEROKEE NATIONAL FOREST: NOLICHUCKY RANGER DISTRICT

 GUM SPRINGS TRAIL: An easy 2½-mile hike that will take you past Gum Springs and upward to Meadow Creek Mountain Ridge, where it intersects with the Meadow Creek Mountain Trail. At that point you have a couple of options: you can either return down the mountain by the same route you came; or you can take the Meadow Creek Mountain Trail to its trailhead off Cave Road some 11 miles south of Greeneville.

From Newport, drive east along Highway 70 to Highway 107 and turn left. From there, drive 3½ miles to the trailhead for Gum Springs at Lanceville.

NOLICHUCKY RIVER TRAIL: A scenic trail along the river, which is somewhat rugged and not well defined, it runs for about two miles from Nolichucky Expeditions Base Camp, then dead-ends; you'll have to hike it both ways. In spring, you might find this trail flooded.

From Erwin, drive south on Highway 23 for almost three miles to the point where the four lanes turn into two lanes. Turn left off the highway onto a small side road marked with a brown sign that says "Cherokee National Forest, Chestoa .75 Miles." A short distance farther on you'll cross a two-lane bridge over the Nolichucky River and immediately turn right onto a paved road. Follow the paved road for about 1½ miles to the Nolichucky Expeditions Base Camp and the trailhead.

HORSE CREEK (COLD SPRING MOUNTAIN) TRAIL: This is also an off-road vehicle trail that can be very busy during the summer months. It's a fairly easy 4½-mile hike along a wide, graded track, offering spectacular views near its end at the Cold Spring Mountain parking area.

Take Highway 107 east from Greeneville, then drive seven miles to Horse Creek Road (County Highway 94) and turn right. Follow the signs to the Horse Creek Campground; the trailhead is three-tenths of a mile further.

CHEROKEE NATIONAL FOREST: UNAKA RANGER DISTRICT

APPALACHIAN TRAIL: Best known of the hiking trails in the Unaka District is, of course, the Appalachian Trail. There are almost 75 miles of the trail within this district, beginning with an entry point in the south at Big Butte, and ending on the crest of Pond Mountain to the north. The main features of this trail section include **Beauty Spot, Pond Mountain, the Nolichucky River, Unaka Mountain, Roan Mountain** and **Laurel Fork**. There are magnificent, open views from many of the balds, and the trail leads through various forest types, including red spruce, and upland and cove hardwoods. Appalachian Trail shelters in the Unaka District are at Flint Mountain, Hogback Ridge, Bald Mountain, No Business Knob, Curly Maple Gap, Cherry Gap, Clyde Smith, Roan High Knob, Yellow Mountain Gap, Roan Highlands, Apple House, Moreland Gap and Laurel Fork. Trailheads are located at Devils Fork Gap (NC Highway 212), Sam's Gap (US 23), Spivey Gap (US 19W), Chestoa Pike (Erwin TN), Indian Grave Gap (TN Highway 395), Iron Mountain Gap (TN Highway 107), Hughes Gap (TN Highway 2680), Carver's Gap (TN Highway 423), Wildermine Hollow (US 19E) and Dennis Cove (FSR 50).

RATTLESNAKE RIDGE: A moderately difficult hike, often quite strenuous, of about 3½ miles. Rattlesnake Ridge begins at the Unaka Mountain Overlook and ends in Rock Creek Recreation Area. There are trailheads at both ends of the trail. Along the way the elevation changes more than 2,700 feet from a high of 4,840 at the Unaka Overlook to a low of 2,100 at Rock Creek. It passes through pine and hardwood forests, follows Rattlesnake Creek, and goes through a section of the Unaka Wilderness. Features of the trail include a lovely view of Beauty Spot.

To begin your hike at the Rock Creek Recreation Area, drive three miles via Highway 395 from the Unaka District Office.

Those starting at Unaka Mountain Overlook should take Highway 395 from the Unaka District Office and drive five miles to Indian Grave Gap, turn left and drive on for another six miles.

LIMESTONE COVE: A fairly difficult trail of about three miles that begins at Rocky Road (FSR 4343) and heads upward for more than 2,100 feet to its intersection with the Stamping Ground Ridge Trail (described later in this section). From there the trail continues for another half-mile to Unaka Mountain Road. Most of the trail lies within the confines of the Unaka Mountain Wilderness.

From the Unaka District Office, take old US 23 to Unicoi, then take Highway 107 and drive four miles to the Limestone Cove Recreation Area and the trailhead.

To start at the trailhead on Stamping Ground Ridge, drive on along 107 for five miles more to FSR 230, Unaka Mountain Road.

STONE MOUNTAIN TRAIL: A moderately difficult two-mile trail that begins on FSR 5340 and leads upward to scenic overlooks on Unaka Mountain and at Limestone Cove.

From the Unaka District Office, take old US 23 and drive five miles to Unicoi. From there, take Highway 107 and drive a half-mile to Scotio Road. Turn left and drive three miles more to FSR 5340.

LACY TRAP TRAIL: This is a moderately difficult trail of almost three miles that connects the Laurel Fork Trail to the Appalachian Trail on White Rock Mountain.

From Hampton, take FSR 50 and drive seven miles to FSR 50F. Follow 50F to its dead-end at Frog Level and take the Laurel Fork Trail for a half-mile.

COON DEN FALLS TRAIL: Although it's only a little more than a mile in length, this is quite a difficult trail. It leads from Forest Development Road (FDR) 50 in Dennis Cove, past Coon Den Falls, and then connects with the Appalachian Trail on White Rock Mountain. It's a steep trail; in places, very steep.

From Hampton, take FSR 50 and drive four miles to a point approximately half a mile from the Dennis Cove Recreation Area.

LAUREL FORK TRAIL: Laurel Fork offers more than eight miles of fairly difficult and often strenuous hiking from the Dennis Cove Recreation Area to its end at Hays Branch. Along the way, the trail, which originated as a fishermen's access route, follows the Laurel Fork Creek, crossing it back and forth – you'll have to wade several times.

From Hampton, take FDR 50 for 4½ miles to the Dennis Cove Recreation Area.

POND MOUNTAIN TRAIL: A relatively easy trail, with a few more difficult sections along the way, that begins at the intersection of FDR 50 and FSR 50F. It enters the Pond Mountain Wilderness and continues to Bear Stand on the crest of Pond Mountain, and from there goes on to US 321.

From Hampton, take FSR 50 for about seven miles to the intersection of FSR 50F.

GRANNY LEWIS TRAIL: This is a fairly difficult trail of almost three miles that begins at the dead-end of Granny Lewis Road and leads to Temple Hill School, following the course of Granny Lewis Creek. The final three-tenths of a mile at Temple Hill School are on private land.

From the Unaka District Office, take old US 23 and drive south to Ernestville. From there, take Highway 19W to Spivey Gap, then FSR 189 to its dead-end.

STAMPING GROUND TRAIL: Stamping Ground is a fairly difficult horse trail of about four miles. It begins at a trailhead on Stamping Ground Ridge (FSR 230) and ends just down the road from Street's Store. It passes through the Unaka Mountain Wilderness, providing grand views of Roan Mountain. The trail is partly on Forest Service land and partly on private land.

From the Unaka District Office, take old US 23 and drive five miles to Unicoi. From there, take Highway 107 and drive on for about six miles to Limestone Cove. For the trailhead on Stamping Ground Ridge, continue along 107 for three more miles to FSR 230 and follow it for five miles to the trailhead.

PATTY RIDGE TRAIL: This is a difficult 2½-mile trail that begins on Highway 136 and ends on FSR 190. It provides a very steep climb from the banks of the Nolichucky River to Patty Creek.

From the Unaka District Office, take Highway 81 to Embreeville and turn left onto Highway 136. Continue on 136 for a mile to FSR 190. Turn onto 190 and drive on for three miles. There is no parking area on the road.

SILL BRANCH NORTH TRAIL: Just a half-mile long, this is an easy trail that leads from Clark's Creek up the north fork of Sill Branch to the waterfalls. There is a trailhead at the intersection of Sill Branch and FSR 25.

From the Unaka District Office, take Highway 81 and drive seven miles to Highway 107. Take 107 four miles more to Clark's Creek. From there, follow FDR 25 for three miles to the trailhead.

SILL BRANCH SOUTH TRAIL: A fairly difficult trail of 1½ miles that leads from Sill Branch North Trail to FSR 5066 on the ridge crest on Rich Mountain.

The directions to the trailhead are the same as for Sill Branch North (above).

CASSI CREEK TRAIL: This 1½-mile trail provides some difficult hiking through the Samson Mountain Wilderness. It leads from a dead-end on Cassi Creek Road to the Forest Service Boundary on Rich Mountain. There is no parking available at the trailhead.

From the Unaka District Office, take Highway 81 for seven miles to Highway 107. Take 107 and drive eight miles more to Cassi Creek Road and follow it to its dead-end and the trailhead.

HELL HOLLOW TRAIL: A little less than a mile in length, Hell Hollow provides an easy walk along the lower slopes within the Clark's Creek drainage. It's a dead-end trail, so you'll have to hike it both ways.

From the Unaka District Office, take Highway 81 seven miles to Highway 107. Take 107 and drive four miles more to Clark's Creek. From there, follow FDR 25 for four miles to the trailhead.

RAVENS LORE TRAIL: A nice easy stroll of just less than half a mile around an interpretive loop that begins and ends at the Unaka Mountain Overlook parking area.

From the Unaka District Office, take Highway 395 five miles to FSR 230. Turn left onto 230 and drive on for six more miles to the Unaka Mountain Overlook.

ROCK CREEK FALLS TRAIL: This is a moderately difficult trail of about 1½ miles that begins south of Loop C in the Rock Creek Recreation Area. It provides a nice though somewhat strenuous walk through the beautiful scenery surrounding Rock Creek Falls.

From the Unaka District Office, take Highway 395 and drive three miles to the Rock Creek Recreation Area. Parking is available.

CHEROKEE NATIONAL FOREST: WATAUGA RANGER DISTRICT

GENTRY CREEK & GENTRY CREEK FALLS TRAIL: This is a four-mile hike rising some 1,200 feet to Gentry Creek Falls, one of the most outstanding scenic areas in the Watauga Ranger District. The trail is well defined and of good quality, at least as far as the falls, from which point it deteriorates significantly. The going is easy to moderately difficult. The hike is a must for serious nature photographers.

From Elizabethton, take Highway 91 north for 7½ miles to Gentry Creek Falls Road (FSR 123) and turn right. Follow the road for 2½ miles; the trailhead is in the back of the parking area on the left.

ROGERS RIDGE TRAIL: This is actually a seven-mile horse trail and is also the main trail to the top of Rogers Ridge. It gains 2,000 feet in elevation along the way. It's a moderately difficult hike along the bald ridgetops that offers spectacular views of the surrounding country. The trail begins at Rogers Ridge and ends at Tri-State Corner.

From Elizabethton, take Highway 91 north for 7½ miles to Gentry Creek Falls Road (FSR 123) and turn right. Follow the road for a little less than 1½ miles to a gravel parking area. The trailhead is in the back of the parking area.

IRON MOUNTAIN TRAIL: A fairly tough trail through some very rugged country. It is rarely used, except during hunting season. In places it is not well defined. It's a fairly difficult hike of about 12 miles and is not recommended unless you're a seasoned hiker and like to blaze trails.

From Mountain City, take Highway 421 and drive northwest for 6½ miles, maybe a little more, to Sandy Gap. You'll find the trailhead on the north side of the road. There are some stone steps that lead up the side of the bank, and there's a parking area on the south side of the road.

BACKBONE ROCK TRAIL: From the trailhead in the Backbone Rock Recreation Area, the trail climbs steadily more than 1,250 feet over about two miles to join with the Appalachian Trail at a trailhead on Holston Mountain. The going can be difficult at times, but the wildflowers and views make it well worth the effort.

From Damascus, Virginia, take Highway 716 south across the Virginia-Tennessee border, where the highway becomes Tennessee 133, to the Backbone Rock Parking Area. (You'll find it on the right just after you exit the tunnel.) The trailhead is on the south side of the parking lot.

HOLSTON MOUNTAIN TRAIL: The trail begins at Holston High Knob Fire Tower and follows the ridge northeast for 7½ miles to its junction with the Appalachian Trail on Rich Knob. It's a fairly level though sometimes difficult hike through hardwood forest. Only occasionally will you have a view of Iron Mountain through breaks in the trees. The view from the fire tower is spectacular.

To reach the trailhead at Holston High Knob, take Highway 91 from Elizabethton and drive north for 10 miles. There, you'll turn left onto Panhandle Road (FSR 56), which shortly turns into a gravel road. Follow the road to the ridgetop and turn right onto FSR 202. The trailhead is on the right just before you reach the tower.

GREAT SMOKY MOUNTAINS NATIONAL PARK

The trails listed below are all within the park. The trailheads are easily located by way of a Park Service map, which is available at the Park Headquarters on Headquarters Road in Gatlinburg.

The park is spread almost equally across Tennessee and North Carolina. The following trails are equally accessible from both states.

ABRAMS FALLS TRAIL (TN): This is a fairly difficult trail that runs alongside Abrams Creek and ends slightly more than five miles from the trailhead at Abrams Falls. The falls are very pretty and well worth a hike. Photographers will find lots of great opportunities along the way, as well as at the falls themselves. The trail dead-ends, so be prepared to hike both ways.

The trailhead is at the western end of the Cades Cove Loop Road.

ALUM CAVE BLUFF TRAIL (TN): The trailhead for Alum Cave is in a parking area off Newfound Gap Road. This is a very popular trail, especially in June when the rhododendrons are in bloom. It's a fairly difficult trail that, for more than 6½ miles, winds its way through the woods to Alum Cave Bluff, a 100-foot overhang covered with alum deposited on the rocks by waters seeping through from underground. It's really quite an interesting sight.

Upper East Tennessee

You can return the way you came, or you can take the **Bullhead Trail** to Mount Le Conte, and then return to the trailhead at Newfound Gap Road; it's quite a hike. Alternatively, arrange for pickup at the Mount Le Conte Trailhead at Cherokee Orchard.

BONE VALLEY TRAIL (NC): A good, stiff trail of about two miles that begins across the bridge from the Bone Valley Campground. It follows the creek, crossing it a number of times, and continues on past the ruins of a pioneer settlement.

CATALOOCHIE DIVIDE TRAIL (NC): An 11½-mile hike that begins at Cove Creek Gap on the North Carolina side at the old NC 284 entrance to the park. The route will take you through Panther Spring Gap to join with the **McKee Branch Trail** for several miles. It then climbs along the ridge to Hemphill Bald and Sheepback Knob, follows the old railroad tracks for three miles, and connects to the Blue Ridge Parkway at Balsam Mountain Spur at Mile Marker 458.2. The going is tough.

COVE MOUNTAIN TRAIL (TN): This is a fairly difficult eight-mile hike leading from a trailhead at the Laurel Falls parking area. It follows the Laurel Falls Trail through pine and oak forest before connecting with the Cove Mountain Trail. It then goes on through virgin hardwood forests, up Cove Mountain Ridge (where the hike can become extremely taxing) and ends at the Sugarlands Visitor Center. It's a very scenic trail offering spectacular views and dozens of opportunities for photography and picnics along the way.

DEEP CREEK TRAIL (NC): The trailhead is in a parking area a little more than two miles up Deep Creek Road, off Highway 19 in North Carolina. The route follows the creekbed and begins a steep but scenic ascent through stands of hardwood and rhododendron to Indian Creek. From there it proceeds upstream to the trail end at Newfound Gap Road. It's a strenuous hike of about 12 miles.

HUGHES RIDGE TRAIL (NC): This is another strenuous hike. You'll ascend Hughes Ridge from the trailhead near Smokemont on Highway 441 in North Carolina. Then you'll hike northward along the ridge with grand views of Raven Fork to the east and Richland Mountain to the west. The trail ends, after more than 12 miles, at its junction with the Appalachian Trail at the Tennessee state line.

JONAS CREEK TRAIL (NC): The trailhead is at the Jonas Creek Backcountry Campground. The path follows an old railroad for 3½ miles alongside Jonas Creek, then switches back to Welch Ridge, crosses the creek, and ends at high rocks. It's a fairly rugged hike and recommended only for the physically fit.

MOUNT LE CONTE TRAIL (TN): The trailhead for this scenic 13-mile hike is in Cherokee Orchard. From there, you'll follow the Rainbow Falls Trail to Le Conte Creek and the 80-foot-high Rainbow Falls, a spectacular cascade that lends itself especially to nature photography. From there, the trail begins to climb steeply upward through the forest to join the **Bullhead Trail**. You'll continue on along Bullhead toward the top of Mount Le Conte, where you'll enjoy spectacular scenic views over the park. You must return the way you came, which makes it one heck of a hike; very difficult in some places, more moderate in others. You'll need to be in good physical condition if you are to make it all the way to the top and back.

SNAKE DEN RIDGE TRAIL (TN): The trailhead for this 10-mile hike is in the Cosby Campground, at the eastern end of the park off Highway 32. It's a difficult, strenuous hike that will take you all the way to the top of the ridge at Inadu Knob and the intersection with the Appalachian Trail. If you're fit, it's an enjoyable and scenic hike; if you're not, don't try it. You can return by the same route or you can continue on along the Appalachian Trail.

OTHER AREA HIKES

MEADOW CREEK MOUNTAIN TRAIL: This is a horse trail of about 14 miles that leads over Chucky and Meadow Creek Mountain Ridges. It's difficult – easy if you're on horseback – but scenic, often climbing steeply for long stretches through woods and forests to its end at FT 2576 near Long Creek. Unless you can arrange for pickup there, you're in for an overnight stay somewhere on the mountain. The round-trip is more than 26 miles, and you can't complete the hike in a single day.

The trailhead is just off Cave Road. Drive south from Greeneville on Highway 70 to its junction with Highway 107 and turn right. From there, drive on to the junction with Collins Road and bear right. Continue for two miles to Cave Road, on the left. Turn left onto Cave Road. The trailhead is less than a half-mile farther on.

Upper East Tennessee

RAVEN ROCK OVERLOOK TRAIL: A two-mile trail in Roan Mountain State Park with its trailhead at the Ranger Station. It follows a number of switchbacks up Heaton Ridge to a scenic overlook at Raven Rock, then loops back to the Ranger Station. A little strenuous, but the view is worth the hike.

STINERS WOODS TRAIL: This is a short trail of a little more than a mile – an easy footpath that loops through an old beech grove and TVA's Small Wild Area. It features lots of wildflowers and great views of Norris Lake. The trailhead is near the cemetery, six miles northwest of Little Barren on Little Barren Road.

■ Off-Road Riding

 ATV (All-Terrain Vehicles) and ORV (Off-Road Vehicles) can offer extreme adventure, especially in the wilderness of the Cherokee National Forest. Unfortunately, they can also be very dangerous and cause extensive damage to the environment. Of the three ranger districts in the upper east Tennessee section of the forest, two have trails set aside for off-road use.

Rules & Regulations

- Street-legal motorcycles and four-wheel-drive vehicles are allowed on all open Forest Service roads.

- Unlicensed motorcycles, four-wheel-drive vehicles, and three- and four-wheel ATVs are not allowed on Forest Service roads.

- All motorized vehicles are prohibited on closed Forest Service roads.

- All vehicles and operators must comply with current state laws.

NOLICHUCKY RANGER DISTRICT

For information, contact the Nolichucky Ranger District Office at ☎ 423-638-4109.

HORSE CREEK 4WD WAY: This road is open to four-wheel-drive vehicles, three- and four-wheelers and motorcycles. The ride, exhilarating, fast and almost five miles long, begins at the end of the paved road at the Horse Creek Recreation Area and ends at the parking area near the top of Cold Spring Mountain.

ROUND KNOB 4WD WAY: A wild ride of more than a mile, open to four-wheel-drive vehicles, three-wheelers, four-wheelers and motorcycles. It begins at the Round Knob Recreation Area and ends at a parking area near the top of Bald Mountain.

BULLEN HOLLOW MOTORCYCLE TRAIL: Although designated a motorcycle trail, Bullen Hollow is also available for use by riders of three- and four-wheeled ATVs. The ride, almost five miles long, is fast, bumpy and exhilarating. It begins at the Doak Cabin site on Shelton Mission Road and ends at Low Gap on Viking Mountain.

New roads are presently under construction in Greene and Cocke counties.

UNAKA RANGER DISTRICT

BUFFALO MOUNTAIN ATV/MOTORCYCLE TRAIL: This trail, almost 13 miles long, is an easy to moderately difficult backcountry route that begins at Horse Cove Gap and ends at Oregon Gap on Buffalo Mountain. It provides an enjoyable ride through some of Unaka's most scenic country; views of Unaka Mountain, surrounding mountains and the "Valley Beautiful" in Unicoi County.

From the Unaka District Office on Main Street in Erwin, take Highway 81 and drive six miles to River Road, then two miles more to Dry Creek Road. Follow Dry Creek Road for five miles to Horse Cove Gap and the trailhead.

■ Snow Skiing

See *Ober Gatlinburg* in the *Sightseeing* section on page 92.

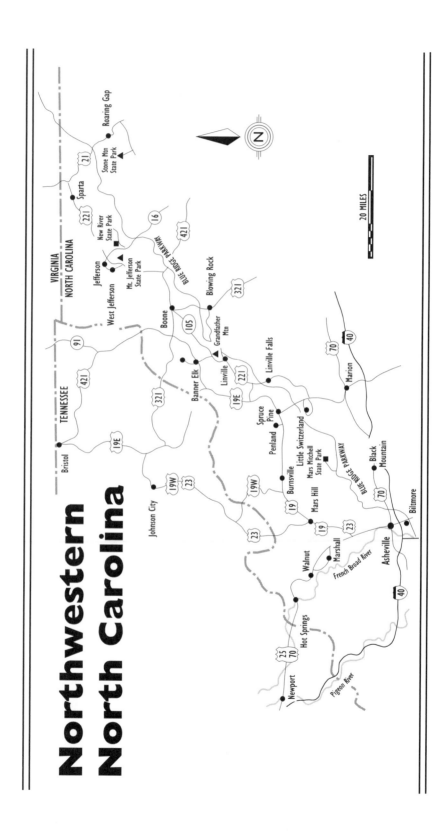

Northwestern North Carolina

The western boundaries of North Carolina are, to say the least, remote. Some of the towns and cities are difficult to reach, quickly. Traveling the Great Smoky Mountains on the North Carolina side means long drives through some of the world's most scenic country along roads that never seem to lead anywhere.

History

 Northwestern North Carolina has a long and often interesting history. The white man arrived in 1670 when a German doctor, under orders from the governor of the English colony, came to explore the land.

Slowly, the area was opened up. Settlers poured in and the population grew. Men like Daniel Boone pushed back the frontiers even further. At first, the settlements were little more than a couple of shacks located in convenient clearings in the woods. Then those little settlements grew to form such towns as Asheville, Boone, Jefferson, and Linville. Next the steam train came, providing speedy access to the north and the great markets there. Finally, the railroads brought a new industry to the rural farmlands of the area: tourism!

The first visitors arrived by rail from the low country. They brought with them their slaves and a new way of life. They explored, traveled, and slowly the inns and hotels were established along lonely woodland routes. By the close of the Second World War tourism had become a major source of revenue.

New roads were built, designed to ease the flow of traffic along the narrow, winding, two-lane highways. America's great scenic road, the Blue Ridge Parkway, was planned to ease the congestion and provide not only a high-speed route through the mountains, but a tourist attraction. And now, more people travel the parkway to view the scenery than they do to get from one place to another.

Then snow skiing came to the mountains of northwestern North Carolina. Today, it is a major industry on the western borders of the state. The resorts – there are more than a dozen of them – are among the best in the nation, and the season is eagerly awaited by locals and visitors alike.

Northwestern North Carolina is now dedicated to tourism, and has one of the most professional tourist support organizations in the Appalachian region.

Getting Here

BY AIR

 The area is served most conveniently by Asheville Regional Airport. You'll have to fly one of the commuter airlines, such as **American Eagle**, ☎ 800-433-7300; **ASA**, ☎ 800-282-3424; **Comair,** ☎ 800-354-9822; or **US Air Express**, ☎ 800-428-4322.

You can also fly into either the Tri-Cities Airport in upper east Tennessee or Charlotte, North Carolina, but that will mean you'll have some driving to do.

BY ROAD

From Tennessee

 Three main routes serve North Carolina from Tennessee. From the north, the easiest passage is via I-40, which leads from Knoxville and all points west to Asheville.

All other routes involve heading east on twisting and turning highways. US 23 heads east out of Erwin, joins 19W, and then goes straight up into the Unaka Mountains toward Asheville.

From Elizabethton, US 19E will take you to 321, one of Tennessee's most scenic, but tortuous, highways, and from there into Boone.

From Virginia

The quickest routes are either I-77 to I-40, and from there turn west toward Asheville; or I-81 to Virginia Highway 91 at Bristol, and then head south and east toward Boone. The most scenic route is, of course, the Blue Ridge Parkway, which is described in some detail later in this chapter.

Getting Around

Well, now that you're here, it's simply a matter of deciding where to go and what to do first. Or is it? Unfortunately, the Blue Ridge Parkway can be an end in itself. Many visitors get on the parkway and never leave it. After all, there's plenty to see and do along the this route. But to fall prey to the parkway's almost irresistible charms is to cheat yourself.

Perhaps the best way to "do" northwestern North Carolina is to get on the parkway, drive a short distance, leave it for a while and explore one or more of the more remote towns and villages, then repeat the process. Don't believe it when you're told you have to see all of the parkway; you don't. In fact, after a hundred miles or so, one can "over feed" on the beauties of the mountains and forests. It is far better to take it in small doses with side trips to relieve the visual feast.

Sightseeing

■ Asheville

Asheville is the heart of the Great Smoky Mountains in North Carolina, and is also the cultural and economic center of the mountain region.

Once again, it was the coming of the railroad that brought prosperity to the town. It arrived in 1880, and preceded New York businessman George Vanderbilt by only nine years. Vanderbilt bought more than 130,000 acres of North Carolina and on it he proceeded to build what was soon to become one of the most visited private homes in America – Biltmore.

Many prominent Americans followed Vanderbilt to the Asheville area; most of them suffering from respiratory ailments such as tuberculosis. They came for the therapeutic mountain air, bought property, and settled down to the quiet life among the beautiful hills and valleys.

Asheville became a center for culture and tourism. Biltmore attracts many thousands of visitors each year and is the hub of the local tourist industry.

The Blue Ridge Parkway and a network of interstates provide easy access to the city, and the overflow of visitors to the Great Smoky Mountains National Park, just 40 miles away, brings even more visitors.

The Asheville Convention and Visitors Bureau, at 151 Haywood Street, is open weekdays from 8:30 am until 5:30 pm, and from 9 am until 5 pm on weekends. ☎ 877-274-0595.

ASHEVILLE ART MUSEUM

Located in the Asheville Civic Center complex, the museum houses a wonderful permanent collection of American art: paintings, sculpture, etc. Well worth a visit, Asheville Art Museum is open weekdays from 10 am until 5 pm, and from 1 until 5 pm on Saturdays and Sundays. Admission is free. ☎ 828-253-3227.

ASHEVILLE CIVIC CENTER & THOMAS WOLFE AUDITORIUM

This is where you'll find all sorts of visiting drama, theater, music and dance groups. The management provides a full program of entertainment that runs throughout the year. The city-owned facility is at Hiwassee and Flint streets. ☎ 828-255-5771.

BILTMORE MANSION

No visit to Asheville would be complete without a look at the city's most famous attraction. The great house and its gardens is a monument to capitalism gone mad. The product of money and power in its ultimate form, Biltmore is like no other home in America. Only the great and ancient houses of England and Europe can compete with its opulence.

Work began on the house in 1890 and took more than five years to complete. It has 255 rooms and occupies 8,000 acres, although in its heyday the estate covered more than 130,000 acres.

The grounds were designed and laid out by Frederick Law Olmstead, who designed New York's Central Park. They feature one of the largest azalea displays in the world. There's even a winery on the grounds.

Tours of the great house include the living and sleeping rooms, the servants quarters, the kitchens, laundry, swimming pool, and the family's recreation rooms, which has a bowling alley.

Allow plenty of time for your visit. Biltmore will take at least a half-day to see; a full day if you do it properly.

Biltmore Mansion and Gardens, on US 25E, are open daily from 9 am until 5 pm. Admission is costly. As of this writing it was $24.95 for adults and $18.75 for youngsters age 10 to 15. Children younger than 10 are admitted free. ☎ 800-295-4730.

COLBURN MINERAL MUSEUM

Located in the Asheville Civic Center, the Colburn Mineral Museum interprets North Carolina's mineral industry and its history. There are a great many exhibits depicting local mineral deposits, as well a number of displays featuring reproductions of the world's most famous jewels.

The museum is open Tuesday through Friday from 10 am until 5 pm, and from 1 until 5 pm on weekends. Admission is free.

CHESTNUT HILL HISTORIC DISTRICT

This area of Asheville, which includes Charlotte and Chestnut streets, provides a look at the city as it was during its early years. This was the city's boom time, when wealthy people suffering from tuberculosis moved into the area to take advantage of the therapeutic mountain air. The district includes more than 200 turn-of-the-century homes.

DOWNTOWN ASHEVILLE

As with Chestnut Hill Historic District above, downtown Asheville depicts city life 150 years ago. The old buildings, some of them built in the early part of the 19th century, comprise one of the largest collections of historic architecture in western North Carolina.

NATIONAL CLIMATIC CENTER

An interesting sidebar to a visit here is this national archive of weather records. It's the largest of its kind in the world. Records on the weather from around the country are collected and stored on the center's computers. You can take a guided tour of the building, see what's going on and how it's done, and watch the staff entering the records. The building itself, which houses several other Federal institutions, is of Gothic architecture and occupies an entire city block. It has many interesting features within, including spiral staircases and gargoyles. The National Climatic Center is next to Battery Park. Admission is free. The center is open weekdays from 8 am until 5 pm. ☎ 828-259-0682.

RIVERSIDE CEMETERY

This cemetery's claim to fame lies buried in two of its graves. They belong to Thomas Wolfe and O. Henry, two of America's most famous writers.

THOMAS WOLFE MEMORIAL: The old boarding house at 48 Spruce Street is said to be the one featured in Thomas Wolfe's most famous work, *Look Homeward Angel*. The house featured in the book was called Dixieland. Today, the old building has been turned into a monument to the writer. Much of the furniture is original and was there when Wolfe wrote the book; some of it was brought in from his New York apartment after his death. The house is open Tuesday through Saturday from 9 am until 5 pm, and from 1 until 5 pm on Sundays. Admission is $1. ☎ 828-255-5385.

UNIVERSITY BOTANICAL GARDENS

These 10 acres on the University of North Carolina campus at Asheville contain more than 25,000 native plants and a sculpture garden for the blind. If you have the time, the gardens are worth a visit. Admission is free. The facility, off US 25N, is open from dawn until dusk year-round.

VANCE BIRTHPLACE

Zebulon Vance was born in a log house just north of Asheville. He was always something of an enigma, but one of North Carolina's most prominent politicians. During his career he became governor and a United States senator. Today, the house where he was born has been restored to its original condition and offers a peek into the life and times of Mr. Vance. You'll find the house in Weaverville on Rheem Creek Road. Open Tuesday through Saturday from 10 am until 5 pm, and from 1 until 5 pm on Sundays. Admission is free. ☎ 828-645-6706.

WESTERN NORTH CAROLINA FARMER'S MARKET

This is a state-owned Farmer's Market that covers more than 37 acres just outside Asheville on Brevard Road. Farmers from around the area bring their goods for the general public to view and buy. These include a variety of home-grown fruits, vegetables, jams, jellies, baked treats, hand-crafted goods, curiosities, and home-grown plants and flowers. The market is open April through December, and is easily reached from either Interstate 40 or Interstate 26; just look for and follow the signs. Admission is free.

WESTERN NORTH CAROLINA HERITAGE CENTER

This is Asheville's museum of local history. Inside you'll find all sorts of exhibits, artifacts, furniture, antiques and bits and pieces that interpret the way of life in this area of North Carolina in general and Asheville in particular. The old brick house, built in 1840, is located on the campus of Asheville-Buncome Technical Community College at 283 Victoria Road. It's open from 10 am until 5 pm, Tuesday through Saturday from May until October, and 10 am until 2 pm, November through April. Admission is $5 for adults, $2.50 for children.

WESTERN NORTH CAROLINA NATURE CENTER

Occupying more than seven acres, the center is one of those places that appeals not only to adults, but to the kids as well. It's a sort of zoo/theme park where the emphasis is on conservation and the preservation of local wildlife. You can see a live bear up close, mountain cats, eagles, deer, skunk, opossum and a variety of snakes and other creepy crawlies. There's also a petting zoo where the children can enjoy goats, pigs, calves and lambs, along with a number of interesting interpretive exhibits. The center, on Gashes Creek Road, is open all week from 10 am until 5 pm. Admission is $5 for adults, $2.50 for children.

■ Black Mountain

Black Mountain, just east of Asheville, is a sort of religious center for the mountain region of North Carolina and is home to a number of retreats. The educational facility that made it famous, Black Mountain College, closed down in 1956, leaving it a quiet little mountain city. It has a fascinating downtown area where you'll find a number of interesting shops, stores and restaurants.

■ Blowing Rock

This is one of western North Carolina's oldest resort towns. Its main claim to fame is the great rock that hangs over the cliff edge above the valley some 3,000 feet below. This rock gave the town its name. The wind, even the smallest breeze, along the valley, hits the cliff and is redirected upward past the rock.

There are many folk tales associated with the rock. One fanciful story features a beautiful Indian princess who is supposed to have asked the great winds to return her lover to her after he jumped from the rock.

The view from the rock is magnificent and well worth the small admission fee. The attraction is off Highway 321, just outside of town, and it's open year-round from 9 am until 6 pm.

The Tweetsie Railroad is one of Blowing Rock's oldest attractions. It's a sort of theme park, now more than 30 years old, where a train that takes visitors on a three-mile ride through "Injun Territory" is the centerpiece. The emphasis is on the "Old West," as seen through the eyes of a child. There's a petting zoo, rides, and all the fun of the fair.

Tweetsie Railroad is on Highway 321 between Blowing Rock and Boone. It is open from 9 am until 5 pm all year. Admission is $14.95 for adults; $12.95 for children. Children under three are admitted free.

Other than the hustle and bustle around the great rock, the quaint little town is a quiet mountain community, heavily dependent on tourism, with a main street lined with all sorts of specialty shops and restaurants. Most attractions are within easy walking distance. If you like craft hunting, this is the place for you.

Other attractions include **Moses H. Cone Memorial Park and Mansion** just off Highway 221; and **Mystery Hill**, a neat little place where the floors are tilted and water seems to flow uphill, open 9 am until 5 pm the year-round.

■ Blue Ridge Parkway

The parkway is the product of a time best forgotten. During the depths of the Great Depression, the federal government, looking for new ways to put the unemployed populace to work, came up with an idea to build a road that would link the Shenandoah National Park in Virginia with the Great Smoky Mountains National Park in western North Carolina. The idea was greeted with enthusiasm and work began to acquire the necessary land. Construction started in 1935. Workers were paid an average of 30 cents an hour and, while the bulk of the construction was to be done by private contractors, those firms were assisted by units of the Civilian Conservation Corps. They built the fences, planted trees and grass along the new way, and worked at controlling erosion caused by the construction work.

It was a massive project and the work was difficult. The crews had to literally blast their way through the mountains. By the time it was finished, they had excavated 27 tunnels and built almost as many bridges.

Today, this is one of the finest scenic arteries in the country. More than 20 million people traveled the parkway every year. All along the way there are sights and overlooks with pull-outs that will take your breath away. Often, you'll find a hiking trail that will take you to an even better vantage point. Roadside picnic tables turn a five-minute stopover into a lunch-time or, better yet, a breakfast to remember. A number of visitor centers scattered along the parkway offer all sorts of information and brochures about the local countryside.

To get the most out of the parkway, take your time. It might look like an interstate, but that's the last thing it is. True, it is the quickest way to get from one point to another, but it's much more than that. Most motorists average 30 miles an hour. Take it slow, stop often and, if you can, spend a little time off the road in the woods or on one of the hiking trails. If you decide to make the parkway an end in itself, pick a spot and stay overnight. Give the kids time to release a little of that pent-up energy that comes from being confined for long hours in a car.

Remember that this is a mountain road, and that winter brings snow. When it comes, the road becomes hazardous and major portions are often closed.

EMERGENCIES & INFORMATION

The parkway emergency number is ☎ 800-727-5928.

For details about the weather and park closings, ☎ 828-298-0398.

BICYCLING

The parkway is ideal bicycling territory. But the hills are hard work for those not in the best shape. They also make for a hazardous, though certainly thrilling, ride down the other side. Over the first 25 miles north of Asheville, the road rises to an elevation of some 3,500 feet. That, even for a pro, is a lot of pedaling.

Before you go, make sure your machine is in proper working order, especially the gears and brakes. Carry an air pump and a spare tire. Take along plenty to drink, and lots of of candy bars for energy. Finally, remember that you will not be alone, and that motorists will have their minds on the mountains and their eyes on the scenery.

CAMPING

There are a number of campgrounds on the Blue Ridge Parkway, most of them simple affairs with only the minimum of facilities: water and toilets, etc. Some are closed for the winter, while others are open year-round, even when it's snowing. For a complete list of campgrounds, see the *Camping Directory*, page 275.

SIGHTSEEING

 There are literally hundreds of places to stop and admire the scenery. You could stop every mile or so if you wished. You could, but the journey would be never-ending. We have listed some of the more popular stop-offs as a guide to the best of the Blue Ridge Parkway. Enjoy.

MILE MARKER 217.5 - CUMBERLAND KNOB: Cumberland Knob was one of the first recreation areas dedicated along the route. More than 1,000 acres have been set aside here. You'll find picnic areas, spectacular views, restrooms, drinking water, a book shop, public telephones and a 20-minute loop trail that provides a pleasant and easy walk. For the dedicated hiker, there's a two-hour loop trail that will take you from the visitor center to Gulley Creek Gorge and back again.

MILE MARKER 237 - AIR BELLOWS GAP: This is the "Crest of the Blue Ridge." At an elevation of more than 3,700 feet, the stop provides a spectacular 180° view of the countryside, including Christmas Tree Valley.

MILE MARKER 238 - DOUGHTON PARK: Doughton Park has over 7,000 acres of magnificent parkland with picnic areas, more than 30 miles of hiking trails, restrooms, drinking water, and a campground (see the *Camping Directory*, page 275).

MILE MARKER 261 - JUMP OFF ROCK: Take the half-mile trail, at the end of which you'll find the sheer drop of several hundred feet from which the stop gets its name. Keep the kids in check.

MILE MARKER 272 - E.B. JEFFRESS PARK: Six hundred acres of prime park land, restrooms, drinking water, and a number of hiking trails. Just the place to stop for a rest and a sandwich on a long trip.

MILE MARKER 281 - GRANDVIEW OVERLOOK: Stop here and enjoy a spectacular view of the Yadkin Valley; it's truly grand.

MILE MARKER 293 - MOSES H. CONE MEMORIAL PARK: Not far from the town of Blowing Rock, this park is one of the most popular stops along the parkway. It was once the residence of the wealthy textile magnate, Moses H. Cone. Today, the 3,600-acre property is open for the public to enjoy. The house has been made into a museum and craft shop selling all sorts of hand-made gifts. The park also offers many miles of hiking and nature trails, including more than 25 miles of carriage roads that old man Cone built for his own enjoyment. Within the park there is a large ornamental lake and a couple of trout ponds where you can try your luck at fishing. The visitor center on the property houses restrooms, drinking water and public telephones.

MILE MARKER 297 - JULIAN PRICE MEMORIAL PARK: More than 4,300 acres of parkland, a trout fishing lake, several hiking trails, a very nice picnic area and a campground (see *Camping Directory*, page 275) make Julian Price a good stopping point. There are restrooms, drinking water, and public telephones.

MILE MARKER 306 - GRANDFATHER MOUNTAIN OVERLOOK: Grandfather Mountain is so named for a distant ridge, the profile of which bears a striking resemblance to the head of an old man. Stop here and decide for yourself what it looks like.

MILE MARKER 304 - THE LINN COVE VIADUCT: Linn Cove Viaduct is one of the many great feats of engineering along parkway. This magnificent bridge was actually built around Grandfather Mountain in order to preserve it. You'll have a certain feeling of other-worldliness as you travel high above the valley.

MILE MARKER 310 - LOST COVE OVERLOOK: An interesting spot to stop at night. Supposedly, you can sometimes see a natural phenomenon known as the Brown Mountain Lights. You can also take a short hike along a trail that leads to some interesting geological outcrops.

MILE MARKER 316 - LINVILLE GORGE: Make time here to hike one of two trails to the falls and you won't be disappointed. The lower trail is easiest on the way down; vice versa for the upper trail. The falls are magnificent, so be sure to take your camera.

MILE MARKER 321 - CHESTOA VIEW: One of the great views along the parkway. Take the short hike along a trail that leads out over Humpback Mountain to a spot where you'll have an incredible view of Table Rock.

MILE MARKER 339 - CRABTREE MEADOWS VISITORS CENTER: A small park is the attraction here. You'll find plenty of room to picnic, several short hiking trails, and a campground (see *Camping Directory*, page 275). If you have the time, you should take a hike along the trail to Crabtree Falls; it's a photographer's dream. There are restrooms in the visitor center, drinking water, and public telephones.

MILE MARKER 355 - MOUNT MITCHELL STATE PARK: At more than 6,680 feet, Mount Mitchell is the highest peak in the eastern United States. Take the easy drive up the mountain to the observation tower, where you'll be rewarded by what is possibly the finest view in the entire region – the hills and valleys of the Great Smoky Mountains. If you have the time and the inclination, you might like to have lunch or dinner in the park restaurant. It's about two-thirds of the way along the road to the summit and is open April through October.

MILE MARKER 363 - CRAGGY GARDENS: There's lots to see and do here. The visitor center has interpretive exhibits, restrooms and drinking water. There are several hiking trails, but one in particular is worthy of note. This well-marked path leads upward through the rhododendrons to the summit Craggy Dome where you'll enjoy a 360° view of the surrounding countryside. It's a strenuous walk.

The best time to visit is in the morning; the dew is fresh upon the ground, everything smells clean and new, and the view from Craggy Dome is one of misty valleys and shrouded peaks.

MILE MARKER 393.8 - THE FRENCH BROAD RIVER: A stop on the banks of this, one of the few north-flowing rivers in the United States, is an absolute must.

MILE MARKER 407 - MOUNT PISGAH: You can see the mountain long before you reach it. At 5,721 feet, it dominates the surrounding countryside. Below, you'll see the vast Biltmore Estate and the Cradle of Forestry, the first school of forestry in America. If you want to reach the top of the mountain, you're in for one heck of a hike. A long, winding trail leads upward from the parking area to the summit. It is only for those who are strong of wind and limb.

MILE MARKER 417 - LOOKING GLASS ROCK: The great, 400-foot-high granite cliff is the "looking glass" for which the stop is named. In winter, when the cliff is covered with ice and snow, it resembles a great mirror.

Be sure to visit the **GRAVEYARD FIELDS**. The short loop trail offers incredible views over Yellowstone Falls. This is the place to take time to walk, picnic and enjoy some of the most magnificent

Northwestern North Carolina

scenery in the eastern United States. It's a very popular stop along the Parkway, so early morning, when the site is relatively quiet, is the best time to visit; later in the day it can get quite busy. In the fall, the colors of the forest make this spot worth a visit all by itself. In the winter, the snow and ice turn it into a wonderland.

MILE MARKER 422 - THE DEVIL'S COURTHOUSE: Old legend has it that this is where the Devil holds court on Judgment Day. Deep in the rocks of the great mountain, there is supposed to be a fantastic cave, the courthouse itself. No one has ever seen it, at least, no one that ever lived to tell the tale. No matter; it's a popular stop along the route with a trail that leads from the parking area to the top of a rocky cliff with rather a nice view.

MILE MARKER 431 - RICHLAND BALSAM: The trail that leads up from here will take you to the highest point on the parkway, some 6,400 feet above sea level. No, it's not as high as Mount Mitchell, but Mount Mitchell is not technically on the parkway.

MILE MARKER 446 - WOODFIN CASCADES: Just a quick stop here is required for you to enjoy the beauty and solitude of these small, but picturesque falls that cascade down from Mount Lyn Lowry. It's a great place for a quiet picnic.

MILE MARKER 451 - WATERROCK KNOB: Yet another magnificent view. Take the short trail to the overlook for a breathtaking panorama.

MILE MARKER 469 - OCONOLUFTEE VISITORS CENTER: When you reach the Oconoluftee Visitors Center, you've reached the beginning and the end of the Blue Ridge Parkway. There's lots to see and do here: a pioneer mountain farm, lots of exhibits, and the Oconoluftee River itself. The park and center are open daily all year from 8 am until dusk. ☎ 828-479-9146.

■ Boone

 The largest small town in western North Carolina, Boone was named for the famous frontiersman who roamed the area from 1760 to 1769. It is close to the headwaters of four great rivers: the Ohio (it's the New River here), the Tennessee (Watauga), the Pee Dee (Yadkin), and the Santee (Catawba). Boone is always a busy town. It's not only the shopping center for the area but, being the home of Appalachian State University, it's also the intellectual capital. More than

10,000 students enroll each year and spend the academic year on either the downtown campus, some 75 acres, or just west of the city on a campus of 180 acres where the Center for Appalachian Studies is located.

Aside from the university, Boone is a typical mid-sized city. The usual malls and museums make it a great place to stop off on the way to wherever it is you're going.

■ Hot Springs

 Hot Springs is quiet, too quiet. Once a bustling little mountain city named Warm Springs, where people came to "take the waters," the town saw its prime times come and go during the 1920s. From then on, except for a short period during the Second World War when it became part of a large German prisoner of war internment center, it went downhill on the road to oblivion. Recently, however, with the spread of tourism into the mountains and some positive interest by local residents, Hot Springs seems to be coming back to life. The old luxury hotels are all gone now, but the spa that once catered to the rich and famous back in the early 1800s is once again open to the public, and neat little bed and breakfast inns are springing up all over the area.

HOT SPRINGS SPA

The mineral springs from which the little city takes its name are, indeed, hot. The water maintains a year-round temperature of 100°. When such places were no longer fashionable, the spa was abandoned and fell into disrepair. In 1990, however, its new owners saw potential in the warm waters of the spring. Today, you can relax in a modern Jacuzzi filled with the special waters of the spa, and receive a therapeutic massage. Rates for the Jacuzzis are determined by the number of people in the party, but it works out to about $12 per head per hour; a massage will cost you another $20 for a half-hour session.

The spa is open all year from 9 am until 6:45 pm. There's a campground on the property with facilities for RVs and tents. 1 Bridge Street, Hot Springs. ☎ 828-622-7676.

■ Jefferson

Named for Thomas Jefferson, this little mountain city is in the heart of the farming community of western North Carolina, close to the Virginia border. The big attractions here are Mount Jefferson and the New River. The mountain rises some 4,800 feet above a state park (which takes its name), and the river provides plenty of water-born action, including rafting and canoeing. Scenic country and the lure of the great outdoors make Jefferson a popular place for adventuring.

MOUNT JEFFERSON STATE PARK

Mount Jefferson rises powerfully from the surrounding countryside and is the center of a 540-acre state park, where naturalists and hikers come to enjoy the scenery and the large variety of plant life: rhododendrons, red maples, tulip trees, yellow birch and aspens. The mountain gained notoriety during the Civil War era when it became a beacon and refuge for runaway slaves. A cave on the mountain provided shelter for them on their way north. There's also a picnic area with tables, several hiking trails, restrooms and drinking water.

The park is open from 9 am until sunset most of the year, but it would be wise to call ahead during the winter months as the roads often become impassable.

The park is on State Highway 1152, just off US 221. ☎ 910-246-9653.

NEW RIVER STATE PARK

New River is a popular destination for those who like to spend time on the water. The river is very old, one of the oldest in North America. It flows through western North Carolina from the Virginia border, through Ashe and Allegheny counties, and provides all sorts of water-related activities along the way, including great fishing.

The state park itself is a remote place, bordered on one side by the great river and by a primitive campground on the other. Aside from its attraction for canoeists and fishermen, the park is also a great place for hikers and naturalists. All sorts of wildlife live along the riverbank: beavers, muskrats, otters, raccoons, and even mink make their homes near the gently flowing waters. Some 14 species of endangered plants can be found within the park boundaries, including rattlesnake rook and Carolina saxifrage.

The park access is on Highway 1590, just off Highway 88 near Jefferson. ☎ 910-982-2587 for information and park hours.

Canoeing The New River

The New River offers long lazy days on quiet waters where you can experience the beauty of a National Wild and Scenic American Heritage River. Said to be one of the world's oldest rivers, its quiet shallows offer a great place for the beginner to learn the art of paddling. The New River State Park, through which it flows, includes pull-ins, picnicking spots, and camping facilities. Local outfitters offer rental canoes and guided trips.

New River Outfitters

This well-established company can look after all your outdoor needs for a day out on the river. They can supply all the necessary equipment for an excursion, including a canoe, and offer a variety of guided tours on the water. ☎ 910-982-9193.

■ Linville

This is a rather exclusive mountain community where tourism in its rawest form clashes somewhat with the classy collection of second homes. For many years, Linville has been a place to "get away to." Today, people are still getting away here, but now the attractions are more commercial than aesthetic.

GRANDFATHER MOUNTAIN

This is Linville's outdoor center. The mountain, a ridge with a rock formation that looks sort of like an old man's face in profile, has been designated by the United Nations as an international biosphere reserve, a place where man and nature are supposed to coexist in perfect harmony. It really is a great place to visit, where you can enjoy the mountain air, hike more than 12 miles of woodland and mountain trails, take scenic walks, and see all sorts of wildlife, including black bears, deer and eagles. There's a gift shop and a restaurant, and you can go picnicking, too.

The privately owned park is open daily except for Thanksgiving and Christmas. Admission is $9.95 for adults and $5.95 for children age four to 12. Children three and under are admitted free.

■ Linville Falls

 Linville Falls, not to be confused with Linville, is a tiny town on the Blue Ridge Parkway. Its main attraction is the falls. Claimed to be the biggest waterfalls in the Southern Appalachians, they are a sight to see. The Linville River cascades through two sets of falls down into Linville Gorge. The attraction, administered by the National Park Service, is not difficult to find. Go to the junction of the Blue Ridge Parkway and Highway 221, then follow the signs. Admission is free.

LINVILLE CAVERNS

Like many other commercial cave systems, Linville Caverns has been doctored and manipulated to provide for public access, but not to its detriment. Located deep inside Humpback Mountain, the caves were first used by Indians as early as 1800, and then by deserters during the Civil War. Today, you can follow the path in company with a guide, deep underground, and walk through the semi-darkness beside a stream filled with trout. The limestone formations are exceptional. The great stalagmites, stalactites, flowstone and calcite formations have been subject to the imaginations of the attraction's owners, though not with much originality. There's the inevitable "Frozen Waterfall" and, of course, a "Natural Bridge." But it's all tastefully done and you won't be disappointed if you decide to visit.

The caverns are on Highway 221, between Linville and Morton, about four miles south of the Blue Ridge Parkway. Hours vary from month to month, but you can be sure they are open daily from 9 am until 4:30, March through November, and on weekends only December through February. Admission is reasonable: $5 for adults; $3.50 for children ages five through 12. Younger children are admitted free.

■ Marshall

This tiny mountain town, 15 miles west of Mars Hill and only 30 minutes from Asheville on Highway 25, sits on a tiny strip of land between the French Broad River and an imposing, rocky cliff. And it's the river that determines the destiny of this small city. The local elementary school sits on an island in the middle of the river, and the entire community is subject to flooding. Be that as it may, Marshall has an atmosphere of quiet well-being and timelessness, where nothing seems to change.

■ Pisgah National Forest

The Pisgah is the third of the large national forest systems in the Great Smoky Mountain region. Covering more than 475,000 acres in two tracts, it includes some of the highest mountain peaks in the eastern US.

Although the Pisgah is not as well known, it is more accessible, and thus more heavily visited than its two sister forests: the Nantahala, farther south, and the Cherokee to the west. Some of the attractions within the Pisgah are better known than the forest itself. Some are spectacular, and almost all are natural wonders of special interest, scattered among mountain towns and villages that are all attractions in their own right.

The Pisgah is administered by the National Forest Service and is broken down into four ranger districts – the Pisgah, Toecane, Grandfather and French Broad Ranger Districts – with the Supervisor's Office located in Asheville.

The **Pisgah Ranger District** is the smallest of the four administrations. It includes a number of natural attractions, not the least of which is the **Shining Rock Wilderness Area**, more than 13,000 acres of natural preserve with numerous hiking trails and primitive campgrounds.

The **Toecane Ranger District** incorporates a vast area north and east of Asheville that stretches as far as the Tennessee state line and includes **Mount Mitchell** (6,684 feet), the highest peak in the eastern United States.

The **Grandfather Ranger District** incorporates the northern section of the forest, including Linville Gorge.

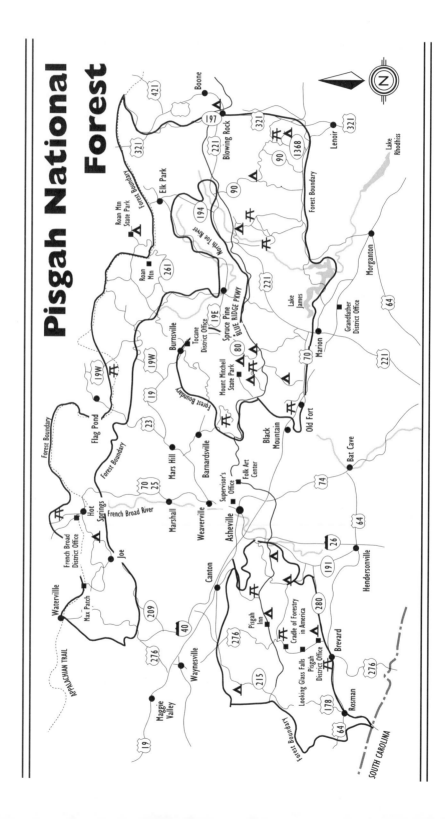

The **French Broad Ranger District** offices are located in Hot Springs and cover the French Broad River to the northwest of Asheville.

 For detailed information, trail guides, maps and brochures, you can write to the Supervisor's Office, or to any of the District Offices. You'll find the addresses and telephone numbers listed under Pisgah National Forest in the *Information* section at the back of this book.

■ Sparta

 Sparta is in Allegheny County, seven or eight miles from the Blue Ridge Parkway and close to the Virginia state line. It is the center of the local tobacco industry; it's also the location of the largest pipe manufacturer (smoking pipes, that is) in the country, Sparta Industries, makers of Dr. Grabow's pre-smoked pipes. It's a busy little town of about 2,000 people and is growing quickly as new industry continues to move into the area. But it still retains its old-world atmosphere, and is worth a little side trip if you are making the drive up the Blue Ridge Parkway into Virginia.

STONE MOUNTAIN STATE PARK

Not to be confused with Georgia's Stone Mountain, this one centers upon a 600-foot-high granite rock with a base more than three miles in circumference. It's a place for mountain goats and humans who like to emulate them. Some of the best climbing in the Great Smoky Mountains is right here on the rocky slopes. The Great Brown Way, Electric Boobs, and Rice Krispies are just a few of the fanciful names awarded to the rocky trails leading to the summit.

If climbing is not your bag, Stone Mountain has plenty more to offer. You can hike the nature trails, view the waterfalls, and try your hand at trout fishing. Or you can take time out and enjoy a quiet picnic among some of the most pleasing scenery in the Smokies.

Stone Mountain State Park is off the Blue Ridge Parkway at Roaring Gap, just to the south of Sparta.

■ Spruce Pine

Arguably the mineral capital of western North Carolina, Spruce Pine is where the finest of ceramic pottery clay, kaolin, comes from. The fine white clay is mined in open pits, along with a number of other valuable minerals, such as mica, feldspar, asbestos and iron. The area is also a source of gemstones and a center for amateur geologists and rock hounds. Spruce Pine is on Highway 19E just a few miles west of the Blue Ridge Parkway in Mitchell County.

Adventures

■ Pisgah National Forest

It seems only right to begin this section with the Pisgah National Forest, even though it's alphabetically out of sequence, because it's the center for adventuring in northwestern North Carolina. Almost every outdoor sport or activity, from hiking to skiing and from horseback riding to off-road vehicle riding, is catered for within the forest.

The forest incorporates 496,000 acres of hard- and softwoods. It's a land of towering mountain peaks, cascading waterfalls, and a wide variety of plant life, some of which is not found elsewhere in the country. Great rivers and historic mountain trails twist and turn through its length and breadth. The Blue Ridge Parkway runs through the eastern section of the forest from north to south. The Appalachian Trail, which crosses the mountains from Maine to Georgia, passes through its western section.

Mount Pisgah

Mount Pisgah was the biblical name for the mountain from which Moses saw the promised land after wandering for 40 years in the wilderness. And it was the inspiration, so the legend goes, for a Scotch-Irish frontier minister by the name of James Hall when he named Mount Pisgah in western North Carolina during an expedition commanded by General Griffith Rutherford in 1776. Apparently he too stood on the mountain and looked down at the French Broad River basin and, drawing from the story of Moses, named the peak. The Pisgah National Forest takes its name from the mountain.

There are four ranger districts within the Pisgah administrative region: the Toecane, the French Broad, the Grandfather and the Pisgah. Within each district are all sorts of attractions, activities and facilities available for most of the year. These include campgrounds, cross-country ski trails, hiking trails, horse trails, off-road vehicle trails, fishing areas, boating areas with public access ramps, and much more, the highlights of which are listed below (by district). You'll find complete contact information for each district listed in the *Information Directory* under Pisgah National Forest, page 329.

Pisgah National Forest Information

Pisgah Ranger District. . . . ☎ 828-877-3265
French Broad District . . . . ☎ 828-622-3202
Grandfather District. . . . . ☎ 828-652-2144
Toecane District . . . . . . ☎ 704-682-6146

PISGAH DISTRICT

More than 156,000 acres in Buncombe, Haywood, Henderson and Transylvania counties come under the jurisdiction of the Pisgah Ranger District of the National Forest Service. There are more than 275 miles of hiking trails within the district – some easy, others not so easy. There are horse trails, trails set aside for mountain biking, and even some reserved exclusively for off-road vehicles.

There are four developed and three group campgrounds (see
Pisgah National Forest in the *Camping Directory* at the end of the
book). And then, of course, there are Pisgah's wilderness areas, of
which Shining Rock and Middle Prong are so busy during the
spring, summer and fall they hardly qualify as wilderness these
days. If you're looking for a place to be alone, you'll be hard put to
find it in either area.

FRENCH BROAD DISTRICT

This is perhaps the one district in the entire forest where you're almost guaranteed solitude. This district is made up of more than
78,000 acres of the Pisgah's most remote and mountainous areas.
The peaks are high, the air invigorating, and the crowds are far
away in more accessible districts. There's only one developed
campground in the area (see *Camping Directory*), but there is a
primitive campground at Harmon Den, a couple of nice picnic areas, and more than 25 miles of hiking trails.

Murray Branch Recreation Area, six miles downriver from
Hot Springs, is a good place for fishing and canoeing, or just spend-
ing a little quiet time out in the open air. Facilities include
restrooms, drinking water, tables and grills, and a couple of picnic
shelters suitable for group or family outings. There's also a nice,
easy one-mile loop trail that offers a magnificent view of the
French Broad River and the surrounding valley.

Max Patch Mountain is a 350-acre tract of open land on a high
knob overlooking the Great Smoky Mountains and, in particular,
the Black Mountain Range. The area sits more than 4,500 feet
above the North Carolina valleys. It is closed to motorized vehicles
of any sort and is, therefore, accessible only on foot. That makes it
less crowded than most areas in the French Broad District, and
you really should make the effort to "go see." You'll find it worth
the walk.

The **Rocky Bluff Recreation Area** is also a neat place to visit.
While the focus is on camping, there are also a number of other
outdoor facilities available for day-use visitors, including an easy
one-mile trail that loops through the forest giving access to a variety of forest vegetation. There's a second trail, an easy three-
quarters of a mile, that takes you along the banks of the creek to
some of best scenery in the area. The recreation area also has

restrooms, drinking water, and campsites. Rocky Bluff is a fee area; campers pay $5 per night.

TOECANE DISTRICT

Named for two rivers that run through it, the Toe and the Cane, this area is administered from a District Office on Highway 19E in Burnsville. It incorporates more than 76,000 acres of National Forest land in four counties: Mitchell, Avery, Yancy and Buncombe. There are several developed campgrounds (see *Camping Directory*), recreation areas, picnic areas and hiking and cross-country ski trails.

Roan Mountain Gardens, located at 6,000 feet on the border of Tennessee and North Carolina, is an outstanding natural display of rhododendrons. Each year, more than 700 acres of the beautiful flowers bloom all across the mountain, drawing visitors from around the nation. The Gardens are off Highway 226 on the Tennessee/North Carolina border.

The **South Toe River Area** is a popular spot for hikers and campers. Swimming and tubing on the river is popular, too, and there are several trout streams and a bear sanctuary.

The **Carolina Hemlock Area** also offers swimming and tubing and is popular for large group recreation. The pavilion can seat up to 100 people, and often does. If you want to use it for a family reunion you'll need to make a reservation. ☎ 828-682-6146. The Carolina Hemlock Area is off Highway 80 about seven miles south of the Blue Ridge Parkway.

Craggy Mountain Scenic Area, a beautiful spot, just west of the Blue Ridge Parkway, about 10 miles northeast of Asheville, is the home of **Douglas Falls**, an area of natural scenic beauty, virgin timber, hemlock, poplar, spruce, oak, and a variety of plant life that does your heart good to see. There are no roads in the area, but there are a number of hiking trails.

Mount Mitchell

At an elevation of 6,684 feet this is the highest mountain in the eastern United States. It's a part of the Black Mountain Range, which has nine peaks rising above 6,000 feet. The ridge is a diverse wilderness area of virgin forest, rugged and, for the most part, inaccessible except via a foot trail that runs the length of the mountain crest. If you want to walk it, enter the Mount Mitchell State Park via Highway 128 north of the Blue Ridge Parkway.

GRANDFATHER DISTRICT

This is one of the most scenic areas of the forest, perhaps in the entire country. It centers on **Linville Gorge**, a fairly remote yet never-quiet wilderness area just off the Blue Ridge Parkway, not too far from the village of Spruce Pine. At the gorge, great falls cascade down the steep, rocky slopes that tower more than 1,000 feet above the river bed. It's an ideal spot for photography, hiking, fishing and rock climbing, but if you want to be totally alone, you'd better go elsewhere.

The **Wilson Creek** area of this district, bordered on the west by Grandfather Mountain, on the southwest by Linville Gorge, and on the east by Brown Mountain, offers just about any outdoor activity that might take your fancy, including hiking. If you love nature you won't want to miss the rhododendron and mountain laurel thickets that seem to spring up almost everywhere.

Brown Mountain Lights

Brown Mountain is the place to find the so-called "Brown Mountain Lights," darting lights that have intrigued the locals and visitors alike for hundreds of years. The lights have been mentioned in Indian mythology, and there have been reports of sightings as far back as pioneer days. The best place to see them, if they appear, is the overlook south of Jonas Ridge on Highway 181, or you can try Wiseman's View on the Kistler Memorial Highway in the early evening.

■ Boating & Canoeing

Northwestern North Carolina is not as well blessed with boating and canoeing opportunities as upper east Tennessee. The difference is the lack of large lakes and navigable rivers. There are, however, one or two bright spots worth checking out.

CATAWBA RIVER

Ideal for canoeing, the river provides a 32-mile stretch of water suitable for beginners. It's a small waterway that moves quite slowly for the first 12 miles or so, but gains speed farther downstream. You'll find the put-in at the Oakdale Road Bridge. The take-out is at Highway 18 in Morganton.

FONTANA LAKE

Fontana is one of the few great lakes in northwestern North Carolina and, as such, it's busy most of the time. It sits in the Great Smoky Mountains National Park close to the Tennessee/North Carolina border. With more than 10,000 acres of water available, though, there's plenty of room for all once you get away from the boat dock. There is a slight shortage of public boat ramps, and the ones in this area are always crowded. There are a couple of ramps in the vicinity of Fontana Dam just off Highway 28, another at Cable Cove, one off Forest Service Road 2550, and another at Evans Knob.

LAKE JAMES

Located west of Morganton and northeast of Marion, just off Highway 70, Lake James is also a popular boating spot. Much better served by public boat ramps, and with more than 6,500 acres of water available, you'll find plenty to do and see. Just as Lake Fontana is busy most of the time, so is Lake James. If you can get out on the water during the week, do so. It's also best if you avoid the lake during the peak of the summer break.

You'll find more than a dozen public boat ramps around the lake, with the most popular ones at Lake James State Park and the Linville Dam Power Plant. The four on the north side of the lake aren't so busy. These you can access from Highway 126. Take Highway 181 going north from Morganton and turn left onto Highway 126; the ramps are signposted along the way. There are two less-used ramps farther west on the north side of the lake. From Marion, take Highway 226 to Hawkins Road and turn right. Follow the road to the lake; the ramps are signposted along the way.

NORTH TOE & TOE RIVERS

Two scenic rivers great for canoeing, but best left to the experts. The run is more than 50 miles from Ingalls to Poplar. The put-in is close to the bridge at Highway 19E.

LAKE RHODISS

This lake is just northeast of Morganton, close enough to town to receive a lot of boating traffic, especially on weekends and during the summer. The lake is accessed by a number of roads, all leading northward from Highway 70. Unfortunately, it's not too well served with public access ramps. There are a couple at Castle Bridge, and two more much farther east close to Hickory. Part of the Catawba River, Rhodiss is a long narrow stretch of water, and that means you'll rarely be out of sight of your fellow boaters. Still, it's pretty country and a worthwhile experience.

SOUTH FORK OF THE NEW RIVER

This river provides more than 90 miles of canoeing from Boone to the bridge at Piney Creek. Some of it is rated as easy, some of it moderate. The run will take you through some of western North Carolina's most scenic areas, wilderness areas, and private land; it also has a section designated "Wild & Scenic." The put-in is at the confluence with the Straight Fork at Boone.

WILSON CREEK

Just a short section of river here, a couple of miles or so, for canoeists with moderate to advanced skills. The river drops quickly down through a scenic, rocky gorge and some fairly difficult sections of whitewater. The put-in is at Brown Mountain, with a take-out at Brown Mountain Beach.

YADKIN RIVER

This river provides a mighty canoe run of more that 150 miles from the bridge at Patterson to the Highway 29/70 bridge near Spencer. Most of it is through easy to moderate waters and is usually runnable all year. The put-in is at the Highway 268 bridge in Patterson.

■ Craft Hunting & Fairs

ASHEVILLE

 Bel Chere Festival, held in the streets of downtown Asheville in July, includes craft demonstrations, mountain music and dancing, games and country cooking.

The Guild Fair is held in July and October at the Asheville Civic Center. It is sponsored by the Southern Highland Handicraft Guild, and draws visitors from all around the region to buy a variety of locally made, hand-crafted goods and mementos.

High Country Christmas Craft Show, held at the Asheville Civic Center in December, is the place to go for unique, hand-crafted Christmas gifts.

Mountain Dance and Folk Festival, held in the Civic Center in August, features mountain crafts and demonstrations, as well as country dancing, music and clogging. ☎ 828-258-6101 or 877-274-0595.

BLOWING ROCK

Goodwin Weavers is where all sorts of hand-woven goods from tablecloths to placemats are made on what once were the water-powered looms of a hundred years ago. Today, the looms use electricity, but the techniques are the same. You'll find the facility on Main Street. Admission is free and the weaving room is open year-round during normal working hours, Monday through Saturday.

Expressions Crafts Guild and Gallery is a cooperatively owned craft shop and gallery on Highway 321. Pottery, basketry, leather goods, woodwork, jewelry, etc. The crafts are exquisite, but the prices are often a little higher than one might expect to pay. Take the turnoff to Appalachian Ski Mountain just outside of town. Open seven days a week. ☎ 828-295-7839.

BLUE RIDGE PARKWAY

The Northwest Trading Post at Mile Marker 258 is a pleasant and authentically rustic craft shop that sells crafts made by local people. Wood carvings, wooden toys, baskets, quilts, jewelry, and even home-baked goods. The Trading Post has handicapped-accessible facilities and is open April through October from 9 am until 5:30 pm. ☎ 910-982-2543.

BOONE

Blue Ridge Hearthside Crafts, on Highway 105 one mile south of Boone, is a cooperative effort with more than 350 crafts people contributing. Wood carving, country furniture, quilts, hand-woven tablecloths, pottery and jewelry. ☎ 828-963-5252.

Doe Ridge Pottery, downtown Boone at 149 King Street, is the place to go for hand-made pottery and stoneware. They also make a fine line of Christmas ornaments. ☎ 828-264-1127.

Hands Crafts Gallery is another cooperative. It's located one mile from the intersection of Highways 321 and 105, on 105 near the High Country Inn. ☎ 828-963-5338.

Morning Glory Craft Gallery, 904 W King Street, ☎ 828-265-4888. Native American art, fancy pottery and hand-made jewelry.

Morning Star Gallery is at corner of Highways 105 and 184. Traditional mountain crafts, including hand-made musical instruments (dulcimers, etc.) and fine art by regional artists. ☎ 828-898-6067.

BURNSVILLE

Mount Mitchell Crafts Fair is usually held over the first weekend in August. Along with more than 200 exhibiting crafts people, you'll enjoy an assortment of country entertainment that includes dancing and mountain music. Burnsville is in Yancey County on Highway 19E. It's quite a journey from almost anywhere, but the crafts fair is well worth the effort. ☎ 828-682-6146.

SPARTA

Blue Ridge Mountain Fair, held over two weeks in late June and early July, includes a crafts fair, a 10-K race, a horse show, and live mountain music and dancing. ☎ 910-372-5473.

SPRUCE PINE

Hensley's Forge is a blacksmith's shop run by Mike and Ben Hensley. They make wrought iron crafts: gates, candelabras, chandeliers, etc. The two craftsmen will take custom orders. The shop is five miles south of Spruce Pine on Highway 226. ☎ 828-524-4204.

Penland School of Crafts is an old establishment opened in 1929 to preserve traditional mountain crafts of western North Carolina. Today, it's the oldest and largest school for arts and crafts in the nation. Students come from around the country to spend two or three weeks learning the old skills of the mountains. They work with all sorts of media, including ceramics, metal and wood. The school is northwest of Spruce Pine, and can be reached by taking either of Highways 19E or 226 and turning off at Penland Road. From there, you simply follow the signs for about five miles to the school. Although it's not generally open to the public, guided tours are available by appointment. ☎ 828-765-2359.

■ Fishing

 Because of its lack of great lakes and navigable rivers, the northwestern section of North Carolina is short on fishing of the customary type. There are one or two exceptions but, on the whole, this is trout fishing country. There must be at least a thousand locations scattered throughout the region where rainbow, brown and brook trout thrive; in small lakes, on mountain rivers and in fast-moving creeks. Pick a spot and give it a try; you won't be disappointed. For a complete listing of trout streams, lakes and rivers, and a list of North Carolina's current fishing rules and regulations, contact the **North Carolina Wildlife Resources Commission** in Raleigh at ☎ 919-733-3633. Below are some of the more well-known locations for traditional fishing.

FONTANA LAKE

Fontana is one of the few great lakes in northwestern North Carolina and, as such, it's also one of the busiest fishing spots. It offers more than 10,000 acres of water, but not many public boat ramps. There are a couple of ramps in the vicinity of Fontana just off Highway 28, another at Cable Cove, one off Forest Service Road 2550, and another at Evans Knob. What sort of sport is available? Well, there's smallmouth and largemouth bass; some white bass; walleye and muskie; and the inevitable crappie. The fishing is considered good.

LAKE JAMES

Located west of Morganton and northeast of Marion, just off Highway 70, Lake James is also a popular fishing spot. This one is much better served by public boat ramps and, with more than 6,500 acres of water, you'll find plenty of action, too. Lake James is busy much of the time, especially on weekends.

Anglers will be pleased to learn that fishing here is good to very good. It's well stocked with largemouth, smallmouth and white bass. There seems to be a strong population of walleye, as well as the usual pan fish, including some sunfish.

See page 163 for details on ramp access at Lake James.

LAKE RHODISS

Located just to the northeast of Morganton, this lake is also very popular with the boating fraternity.

Rhodiss, part of the Catawba River, is a long narrow stretch of water, and that means you'll rarely be out of sight of your fellow anglers. Still, the fishing for largemouth bass, crappie and sunfish is good.

You'll find the lake by taking any one of a number of roads that lead northward from Highway 70. Unfortunately, it's not too well served by public access ramps. There are a couple at Castle Bridge and a couple more much farther east close to Hickory.

■ Rock Climbing

STONE MOUNTAIN STATE PARK

 Said to have something for everyone, Stone Mountain State Park offers several routes rated from easy to moderate. These include the South Face and the North Face. Ratings range upward from 5.4. No new bolting is allowed. Existing bolts are all considered safe, but check with the local authorities before taking anything for granted. ☎ 336-957-8185.

LINVILLE GORGE WILDERNESS AREA

The gorge offers a number of interesting and challenging climbs. In places, the gorge reaches depths in excess of 2,000 feet. The climbing areas, and there are more than 100 routes, include The Chimneys, Table Rock, Little Table Rock, Hawksbille, Sitting Bear, and Shortoff Mountain. Ratings range from 5.4 to 5.12. Most are bolted. Hawksbill is a fairly difficult overhanging climb. ☎ 828-652-2144 for more information.

PISGAH NATIONAL FOREST

Looking Glass Rock is one of the best-known climbing areas in the Great Smoky Mountains. There are some 80 routes available, ranging in difficulty from 5.5 to 5.11 and A2 to A5. The white granite mountain rises out of the forest and offers some spectacular views. The climbs include overhangs, cracks, and faces. The five main areas include the South Face, North Face, Hidden Wall, Sun Wall, and the Nose Area. Looking Glass Rock is just off Highway 276 some seven miles from Brevard. ☎ 828-877-3265 for more information.

■ Hiking

There are literally hundreds, if not thousands, of hiking and walking trails within the Great Smoky Mountains in northwestern North Carolina. To list them all would require a book much larger than this one. We have profiled a few of the better-known trails. Some of them are, because of their location and character, very busy most of the year. If you need more information, you have only to contact any of the ranger districts listed in the *Information Directory* under the Pisgah National Forest. They will be happy to supply you with detailed listings and maps.

AREA HIKES

BABEL TOWER TRAIL: This is a fairly short trail within the Linville Gorge Wilderness Area. It is heavily used through the summer and on weekends. It has a lot of steep grades and switchbacks and the going is often difficult. Although it leads to one of the most scenic areas in the gorge, this trail is probably best left to more experienced hikers. The trail rises more than 900 feet over 1.2 miles and enjoys some great views of the river and rapids.

CRAGGY PINNACLE TRAIL: This trail, a little more than a mile long, is on the Blue Ridge Parkway at Mile Marker 364. It's a switchback trail that starts in the parking lot of the Craggy Dome Overlook and winds its way on upward through stands of rhododendron and wildflowers, to the pinnacle of the mountain. Again, the going can be quite strenuous, and there's always the possibility of high winds, especially at the pinnacle. The view from the top is fantastic.

GREAT SMOKY MOUNTAINS NATIONAL PARK

The park lies almost equally in Tennessee and North Carolina, and can be accessed from both states. That being the case, you'll also find trails on both sides of the state line. Some have already been listed in the chapter dealing with upper east Tennessee. These include Abrams Falls Trail, Alum Cave Bluff Trail, Bone Valley Trail, Cataloochie Divide Trail, Cove Mountain Trail, Deep Creek Trail, Hughes Ridge Trail, Jonas Creek Trail, Mount Le Conte Trail and Snake Den Ridge Trail.

LOVER'S LEAP-PUMP GAP TRAIL: This area offers several loop trails ranging from a little more than a mile to one of more than 7½ miles. Lover's Leap is a rocky ledge high above the French Broad River overlooking Hot Springs and the French Broad River Valley. The trails, during spring and early summer, are alive with wildflowers. The Leap Trail is often quite busy. If you want to get away from the crowds, take the Pump Gap Trail Loop.

From Hot Springs, go east on Highway 25/70 across the French Broad River Bridge. Immediately after crossing, turn left at the first intersection onto River Road and follow the signs to the Silvermine Trailhead.

MOUNT MITCHELL TRAIL: This is a strenuous hike through virgin stands of hardwood forest, across several mountain streams, and on for more than 5½ miles to the summit of Mount Mitchell. The view is spectacular and well worth the haul up more than 3,600 feet from the trailhead. Not for the faint of heart or weak of wind.

The trailhead is at the Black Mountain Campground on the South Toe River. From Burnsville, take Highway 19E and then head south on Highway 80. Turn right onto Forest Service Road 472 at Mount Mitchell Golf Course and follow it to the Black Mountain Campground.

LOST COVE TRAIL: This is a 7½-mile loop trail with its trailhead at the Old Warden Station near Roseborough. The route climbs westward on the crest of Timber Ridge to the summit of Bee Mountain, then descends steeply into Lost Cove Creek. It follows the creek and then ascends once more to Timber Ridge before dropping to Gragg Prong Creek and back to its starting point. The going is moderately difficult and often strenuous.

From Highway 221, take Roseborough Road and drive east to the village; the trailhead is on your right.

SHORTOFF MOUNTAIN TRAIL: This 11½-mile trail takes hikers into the Linville Gorge Area. It follows the ridgecrest southward, steeply, and provides spectacular views of the Chimneys and Linville Gorge from Shortoff Mountain. At one point, it connects with the **Mountains to the Sea Trail**, continues on along Old NC 105, and then on to NC 126.

The trailhead is near the Table Rock Picnic Area. From Highway 181 just to the south of Piedmont Spur, take Rose Creek Road and follow it westward past Table Rock to the trailhead.

SHUT-IN TRAIL: This trail was originally constructed in the 1890s by George Vanderbilt to provide horse access from the Biltmore Estate to his hunting lodge on Mount Pisgah. Today, more than 16 miles of hiking trail leads through assorted woodland, forest and rhododendron fields to the Walnut Cove Overlook. It then takes a steep and long descent into Chestnut Grove. From there it continues to the summit of Little Pisgah Mountain and the trail end at the Mount Pisgah Trailhead.

You'll find the trailhead on the Blue Ridge Parkway at Mile Marker 393.6.

WHITE OAK-HICKEY FORK TRAIL LOOP: This is a complete loop trail of about 7½ miles through some of the most beautiful scenery in the mountains. The trail has been designated "most difficult" due to its length and steepness. Experienced hikers, however, will enjoy the challenge. The area is scattered with sparkling mountain streams, a cascading waterfall, and a variety of woodland species. A great trail, if ever there was one.

From Hot Springs, go east on Highway 25/70 to Highway 208. Turn left onto 208 for 3½ miles to Highway 212, which you take for seven more miles to NC 1310. Turn left onto 1310 and go 1½ miles to a fork in the road. Bear left and go to the end of the road; parking is available on the right.

■ Mountain Biking

BOONE

Greenway Trail

 This is a fairly easy six-mile trail on gravel and dirt. It begins and ends in Boone itself and, along the way, crosses the South Fork of the New River by way of rustic wooden bridges several times. Once out in the country, it narrows and wends its way through miles of beautiful western North Carolina scenery. The trail is bordered by lush vegetation, wildflowers, rhododendrons and stands of ancient oak trees. From the junction of Highways 321 and 221 in Boone, go south on Highway 221 for about a half-mile then turn east onto State Farm Road. From there, ride one mile and turn left into the Watauga Recreation Area.

Linville Gorge Loop

This is a bit of a tester. You'll need plenty of stamina to ride the almost 50 miles that make up the Linville Gorge Loop. The trail leads over paved and dirt roads, up hill and down into valleys, but rising inevitably through more than 4,000 feet. It's not a ride for the Sunday afternoon cyclist. If you're up to it, it's a real adventure, exciting and exhilarating. Much of the way you'll spend in low gear, standing on the pedals; then it's downhill, freewheeling with wind blowing in your face, only to turn upward again, straining hard just to keep the machine in motion. Beyond that, it's a ride of beauty and broad vistas, of wildflowers on the mountains, with the Linville River, sometimes several thousand feet below at the bottom of the great gorge. There's little in the way of facilities along the way, so you'll need to take along plenty to eat and drink. Plan to spend eight to 10 hours on the trail. From Linville Falls, take NC Highway 183.

Watauga River Road

The name truly reflects the nature of the adventure. It follows along the easy dirt surface on the banks of the river. If you're a lover of all things pastoral, you're in for a rare treat. The trail meanders along beside quiet waters as well as a stretch of whitewater where you can watch the frolics of the rafters as they maneuver the big rubber boats through one set of rapids after another. The road winds onward beyond the riverbank, through open fields where black and white cows chew contentedly through the day, and on to Blowing Rock. You can make it as long or short a visit as you like, for the area offers a number of quaint little bed-and-breakfast inns where you can spend hours of sightseeing and a pleasant evening before riding onward the next day. Take Highway 105 south from the junction of Highways 194 and 105 toward Blowing Rock; the ride is well posted.

THE FONTANA VILLAGE TRAILS

There are several interesting trails in and around Fontana, most of them short, less than five miles, but often testing. Some are on TVA property, some in the Nantahala National Forest. The **Lewellyn Cove Loop** is a three-mile trail that intersects with three other trails. The four trails can be cycled as one, or individually. The dirt trails – steep, rocky climbs – provide something more than an aerobic hour or two; the rides offer an interesting cross-section of the area as they meander, often through dense woodland, then open fields, and on across woodland creeks and mountain streams. Be sure to drop in at the bike shop at the Fontana Village Resort for supplies and camping information. For more information on Fontana Village, see pages 198 and 216, and page 324 for accommodations.

Clawhammer Trail, Black Mountain

Black Mountain is a small town some 20 miles east of Asheville. Famous for its arts and crafts community, the little settlement also boasts a testing bike ride. From Black Mountain itself, the trail twists and turns over seven tortuous miles and rises more than 2,000 feet to make the heart pump and the muscles ache. It's a creek side trail, crossing back and forth across the water a half-dozen time, through some of North Carolina's most beautiful mountain country. It's a bit out of the way, but well worth a visit.

TSALI TRAILS - NANTAHALA NATIONAL FOREST

The Nantahala National Forest is just off Highway 28 near Bryson City. Inside the park are some of the most popular biking trails in the mountains. Four trails, together more than 35 miles of riding, offer a diversity of pedaling: moderate to steep climbs and exhilarating downhill dashes on trails that run from smooth to bumpy. Along the way you'll pass through pine forest and hardwood stands. It's a popular area, so try to pick a time when it's less likely to be crowded. If you're interested in camping, the park has plenty to offer: more than 40 units, drinking water, showers and even flush toilets. Fishing is available, too.

■ Horseback Riding

Journeying on horseback through a forest brings spectacular views. Both national forests in western North Carolina offer a selection of experiences for riders of all skill levels.

Many of the hiking trails listed for the Pisgah and the Nantahala are open for equestrian use (check the listings here and in the southwestern North Carolina section under *Hiking*). Those that are are marked with a horse-use sign (like the one you see here) may be used by horses. If a trail is unmarked, or if it's marked with a red slash through the horse, then the trail is reserved for hiking only. All Forest Service roads are open for horseback riding, unless there is a sign indicating otherwise.

Riders in both of western North Carolina's national forests must observe the rules detailed on pages 38-39.

PISGAH NATIONAL FOREST

Toecane Ranger District (South Toe River Area)

This area features two major trails, the **Buncombe Horse Range** (17 miles) and **Camp Alice** (two miles). Both are set among numerous streams and creeks that flow down the steep slopes of the Black Mountains. The Buncombe is recommended only for riders with advanced skills. The trail is long, hard going, and physically challenging. Aside from the two designated trails, there are also more than 10 miles of gated Forest Service roads that provide easy to moderate riding.

From Burnsville, take Highway 19E and head south on Highway 80. Turn right onto Forest Service Road 472 at Mount Mitchell Golf Course and follow it past the Black Mountain Campground to a parking area set aside for horse transports about four miles past the campground.

VICTOR FIELDS: Victor Fields is a part of Sevenmile Ridge, adjacent to the Blue Ridge Parkway. It's an area of gentle ridgetops, hardwood forests, and open fields. Riders enjoy some fine views, including the Black Mountains in the distance.

From the intersection of NC 80, head north on the Blue Ridge Parkway for two miles and turn onto an unsigned gravel road, Forest Service Road 5511. You'll find parking available in several pull-offs along the way.

COLEMAN BOUNDARY: This area is also known as Big Ivy. It is a scenic area that sits high on the northwestern slopes of Great Craggy Mountain below the Blue Ridge Parkway in Buncombe County. There are seven designated horse trails, all fairly short, that provide a variety of riding opportunities:

Bear Pen runs along an old road for almost 1½ miles and features a number of stream crossings. **Corner Creek** also runs along an old road, but provides several switchbacks along its 1½ miles. **Elk Pen** is a stream-side trail of almost two miles that features switchbacks. **Hensley Fields** is an old road on the side of a hill with some physically challenging steep sections over its two miles. **Perkins** is a steep old road trail of a little more than a mile. **Stair Creek** is another old road that runs by the side of a stream for one mile and features a number of switchbacks. **Walker Creek,** another old road, runs alongside a stream for most of its 1½ miles, and it, too, features switchbacks.

Beyond the designated trails, Coleman Boundary also offers more than 16 miles of easy to moderate riding on Forest Service Roads 74 and 5548. Some routes wind in and out of coves, while others provide grand views of the surrounding country.

From Asheville, take US 19/23 north to NC 197. Turn east and drive to the Barnardsville Exit; turn right onto SR 2173. Go five miles to Forest Service Road 74 at the forest's boundary and park along the side of the road.

Toecane Ranger District
(Flattop Mountain Area)

Flattop is the prominent mountain range that separates the Nolichucky River and Big Creek drainages near the Tennessee/ North Carolina border. There are about 10 miles of riding on Forest Service Road 278. This road skirts the main ridgetop and is open to horses and vehicles for most of the year. Openings in the forest along the roads provide some nice views. The going is easy to moderately difficult.

From Burnsville, go west on US 19E and then north on 19W. Forest Service Road 278 begins at Spivey Gap on 19W near the state line, or at the end of SR 1415, which is a dirt road also on 19W.

Pisgah Ranger District
(South Mills River Area)

This is one of the most popular hiking and horseback riding areas in the Pisgah National Forest and is also one of the busiest. There are numerous trails scattered all over the area. Many are loop trails. All provide riding opportunities of varying types; most are moderately easy. The majority of trails follow old logging roads and railroads that run alongside the forest streams and creeks. It's a very beautiful area of mountain streams, hardwood forests and wildflowers.

Most of the trails connect to the **South Mills River Trail**, which begins at the end of Forest Service Road 476 and at Turkey Pen Gap Trailhead. From US 276, southeast of Waynesville, turn onto Forest Road 1206 (Yellow Gap Road) near the Pink Beds Picnic Area, and then turn right onto Forest Road 476. Go for a little more than a half-mile and park in the roadside campsite on the right. Do not take trailers beyond this point; there is no turnaround.

The **Turkey Pen Trail** starts at the end of Forest Road 297 off NC 280, northeast of Brevard. Riders should stay away from this trailhead on weekends; it's very busy. Also, there's no turnaround space for trailers when the parking area is full.

Pisgah Ranger District (North Mills River Area)

This is an area of the Pisgah southwest of Asheville where numerous tributaries of the North Mills River flow through the basin that borders the Blue Ridge Parkway between Mount Pisgah and bent Creek Gap in Henderson County. A number of trails combined with gated forest roads provide some interesting and sometimes challenging, multiple-loop riding opportunities.

> *Be very careful; these routes are shared not only with hikers, but with mountain bikers, too.*

All trails begin from the **Trace Ridge Trailhead**, a busy intersection for hikers and horses. From Asheville, take Highway 191/280 and go to its intersection with Forest Road 5000. Follow 5000 (Wash Creek Road) for 1½ miles north from the North Mills River Campground. Turn left across a low concrete bridge and continue for a half-mile more to the parking area. Parking is set aside for horse trailers but, as already mentioned, you may find the area very crowded on weekends.

French Broad Ranger District (Harmon Den Area)

You'll find several nice horse trails here that range in length from one to five miles. Cold Springs Creek flows through dense woods and grassy fields on its way to the Pigeon River, and the entire area shows the remains of its history: farming, logging, narrow gauge railroads, settlements.

The grassy ridges of Max Patch Mountain near the Tennessee border are the high points in the area, and the woodland trails combine with a number of Forest Service roads to provide loops, some of which are open to motorized vehicles.

Take the Harmon Den Exit off I-40 near Tennessee and head northeast on Cold Springs Road (Forest Service Road 148) for three miles to the Harmon Den parking area on the left. Parking for horse trailers is also available at the lower junction of FRs 148 and 3526, Robert Gap Trailhead at the junction of FR 148 and SR 1182, and at the Cherry Ridge Trailhead on SR 1182. The trailheads are all about seven miles from one another.

■ Llama Trekking

That's right, the word is llama, and llama trekking is the latest rage to hit the Great Smoky Mountains in western North Carolina. It's a combination of hiking, backpacking and pony trekking made all the more interesting, and exciting, by the strange but lovable creatures that carry the load for you. These gentle animals transform what can be for many a long and arduous hike through some of the most rugged mountains into little more than a long, relaxing, walk in the sunshine. Several outfitters now have herds – maybe that's not the right word – of lovable pack animals with an available guide to take you on an adventure where your hairy companion is right at the center of the experience. The Pisgah National Forest has hundreds of miles of hiking trails open to llama trekking, and the adventure usually lasts over a weekend or several weekdays; you choose.

Speaking of choosing, when you arrive at the jumping-off point of your adventure, you'll be introduced to the team – llamas, that is – and you'll choose one to be your sidekick for the duration. Personality – theirs, not yours – will play a big part in the choice, although they say that the choice is really made by the llama. These friendly creatures with their big brown eyes seem to have a way of pulling you in. Next, it's time for a little orientation: you'll learn about the habits and idiosyncrasies of the llamas, and your itinerary – the trail, terrain, etc. Once that's finished it's time to move out. You'll feel a little strange at first; after all, your new buddy is unlike anything you've every come across before. But you'll soon get used it.

Lunchtime follows about an hour into the trek, and it's quite an experience. The tour guides never do anything by halves, and the food is no exception: turkey sandwiches, pasta salad, and homemade brownies are the usual fare.

The trail wends its way through woodland and meadow, along the riverbanks up rocky inclines. The scenery is often spectacular, the weather wonderful, and the atmosphere one of total relaxation – a far cry from the usual backbreaking, sweaty experience that backpacking can become in these mountains. Camping for the night is another unusual experience. A shady spot somewhere on the banks of a river is the usual locale of choice. The llamas are tethered close by, where they can see what's going on, and then it's time for a little local sightseeing: a walk through woods and up the trail to a local waterfall, perhaps, or maybe nothing more than a quiet evening walk along the river bank, or an hour or two of fishing.

Then it's dinner time. There's nothing quite like a meal in the open air around the campfire to set the mood for an evening of storytelling and singing. And so it goes, the next day continuing much the same as the one before, but maybe taking in a little swimming, rock climbing or exploring. At the end of the trek you'll have enjoyed a unique experience you're not likely to soon forget. Perhaps you'll do it all again next year.

Llama Trekking Outfitter

Wind Dancers Lodging and Llama Treks
1966 Martins Creek Road, Clyde, NC 28721
☎ 828-627-6986

Lunch, dinner and overnight llama treks on peaceful, secluded woodland trails near the Great Smoky Mountain National Park. Unique log chalet-style B&B lodging. Open year-round.

■ Snow Skiing

The first ski resort in North Carolina opened 35 years ago at Cataloochee, in the Maggie Valley area. It was quickly joined by the Blowing Rock Ski Lodge, and then by Hound Ears. Since then, skiing has become the premier outdoor winter sport. More than a dozen major ski resorts cater to an ever-increasing number of enthusiasts, and the service they offer continues to improve with each passing year. Today, the ski lodges are reminiscent of the European lodges and, while the area can't really compete with the ski establishments of Colorado and northern California, they certainly do provide a quality that's hard to beat. Beyond regular skiing, the new sport of snowboarding is becoming increasingly popular, as is cross-country skiing. The season usually runs from mid-November through March.

CROSS-COUNTRY SKIING

This sport is becoming more and more popular. It's still restricted mainly to national park areas here, and then only in some specially designated sections, such as certain trails on the Blue Ridge Parkway: Roan Mountain, Doughton Park, etc., and to one or two of the major ski resorts, like Beech Mountain. It's a very invigorating, taxing sport, but an exciting outdoor experience like no other. To be alone on the mountain when the air is cold and crisp, with only the sound of the snow whispering beneath your skis, is an experience you'll never forget. For cross-country skiing information in North Carolina, call the Ranger's Office on the Blue Ridge Parkway. ☎ 828-295-7591.

APPALACHIAN SKI MOUNTAIN

Located in Blowing Rock, the Appalachian Ski Mountain is a family-owned resort with eight major slopes of varying difficulty. It has a peak elevation of almost 4,000 feet, and a vertical drop of more than 360 feet. A lot of thought and effort has been put into this resort. There's a great Bavarian-style ski lodge with a huge fireplace and an atmosphere very like those found in European alpine resorts.

The slopes are serviced by three chairlifts and a rope tow. The lodge incorporates rental and nightly accommodations, a restaurant, a gift shop and a ski shop. Rental equipment, clothing and lessons for skiers of all skill levels are available, and the management provides instruction for young skiers aged four to 12. For rates, brochures and information, ☎ 800-322-2373 or 828-295-7828.

BEECH MOUNTAIN SKI RESORT

At an elevation of more than 5,500 feet, this is the highest ski area in the eastern United States. It's a full-service resort with a large complex that includes a variety of accommodations and a number of shops, stores, ski schools and restaurants. Beech Mountain has 14 ski slopes of varying difficulties: five for beginners, six for skiers of intermediate skill, and three more reserved for advanced skiers. The vertical drop is more than 830 feet, and the mountain is served by a high-speed chairlift, a J-bar tow and a rope tow. Ski packages are available. For information, reservations and brochures, ☎ 800-438-293 or 828-387-2011.

HIGH MEADOWS

Just off Highway 21 near Roaring Gap, High Meadows is one of the smaller skiing areas in the northwest. There are two slopes, each with a surface lift and a vertical drop of about 80 feet. Write PO Box 222, Roaring Gap, NC 28668 for information. ☎ 910-363-2622.

HOUND EARS

Another smaller ski resort, Hound Ears has three slopes with a vertical drop of about 110 feet. The resort caters mainly to families, beginners and cross-country skiers. There's a chairlift and a surface lift. The ski area is located near Blowing Rock. ☎ 828-963-4321.

MILL RIDGE

Located in the Banner Elk/Boone/Blowing Rock area, Mill Ridge has often been called the South's "Biggest Little Slope" and is often very busy. The area has three slopes with a vertical drop of more than 225 feet, a chairlift and a surface lift. It caters mostly to families and beginners. Route 1, Banner Elk, NC 28604, ☎ 828-963-4500.

HAWKSNEST

This is one of North Carolina's premier ski resorts. It is very busy, often to the point of distraction, for most of the season. Once you get out on the slopes you'll understand why it's so popular. There are 11 ski slopes: two for beginners, five for intermediates and four more for advanced skiers. The elevation at the peak is 4,800 feet, and the vertical drop is around 620 feet. The mountain is serviced by two double chairlifts and two surface lifts. There's also a special snowboard park reserved exclusively for those who prefer one board to two. They offer a couple of special programs; Kiddy Hawk, which caters to kids aged from five to 12; and Nighthawk, a program for advanced skiers capable of nighttime skiing. The resort offers all sorts of facilities and special services, including a good restaurant, a lounge, coffee shop, and a ski shop where you can rent equipment, clothing and snowboards. You can also take ski and snowboarding lessons. The resort is in the town of Seven Devils at 1800 Skyland Drive. ☎ 828-963-6561. For a snow report at the resort, ☎ 828-963-6563.

SUGAR MOUNTAIN

This is one of the state's most popular resorts and rarely will you find the slopes deserted here. It is estimated that, at peak periods, more than 9,000 skiers per hour descend the slopes. With an elevation of more than 5,300 feet and a vertical drop of over 1,200, it's one of the highest resorts in the state. There are 18 ski slopes operating on Sugar. Seven are for beginners, nine for skiers of intermediate skills, and two are designated as expert runs. The mountain is serviced by five chairlifts and three surface lifts. There's lots of family-oriented fun, including a special program for kids called Sugar Bears. There's also a restaurant, coffee shop, a nursery for the little ones, and a ski shop offering rental equipment and lessons. The resort is not far from Banner Elk, just off Highway 184. ☎ 828-898-5421. For a snow report, ☎ 828-963-5265.

WOLF LAUREL

Situated 40 miles north of Asheville, close to Mars Hill and Highways 19 and 23, Wolf Laurel is one of the state's newest resorts. The peak elevation is 4,600 feet, providing a vertical drop of 650 feet. There are 16 ski slopes in operation, catering to skiers of all skill levels, and more are planned. The mountain is serviced by four lifts. The lodge incorporates a ski shop where you can rent clothing and equipment, take lessons, and purchase season passes. Several special ski programs are on offer, including night skiing and the SkiWee children's program. ☎ 800-817-4111.

Shopping

■ Asheville

 Asheville is the shopping center for all of western North Carolina. Unlike so many downtown areas that have decayed and fallen victim to perimeter malls, its city center has undergone something of a renaissance. Today, downtown Asheville is very pedestrian-friendly. There are several conveniently located municipal parking areas and plenty of neat little restaurants and coffee shops.

Biltmore Avenue is the place to start if you're into upscale shops and art galleries. Antique hunters will not want to miss **Antiques**

at the Square, at 4 Biltmore Avenue, or **King-Thomasson Antiques**, just a few blocks further on.

Fain's Department Store is a must downtown stop, and then there's the **Corner Cupboard Antique Mall** at 43 Rankin Avenue; **Lexington Park Antiques** at 65 West Walnut; and the **Asheville Antique Mall** at 43 Rankin Avenue.

■ Biltmore Village

Just outside Asheville, Biltmore Village, with its cobbled streets and tiny shops, is reminiscent of an Old-English county town. If you're a dedicated shopper, you won't want to miss it. You'll find all sorts of interesting places to browse. Book lovers could spend hours at **Once Upon a Time**, 7 All Souls Crescent. **The Biltmore Magic Company**, at 1 Swan Street, really is a shop with a difference, and **The Complete Naturalist**, at 2 Biltmore Place, offers all sorts of bits and pieces of interest to nature lovers. A **Christmas House**, at 10 All Souls Crescent, is the place to go for special Christmas ornaments and goodies, while **Fireside Antiques and Interiors**, at 5 Boston Way, specializes in English antiques. **Interiors Marketplace**, just one block north of the village near the former railroad depot, is a unique shopping experience. Inside you'll find all sorts of unusual, one-of-a-kind merchandise – all upscale, and presented in a way that's designed to make you feel right at home.

■ Black Mountain

Black Mountain is just 15 miles east of Asheville. It's a tiny little mountain village that seems to be dedicated almost exclusively to the antique hunter.

In the Historic District, near the old railroad depot, you'll find a number of antique stores and malls, including the **Cherry Street Antique Mall** at 139 Cherry Street; the **Black Mountain Antique Mall** at 100 Sutton Avenue; and **Howard's Antiques** at 121 Cherry Street.

■ Blowing Rock

Once again, it's the main street that provides most of the shopping opportunities in this quaint little mountain town. The street is not too long and is well within walking distance of the parking areas and accommodations.

You'll find a variety of specialty shops scattered along both sides, including a number of gift and antique stores. Of special interest are the **Shops of Martin House**, an assortment of small shops in a one-time residence on Main Street, where you will find all sorts of curios, from gourmet coffee to candles and from clothing to candy.

■ Boone

Most of the shopping in Boone is done on West King Street. Outlets and stores here sell everything from fine clothing to ski equipment, jewelry to fine art and gifts. A couple are worthy of a special mention. At 487 W. King, the **Blue Planet Map Company** is one of those places you always wish you could find, but never seem able to. Inside you'll find maps of every shape and size covering all points around the globe, atlases, children's books, globes and clothing – all with a map theme.

The **Boone Antique Mall** at 631 W. King is just the place for those who like to browse. More than 27,000 square feet of floor space on three levels and over 75 dealers offer everything from antique jewelry to furniture to fine china. A must for any antique hunter.

■ Hendersonville

The Main Street downtown is Hendersonville's most popular shopping spot. The old storefronts and historic buildings have been renovated and given new life, and the sidewalks are lined with trees, flowering plants, and park benches, making for a very pleasant outdoor experience. Unfortunately, parking does not seem to have been given the same consideration and Main Street can be a hike of several blocks from your parking spot. Even so, it's a pleasant walk and the end more than justifies the means; the downtown area is a microcosm of antique shops, clothing stores, outlets, and specialty and gift shops.

The Curb Market, inside at the corner of N. Church and Second Avenue, boasts more than 135 merchants who make or grow everything they sell. For antique hunters, there's **Mehri & Company** at 501 N. Main; the **Main Street Antique Mall** at 429 N.

Main; the **Village Green Antique Mall** at 424 N. Main; and **Wagon Wheel Antiques** at 423 N. Main. If your kids love teddy bears, don't miss the **Teddy Bear Cupboard** at 442 N. Main. **Honeysuckle Hollow** is a quaint shop that's difficult to hang a tag on, but it is filled with all sorts of nifty goods.

If it's mall shopping you enjoy, just head out on Highway 64E from Main Street and you'll find the **Blue Ridge Mall** at 1800 Four Seasons Boulevard. There's not much to be said about it. It's a typical large mall with most of the big stores represented, including J.C. Penney, Belk, and Kmart. (Also see page 229.)

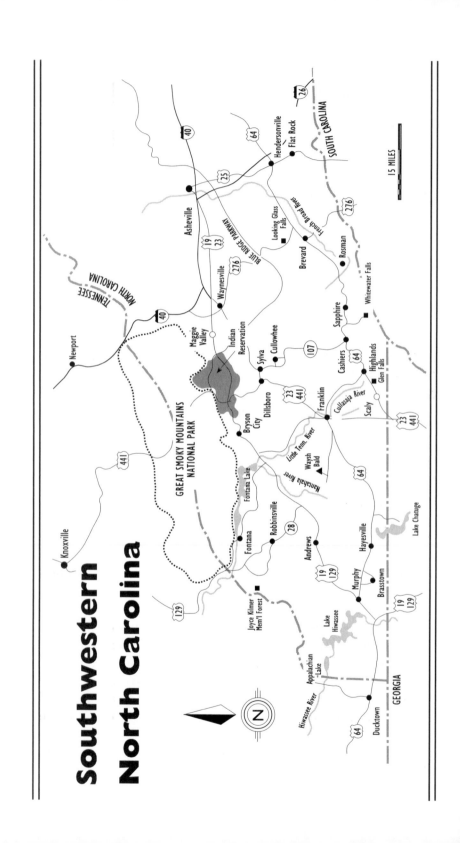

Southwestern
North Carolina

Southwestern North Carolina

Southwestern North Carolina is a remote, mountainous area where two great forests meet and beautiful rivers flow through a wild and lovely countryside. It is, for the most part, as unspoiled as it was when the white man first set foot among the hills and valleys at the very edge of what was then the known world.

History

 The area was first populated mostly by **Cherokee Indians**, bear, bison and deer. And it is for those Indians, though they are mostly long gone, that many of the beautiful places in the southwestern mountains are remembered. Ancient Indian names given to the mountains peaks, great forests, and fast-flowing rivers still conjure images of the area's distant past: peaceful Cherokee villages where, for a thousand years, Indians lived out their lives.

In 1540, Spanish explorer **Hernando De Soto** arrived. He was looking for the fabled "city of gold" that the Indians in one village after another told him was just beyond the next ridge. Needless to say, De Soto didn't find what he was looking for. So, instead, he set his force of 600 soldiers to pillaging and plundering. The Cherokees were enslaved and forced to carry the Spanish supplies and equipment, while their crops were ravaged and destroyed. De Soto set the Cherokees upon the downward path of exploitation and destruction they would travel for almost 300 years. De Soto was followed by settlers from the east, pioneers who were continually pushing back the western boundaries of the New World. Some settled in the valleys among the mountains, building small-holdings, villages and churches; others moved on, restless. Then came the infamous "Trail of Tears" that took the Cherokees out of the ancestral hunting grounds in the 1830s. And it was around that time when a new breed of white man began arriving. They came from the east, an affluent people looking for relief from the summer heat of the eastern lowlands. They brought their slaves with them, bought up huge tracts of land, built fine summer homes, and introduced a new social, but seasonal, society to the mountains. In a way, it was the beginning of the tourist industry here.

The Civil War had little effect on the southwestern mountains, except that the summer influx of wealthy southerners came to an end. Things were quiet for a while after the war, and then the railway came, bringing with it another new breed: the entrepreneur. Timber, coal and other minerals were taken from the hills and exported to the ravenous east. Money flowed into the mountains. Then came tourists, naturalists, and outdoorspeople and, along with them, more money and a new industry – **tourism**. Hotels, inns and resorts sprung up everywhere.

Today, the federal government, along with the state government and a number of local agencies, has taken steps to see that development doesn't get out of hand. Much of the land is protected, with thousands of acres placed under the protection of the National Park Service and the National Forest Service. Other land has been set aside for use as state parks, and still more is under the control of massive federal agencies such as the Tennessee Valley Authority (TVA), which has gone to great lengths to preserve and develop outdoor parks and remote mountain getaways.

Of the Cherokees, only a few remain on a small reservation appropriately called Cherokee, in North Carolina. They are the descendants of the few that refused to leave their ancestral homes. When the time came for them to move, they hid in the forests, waiting for better times. Eventually those times did arrive, and the Indians were allowed to stay. The result is a tiny Indian township in the mountains, one of the richest communities in the state. Money flows into Cherokee in the form of tourists looking for something different. There's even a little action; bingo is big business in Cherokee.

Southwestern North Carolina is a beautiful area; a land where tiny mountain towns are scattered like pearls on the land. It is the great outdoors of the Southern Appalachians.

Getting Here

BY AIR

 The area is served most conveniently by **Asheville Regional Airport**. You'll have to fly one of the commuter airlines such as **American Eagle**, ☎ 800-433-7300; **ASA**, ☎ 800-282-3424; **Comair**, ☎ 800-354-9822; or **US Air Express**, ☎ 800-428-4322.

Alternatively, you can fly into Chattanooga or Knoxville, Tennessee; the Tri-Cities Airport in upper east Tennessee; or from Charlotte or Raleigh-Durham, North Carolina. All of these gateways will require that you drive awhile to reach the Great Smoky Mountains.

BY ROAD

From Tennessee

Three main routes serve North Carolina from Tennessee.

From the south, you'll travel into Chattanooga by one of three interstates: 59 from Birmingham, AL; 24 from Nashville, TN; and 75 either from Atlanta, Georgia, or Knoxville. From Chattanooga, go north on I-75 to Exit 20, and then take US 64, a tortuous route, east to Murphy, North Carolina.

From the north, the easiest way is via I-40 that leads from Knoxville and all points west to Asheville. Then travel south either on I-26, or Highways 19 and 23.

All other routes involve heading east on some of the most twisting highways in the nation. US 23 heads east out of Erwin, joins 19W, and then goes straight up into the Unaka Mountains toward Asheville.

From Elizabethton, US 19E will take you to 321, one of Tennessee's most scenic highways, and from there into Boone.

From Eastern North Carolina

From Raleigh-Durham, follow I-85 and I-40 west to Asheville; **from Charlotte**, take I-85 west to Gastonia, then Highway 74 west to the junction with Highway 64, which you follow all the way in.

From Georgia

The primary route is US 23/441 north from Tallulah Falls. It's a picturesque route, and a delightful driving adventure all its own.

Getting Around

The southwestern corner of North Carolina is still a very remote area. In the extreme west, the few hotels and restaurants are mostly located in Murphy, and there aren't that many. The farther east you go, the more choices you'll have. You might like to base yourself somewhere within a triangle comprised of the three cities of Asheville, Franklin and Hendersonville, where you'll find plenty of good hotels. From there, you can visit most of the interesting places by day trips. The secret is, of course, to plan your stay. This book will help you do that, but you'll also need to obtain a good map, preferably a topographical one.

If you like to camp, this is the place for you. There are plenty of campgrounds of all sorts and sizes from which to choose. The Nantahala National Forest provides good opportunities; there are more in the state parks; and, of course, there are the commercial campgrounds.

Sightseeing

■ Brevard

Brevard is a popular retirement community just off Highway 64 on the edge of the Nantahala National Forest, and only about a dozen miles from Hendersonville. It's a clean, pleasant little town that ranks high on lists of best places to live. Brevard is the seat of Transylvania County. Asheville Airport is less than 20 miles away via the new I-26 connector, and Transylvania's two other small communities, Lake Toxaway and Rosman, are only minutes away.

Brevard is set in one of the most beautiful areas of the Southern Appalachians. Transylvania County, the "Land Of Waterfalls," is more than 80% national forest and its residents boast of more than 150 waterfalls along its hundreds of miles of rivers, creeks and streams. No visit would be complete without at least a look at the rivers and waterfalls near Brevard; you'll find the well-known ones listed a little later in this chapter.

CRADLE OF FORESTRY

The Cradle of Forestry is the result of George Vanderbilt's devotion to his estate and the great forests thereon. To ensure that his wishes were carried out to the letter, he hired a German-born forester of international repute, Dr. Carl A. Schenk. He became Vanderbilt's estate manager, and it was he who opened the famous school, the first of its kind, that we know today as the Cradle of Forestry. Unfortunately, the school closed in 1913, but visitors can stroll the reconstructed campus grounds, visit a ranger's dwelling of the period, and a lodge built in the German Black Forest style.

The Cradle of Forestry is three miles south of the Blue Ridge Parkway on Highway 276, 14 miles north of Brevard. It's open seven days a week year-round, from 10 am until 6 pm. Admission is $2 for adults, $1 for seniors and youngsters aged six to 17; children under six may enter at no charge. ☎ 828-877-3130.

PISGAH FOREST NATIONAL FISH HATCHERY

This, the largest trout hatchery in the eastern United States, was once a logging camp. It then became a camp for the workers of the Civilian Conservation Corp. Today, it's operated by the North Carolina Wildlife Resources Agency to raise thousands upon thousands of fingerlings to stock regional streams, creeks and rivers. It's a really neat place to visit, especially so for children, who take great delight in watching the waters bubble with fish at feeding times; they even get to feed fish themselves.

The hatchery is open daily from 9 am until 5 pm and there's no charge for admission. From the Brevard entrance to the Pisgah National Forest, take Highway 276 to Forest Road 475. The Hatchery is less than a mile along 475. ☎ 828-877-3121.

SLIDING ROCK

Water slides. We've all see those great plastic monstrosities, usually blue or garish yellow, that seem to spring up in the most unlikely places. Well, North Carolina is no exception; you'll find them everywhere. But sliding rock is a water slide unique among its peers; it's a natural one, and great fun, too. If you have what it takes, you can ride the slippery rock slope, which sits at an angle of 50 to 60°, for a wild and watery 60 feet and splash down in a six-foot-deep pool of crystal-clear water below. More than 11,000 gallons of water cascade down the rock each minute, making for an exhilarating, if not hair-raising ride. If you find the thought of riding the rock a little scary, you can stand and watch from the bottom, close to the pool.

Needless to say, this is one of the most popular spots in Transylvania County. The parking lot is often full, especially on weekends and during school holidays, but you can usually find a quiet time in the early morning on weekdays. Lifeguards are on duty from 10 am until 6 pm, Memorial Day through Labor Day.

You'll need to wear something more substantial than a regular bathing suit. The rock, though slick, can quickly take the seat out of your swimsuit. Try an old pair of cut-off jeans. Also, you'll need to be very careful while walking or standing on the rock as it's easy to slip and fall.

From its junction with Highway 64, take Highway 276 and drive 7½ miles to Sliding Rock.

■ Bryson City

This small mountain city in Swain County, just 60 miles southwest of Asheville on the edge of the Great Smoky Mountains National Park, remains one of North Carolina's undiscovered gems. Even though it's more easily accessed than many of the mountain cities, tourism has yet to make its mark on Bryson City. The tourists that do visit finvd, to their delight, a completely unspoiled small town in the heart of a beautiful landscape. Swain County is more than 550 square miles of mountains, forests, rivers, creeks and wilderness, most of it on federal land, all of it unspoiled. Within the boundaries of

Swain County flow three of the nation's great rivers: the **Nantahala**, the **Oconoluftee** and the **Tuskeegee**. Needless to say, Bryson City is a major center for whitewater sports. But there's more. There are hundreds of miles of hiking trails; **Fontana Lake** is just to the west; it is the headquarters of the **Great Smoky Mountain Railroad**, which offers excursions through the area; the **Cherokee Indian reservation** is only a few miles northeast; and then there are the forests. The **Nantahala National Forest** stretches away to the west, south and east, while the **Great Smoky Mountains National Park** takes care of the north.

Bryson City is on Highway 19, southwest of Asheville. Alternatively, take Highway 441 from Gatlinburg to Highway 19 and turn south; it's only 40 miles.

OUTFITTERS

High Country Outfitters

This company is only one of many outdoor adventure companies. You can rent all sorts of equipment, canoes and kayaks from them, and you can take a raft ride down the Nantahala. ☎ 828-488-3153.

Nantahala Outdoor Center - USA Raft

This is one of the oldest of the many outdoor adventure companies that have sprung up on the banks of rivers in the mountainous regions of Tennessee, North Carolina and Georgia. It's a full-service company with an excellent reputation for safety and service. They will take you down the river on a guided rafting trip, or supply you with rental canoes and the necessary instruction, bicycle tours and a number of other custom-designed packages, as well as outdoor clothing, and even accommodations. ☎ 800-232-7238.

■ Cherokee

Set on the edge of the Great Smoky Mountains National Park, it's no wonder that the capital of the Cherokee Nation in the east is one of the most popular stops on the tourist circuit. Cherokee is the largest Indian reservation in the eastern United States. It is the direct result of the great roundup of 1838 when General Winfield Scott set his army to move the Cherokee out of the area, along the Trail of Tears, and onto the new reservations in Oklahoma. Many thousands of Cherokees decided they wanted to stay right where they were and slipped away into the great forests to hide. Scott's men ran many of them down, but a large number managed to escape. Those that did were left poor and without a home. Eventually, however, through the efforts of a local trader and self-taught attorney, they received some of the money that the Cherokees in Oklahoma had been paid for their lands in the mountains. They used it to buy back some 57,000 acres of their one-time homeland.

Today, Cherokee is a strange place. The Indians have overcome the adversities of the past and now blatantly exploit their culture and heritage.

The town, always busy and crowded, is more theme park than residential community. Visitors, who arrive in Cherokee by the hundreds of thousands, are met by canvas teepees, plastic totems, Indians in full regalia, and dozens of little shops pushing all sorts of cheaply made Indian souvenirs: tomahawks, pipes and such. And then, of course, there's the bingo – Cherokee's answer to the great casinos of Nevada and Atlantic City.

But you can still find remnants of genuine Cherokee culture, if you hunt. Cherokee, commercial though it is, is a fascinating stop on any tour of the Great Smoky Mountains, and one that really shouldn't be missed.

CHEROKEE BINGO

Like high-stakes bingo? This is the place for you. The cost to play is high, but so are the winnings. Jackpots exceeding $100,000 are commonplace, and some exceed $500,000. The facility holds more than 4,000 people and games are held twice a month. Cherokee Bingo is on Highway 19N, about three miles out of town. ☎ 800-368-2464.

TRIBAL BINGO

This is bingo priced so that anyone can play. Games run nightly at 7 pm, Monday through Saturday, and jackpots can range from $100 to $500. The hall is on Acquoni Road in Cherokee, close to the Civic Center. ☎ 828-497-4320.

BOTANICAL GARDENS

This is a nice, quiet place with many wildflowers. Just the right spot to get away from the hustle and bustle of town. You'll find it next to the Oconoluftee Village. It's open in spring, summer and fall. Admission is free. ☎ 800-438-1601.

MINGO FALLS

This is one of those fabulous spots in the mountains where modern society has had little effect. Still unspoiled, and a rare sight to behold, the falls and the surrounding mountains provide a not-to-be-missed side trip just a few miles away from the busy Cherokee tourist center.

From Cherokee, take 441 to its junction with the Blue Ridge Parkway. Drive on for one mile to the Job Corps Center. Turn right there and drive a half-mile to Big Cove Road. Turn left onto Big Cove Road and drive three miles to the Mingo Cove Campground. The trail to the falls begins there.

MUSEUM OF THE CHEROKEE INDIAN

This is a modern museum and now the heart of what once was the great Cherokee Nation. Once inside, you'll embark upon a self-guided tour of exhibits and artifacts that depict the history and culture of the Indian Nation from the earliest times. To do it properly will take about two hours. The gift shop sells gifts, crafts and artwork that are much more authentic than the plastic foibles you'll find in the gift shops on the streets of Cherokee.

The museum is on Highway 441 at the junction with Drama Road. ☎ 828-497-3481. It's open all year, except for the usual public holidays, from 9 am until 8 pm during the summer, and from 9 until 5, September to June. Admission is $5 for adults, and $3 for children aged six to 12.

OCONOLUFTEE INDIAN VILLAGE

This is the most genuine Indian attraction in Cherokee. Oconoluftee will take you on a journey back to the mid-1700s, when the Cherokee Nation occupied the surrounding mountains and forests. Tours of the village are given by authentically garbed Indian guides, and you'll see the everyday life of a Cherokee Indian family played out much as it would have been more than two centuries ago.

Indians show their traditional skills: pottery, weaving, basket-making, bread-making and canoe building. There's a typical Indian home of the times and the all-important, seven-sided council building. When your tour is over, you can wander around at will and ask questions. The village is open daily from 9 am until 5:30 pm, mid-May through October. Admission is $10 for adults and $5 for children aged six to 13. The village is at the junction of Highway 441 and Drama Road. ☎ 828-497-2315.

UNTO THESE HILLS

This is an outdoor drama that tells the history of the Cherokee Nation from the time when Hernando De Soto arrived right through to the tragic Trail of Tears. It's a colorful event, well worth the price of admission.

The play is performed at the Mountainside Theater on Drama Road, just beyond the junction with Highway 441. Admission is $10 for adults, $6 for children to the age of 12, and reserved seats cost $12.50. Performances are given from mid-June through August and begin between 7 and 8:45 pm, depending upon the month. Tickets are available at the box office on Drama Road (9 am until 6:30 pm, Monday through Saturday) or you can order by phone. ☎ 828-497-2111.

■ Cullowhee

This little town, about 10 miles west of Waynesville on Highway 74, is most famous as the home of Western Carolina University. There are a couple of other noteworthy attractions in the area, but it's the university, which houses the largest library in southwestern North Carolina, that attracts most of the attention.

JATACULLA ROCK

This big rock is something of an enigma, for it's covered with a mass of old Indian carvings that have never been interpreted. The rock is in a field not far from East LaPorte, south of Cullowhee on Highway 107. Just take the road south to State Road 1737 and follow the signs. Admission is free.

MOUNTAIN HERITAGE CENTER

This small, attractive museum is dedicated to the preservation of the area's mountain culture and its Scotch-Irish roots. Here, you'll learn all about the mass migration of settlers from the "Old Country." The story is told through a number of exhibits, murals, artifacts, a life-size replica of an 18th-century Irish cottage, and a range of special programs and audio-visual presentations. The museum is on the campus of Western Carolina University, and is open Monday through Friday from 8 am until 5 pm. Admission is free. ☎ 828-277-7129.

WESTERN CAROLINA UNIVERSITY

This is the cultural center of the area, offering lectures, theatrical productions and concerts throughout the year. The university also has a strong sporting tradition, especially in basketball. ☎ 828-227-7317.

■ Flat Rock

 This is a very attractive neat little town set among the mountains just a couple of miles south of Hendersonville on Highway 25. The community was formed by planters from the Charleston (SC) area who came looking for relief from the summer heat. With them came money, slaves and a luxurious way of life previously unknown in the area. Back then, the summer season in Flat Rock began in May and lasted through October. It was a time for relaxation and gentle living that was brought abruptly to an end by the ravages of the Civil War.

Today, Flat Rock still attracts those running from the heat, but it's a quiet place, a historic town of fine architecture with beautiful countryside. The downtown historic district is listed on the National Register of Historic Places.

CARL SANDBURG HOME
NATIONAL HISTORIC SITE

Although it once was the home of Christopher Memminger, the one-time Secretary of the Treasury for the Confederacy, this stately old house and estate is much more famous as the home of

Carl Sandburg, poet and Pulitzer Prize-winning biographer of Abraham Lincoln.

It was in 1945 that Sandburg and his wife Paula moved into the old house. He came to write and, for 22 years, that's exactly what he did.

Today, the house remains in much the same condition as it was when Sandburg made his home there. His study is intimidating and has the air of a very private domain. It's as if Mr. Sandburg has just stepped out, but will return at any moment.

The house is near the Flat Rock Playhouse off Highway 25 on Little River Road; just follow the signs. ☎ 828-693-4178. Admission is free.

■ Fontana Dam & Fontana Village Resort

Fontana is the highest dam in the eastern United States. At more than 480 feet, it presents an awesome spectacle, holding back the Little Tennessee River to form a magnificent lake of more than 10,000 acres. The dam was built by the TVA at the end of World War II to provide hydroelectric power to towns and cities over a wide area. As the dam grew, so did Fontana Village. Once the home of the construction workers who built the dam, it now is a remote place where people who like to be one with the great outdoors go to play, relax, and live.

Fontana Village is a resort with 250 cabins and a modern hotel. Visitors can enjoy every type of outdoor activity from golf to hiking, and from tennis to fishing.

Fontana Village is on the lake on Highway 28 at the southern edge of the Great Smoky Mountains National Park, north of Robbinsville, which is on Highway 129. ☎ 800-849-2258.

■ Franklin

The seat of Macon County, Franklin's claim to fame is the unusually rich mineral and gemstone deposits in the surrounding hills. Located geographically almost at the heart of the Nantahala National Forest, and at the junction of four major highways, the little town is a stop along the way to almost anywhere else. For instance, if you're arriving in southwestern North Carolina from Chattanooga, Tennessee, you'll drive in on Highway 64 to Murphy. From there it's only a stone's throw along 64 to Haysville, Chatuge Lake and the junction with Highway 441, which will take you all the way north to Cherokee and the Great Smoky Mountains National Park.

Hernando De Soto was probably the first to stop here and, although his motives were purely commercial, he missed out on the wealth that was lying in the ground beneath his feet.

Settlers began arriving in Macon County in 1817. A trading post was established and Franklin began to swell. By the outbreak of the Civil War, the county population had grown to more than 7,000, and the little mountain city was staunchly Confederate. It sent more than a third of its male population to fight for the cause; less than 50% of them returned.

Franklin is set deep among the highlands of the Nantahala. At an elevation of almost 3,000 feet the air is crisp and invigorating. A few miles west, the Nantahala Mountains rise above the Little Tennessee River Basin. Everything here is dominated by the peak of Standing Indian Mountain at 5,500 feet.

Gems & Mining For Fun

It's thought there are large deposits of precious stones still to be found in the rocky areas around the city. Tiffany's once owned an emerald mine in the area. Today, it's become a popular hunting ground for rockhounds, who come in large numbers from all around the country, bringing with them an assortment of battered equipment and camping gear. Having established a base, they spend their time at the mines in Cowee Valley, washing great quantities of mud in search of the "big one." And find it they do, though not very often.

 In 1992 a teenager found a 1,497-carat sapphire – that discovery will keep visitors coming for many years.

Western North Carolina offers mineral and gem enthusiasts – rockhounds, as the aficionados are called – a whole bundle of unique opportunities. For those who've never done this before, now's the time to consider it – a new adventure to try. Most venues require a trek into the wilderness and time spent on hands and knees or up to your elbows in water and mud. Obviously, it's perfect for kids.

There are several areas around the state where you can get hooked into this fascinating and educational hobby. There's the **Spruce Pine Mining District**, which includes parts of Avery, Mitchell and Yancy counties; the **Hiddenite District** in Alexander County; and the area we are concerned with here – **Franklin** in Macon County in Southwestern North Carolina. The mines in the Franklin district are, for the most part, located in an area known as the **Cowee Valley**.

Most of the richest deposits are now on private land. Some, however, are open to the public and welcome rookie rockhounds, as well as those with more experience. Often, an hour or two spent sifting through 100 pounds of gravel, rubble and clay can be time quite profitably spent, and, as always, there's a chance you might luck into a big one. So, what can you find? You might come across aquamarines, saphires, garnets, rhodolites, emeralds, even rubies. It's hard to predict what the quantities or quality will be. Still, the hunt's the essence of the adventure.

COWEE VALLEY GEM MINES

There are more than a dozen mines in the valley. Most of them are commercially operated and cater to visitors. You'll pay a small fee to visit and prospect, usually $4 or $5, and a little more for the bucket rental, although you can bring your own.

The majority of mines are open seven days a week from 8 am until sundown from April though October, and most are very busy during the summer months. Try to vsit early or late in the season to avoid the crowds.

Head north from Franklin on Highway 28; you can't miss Cowee Valley.

Mines You Can Visit and Work

Jacobs Ruby Mine

269 DeForest Lane, Franklin, NC 28734

Cowee Valley is one of only two place in the world where sandy gravel will yield blood red rubies; the other is the

Mogok Valley in Burma. Open May through October, Monday through Saturday, from 9 am until 5 pm. Call for rates. ☎ 828-524-7022.

Gold City Gem Mine

9410 Sylva Road, Franklin, NC 28734

Gold City is more a miniature theme park than it is a mine. "There's something here for the whole family." There's a chairlift rising more than 5,000 feet to an observation platform high on the mountain; a gem store where, if digging for gems is not for you, you can buy that little something special; a gift shop where you can buy hand-crafted goods, such as quilts and the like; and there a place where you buy lunch, or a snack. Call to get current information. ☎ 800-713-7767.

The Old Cardinal Gem Mine

71 Rockhaven Drive Franklin, NC 28734

Hey, they even have "dirt to go." A great place for beginners to try their hand at gem mining. The Old Cardinal offers group rates, expert help, a picnic area, snack and cold drinks, and all the equipment you need to strike it rich. What can you find? Rhodolite, rubies, sapphires, and moonstones. Call for current rates. ☎ 828-369-7534 and ask for Jim or Edna.

Mason Mountain Rhodolite & Ruby Mine

5315 Bryson City Road, Franklin, NC 28734

Owners Brown and Martha Johnson have been in the business more years than they can remember, and they are, so they say, ready and willing to help you get started. Admission is $5 for adults, $3 for children under 12. Mining cost is extra: you pay by the bucket or bag. A bucket full of dirt, including the equipment needed to search it, costs $1 or $2, depending upon the size of the bucket. A "special bag" full of dirt costs $10, and a "super bucket" costs $25. Look for rhodolites, kyanite, garnets, moonstones, rubies, sapphires, crystal quartz and smoky quartz. The mine is open seven days a week, but call first to make sure. ☎ 828-524-4570.

Southwestern North Carolina

The Hudsons of Cumming, GA, got the surprise of their lives at the Mason Mountain Rhodolite & Ruby Mine. Sifting through the contents of a five-gallon bucket, they came across a blue sapphire that weighed in at 1½ pounds; it was valued at $30,000.

GEM & MINERAL MUSEUM

This museum is situated in the old Macon County Jail on West Main in downtown Franklin. The exhibits include some very large gemstones and interpret the story of mining in the area. It's open Monday through Saturday from 10 am until 4 pm. Admission is free. ☎ 828-369-7831.

■ Wayah Bald

Although it's not in Franklin, Wayah Bald is well worth the extra time it will require for you to visit. It's a high bald, a mountain without trees, set at more than 5,300 feet. During springtime the mountain is a riot of color from the profusion of wildflowers and azaleas that cover it. That, and the view from the top, make it one of those special places not to be missed. Just drive west from Franklin on Highway 64 to NC 1310, turn right and drive to Forest Service Road 69, then turn right again.

■ Hendersonville

The seat of Henderson County, Hendersonville has always been an important stop for tourists, at least since 1830. Back then, it was the wealthy refugees from the summer heat of the coastal lowlands of the Carolinas who travelled to the area. Today, tourists still arrive in Henderson in large numbers. They come to see the spectacular mountain scenery and to shop Hendersonville's unique downtown open to pedestrians only.

HOLMES STATE PARK

Not a large state park as state parks go, but interesting just the same. Here you'll learn all about forestry. The park includes three types of terrain: bottomland, hillside and mountaintop. And it's those and the proper use of a forest that are explained through interpretive exhibits and two nature trails: the **Forest Walk** and the **Forest Demonstration Trail**. It's a day-use park, so camping is not allowed. Picnicking is permitted. The park is just 10 miles west of Hendersonville on State Route 1127.

JUMP OFF ROCK

Jump Off Rock, subject of a dozen or more Indian legends, is a promontory 3,500 feet in elevation overlooking Hendersonville. All of the legends tell of suicide or unrequited love. The drive and the views are wonderful. To visit the rock, drive out of town along Fifth Avenue to Laurel Parkway and follow the signs.

■ Highlands

At an elevation of more than 4,100 feet, Highlands really lives up to its name. It's the highest incorporated town east of the Mississippi. The journey to Highlands along Highway 64 is, in itself, quite an adventure. The route leads through the Cullusaja Gorge and some of the most spectacular and most photographed mountain scenery in the world. Hewn from the mountains by the fast-flowing river, the gorge also features some of North Carolina's most famous waterfalls.

The little mountain town is the creation of two men, Sam Kelsy and Clinton Hutchenson, who bought land on speculation in 1875. They advertised the location by sending out handbills all around the country. These told of a new town where the climate was gentle and the air clean and invigorating. Their speculation paid off. By 1883 Highlands boasted more than 300 residents. Today, the permanent population is around 2,000, but that grows to more than 20,000 during the peak tourist season.

Highlands is a botanist's dream. With more than 70 inches of rainfall each year and a gentle climate to boot, the mountains and valleys surrounding it are covered with wildflowers and other plant life. So conducive are the conditions for healthy plant life that the area is home to one of the oldest research centers in the country, the Highlands Biological Research Station, which is world-renowned for the study of flora and fauna.

Southwestern North Carolina

HIGHLANDS BIOLOGICAL RESEARCH STATION

Now under the protective wing of the University of North Carolina, the Highlands Biological Research Station was established in 1927 to take advantage of the unique conditions of the Highlands area, and to study the area's wildlife. It's an interesting place to visit, as is the Highlands Nature Center, also on the property.

The **Highlands Nature Center** is, in fact, a small museum of local history, as well flora and fauna. Inside you'll find all sorts of interesting exhibits, including a collection of Indian artifacts and a cross-section of a hemlock tree that was some 425 years old when it was cut down.

Located on Horse Cove Street in Highlands, the Biological Station and Nature Center are open April through Labor Day, from 10 am until 5 pm, Monday through Friday, and on Sunday from 1 until 5 pm. Admission is free. ☎ 828-526-2112.

SUNSET ROCK

From downtown Highlands, take the road leading up to Ravenel Park. There, on the mountaintop, is one of the finest panoramic views in the entire region. As its name suggests, the best time to visit is at sunset, when the peaks to the west are silhouetted against the deep red glow of the evening sun.

■ Murphy

 Murphy was, and is, the last civilized stop in North Carolina on the road west into Tennessee. It was here, at Fort Butler, that General Winfield Scott had his headquarters. It was from here, too, that he supervised the great roundup of the Cherokee Nation for their enforced march westward to Oklahoma. Strangely, it's also the site of the last battle of the Civil War east of the Mississippi, a battle which, ironically, the Confederacy won. Compared to the great battles that had gone before, it wasn't much of an event. It seems a large group of Confederate deserters had switched sides and formed themselves into a Federal unit. As they were all deserters, they all had cases pending against them. The papers pertaining to their crimes, so they thought, were housed in Murphy's courthouse. They simply burnt the place down to destroy the incriminating paperwork. Retribution was swift. On May 6th, 1865, the quasi-federal unit was set upon at Hanging Dog Creek by a well-organized veteran Confederate regiment and was quickly defeated.

Today, Murphy is a small, very quiet place set deep among the hills and woodlands of the Nantahala National Forest. It's God's Country, so the locals say, and who could disagree? Cherokee County, of which Murphy is the seat, has fine scenery. It's an area of river valleys and mountain peaks, of the great wilderness and vast lakes, and it's a sportsman's paradise.

APPALACHIA LAKE & DAM

This TVA-constructed dam is unique in its operation. Instead of hydroelectric power being generated at the dam itself, as it is in most cases, water is transported underground along an eight-mile tunnel to the Appalachian Powerhouse, downstream in Tennessee near the town of Reliance. The TVA has always been creative in this sort of effort, as is evidenced by its construction of a similar project on the Ocoee River in Tennessee. At the Ocoee, however, rather than a tunnel, it's a flume that transports the water along the mountainside.

CHEROKEE COUNTY HISTORICAL MUSEUM

This little museum in Murphy is dedicated to local history, and particularly to its Indian heritage. Inside you'll find displays of Indian pottery, artwork and the tools that made life for them a little easier. You'll also see artifacts left behind by Hernando De Soto's expedition of 1540, along with those of the early pioneers that found their way into the mountains around Murphy. The museum, on Peachtree Street, is open Monday through Friday from 9 am until 5 pm, and on Saturdays from 9 until noon. Admission is free. ☎ 828-837-6792.

FIELDS OF THE WOODS

Fields of the Woods is a theme park with a difference. Christianity, as interpreted by the Church of God of Prophecy, is the focus of the 200-acre park. Here you'll find the world's largest cross, 150 feet tall and 115 across the arms; the world's largest display of the Ten Commandments, 300 feet square with letters five feet high; a depiction of the New Testament open at Matthew 22:37-40, some

Southwestern North Carolina

34 feet wide and 24 feet high; and a replica of the tomb in which Jesus was laid to rest.

The park is on Highway 294 near Murphy. It's open year-round and admission is free. ☎ 828-494-7855.

HIWASSEE LAKE & DAM

Built in 1940, the Hiwassee Dam is one of the highest of its kind in the country. Set across the Hiwassee River, it creates a lake more than 20 miles long with at least 180 miles of shoreline. Needless to say, this is a center for fishing and watersports in the region. Surrounded by Nantahala National Forest, Hiwassee is a remote place where dedicated sportsmen and women can enjoy their sport away from the hustle and bustle of the more centrally located lakes.

■ Nantahala National Forest

 The Nantahala is southwestern North Carolina's answer to the Great Smoky Mountains National Park. But the Nantahala is, for the most part, less traveled. Within the 515,000 acres that make up the Nantahala are many unique attractions, recreation areas, and outdoor sporting opportunities, many of which are not found in its big brother to the north. Then again, there are some things you will find in the Great Smoky National Park that you won't find in the Nantahala, most notable of which are the roads clogged with stalled or slow-moving traffic.

The Nantahala, especially at its westernmost reaches, has long been an important outdoor sporting center, yet it remains largely undiscovered by the touring public. In the west, it's a wild and remote region, administered by the National Forest Service for the good of forestry in general and outdoor recreation in particular. Farther east, the public at large is slowly becoming aware of the great opportunities and possibilities offered by the wilderness areas of the Nantahala.

Within the forest boundaries you'll find more than a thousand miles of hiking and nature trails, including the **Bartram Trail** that runs through Franklin's city limits, and more than 80 miles of the most rugged section of the **Appalachian Trail**.

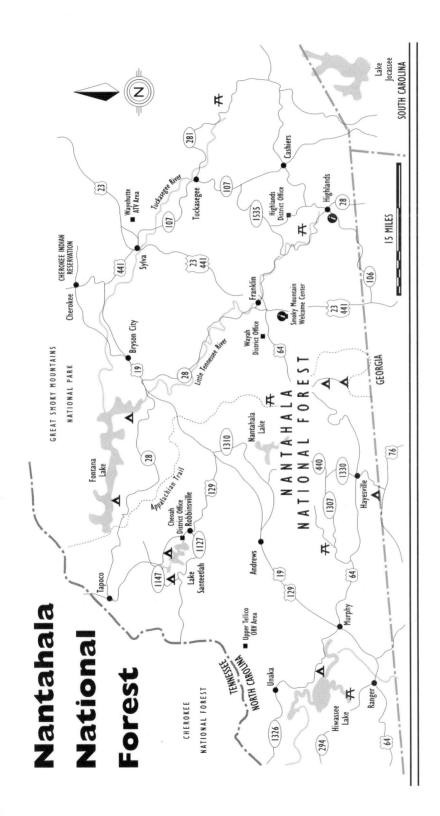

Nantahala National Forest

Southwestern North Carolina

GREAT SMOKY MOUNTAINS
NATIONAL PARK

CHEROKEE INDIAN
RESERVATION

CHEROKEE
NATIONAL FOREST

NANTAHALA
NATIONAL FOREST

TENNESSEE
NORTH CAROLINA

GEORGIA

SOUTH CAROLINA

Fontana Lake

Lake Jocassee

Hiwassee Lake

Nantahala Lake

Lake Santeetlah

Tuckasegee River

Little Tennessee River

Appalachian Trail

Wayehutte ATV Area

Upper Tellico ORV Area

Cheoah District Office
Robbinsville

Highlands District Office

Wayah District Office

Smoky Mountain Welcome Center

Tapoco
Unaka
Ranger
Murphy
Andrews
Hayesville
Franklin
Highlands
Cashiers
Tuckasegee
Sylva
Cherokee
Bryson City

23, 28, 281, 107, 1535, 441, 1310, 1147, 1127, 1326, 294, 1330, 1307, 440, 76, 64, 129, 19, 106, 28, 108

15 MILES

N

Also within the forest you'll find the Joyce Kilmer Memorial Forest, a 3,800-acre tract of virgin timber, with some trees towering more than 100 feet high. Even more awe-inspiring is Whitewater Falls on Highway 281 close to the North Carolina/South Carolina border in Transylvania County.

> *Whitewater, at 411 feet, is the highest unbroken waterfall in the southeastern United States.*

Unfortunately, Nantahala's undiscovered beauty comes complete with its own drawbacks. There are few tourist centers within its boundaries, and that means there are few amenities. Good hotels are few and far between. Good restaurants are even more scarce. Forest campgrounds, though improving, are somewhat primitive, and commercial grounds are almost as rare as luxury hotels. If you're a true outdoorsperson, the lack of essentials won't bother you too much. If you do your camping in a motorhome, you'll definitely want to travel in busier regions.

Nantahala National Forest Information

Highlands District	☎ 828-526-3765
Cheoah Broad District	☎ 828-479-6431
Tusquitee District	☎ 704-837-5152
Wayah District	☎ 704-524-6441

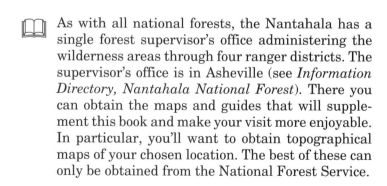

As with all national forests, the Nantahala has a single forest supervisor's office administering the wilderness areas through four ranger districts. The supervisor's office is in Asheville (see *Information Directory, Nantahala National Forest*). There you can obtain the maps and guides that will supplement this book and make your visit more enjoyable. In particular, you'll want to obtain topographical maps of your chosen location. The best of these can only be obtained from the National Forest Service.

Waterfall Country

The following is a guide to some of the most spectacular scenery in the area. Before you embark on your tour, however, there are one or two considerations you should keep in mind.

Warning

Waterfalls have an enchantment all their own. The tumbling, rushing, roaring waters are hypnotic. The noise and the speeding torrents draw you ever closer to the edge, and even onto the slippery rocks. Perhaps it's just that once-in-a-lifetime photograph that makes the risk seem worthwhile. Whatever it is, there's a real danger in getting too close. Wet rocks are always slick, and a slip from the top of a waterfall can be fatal. Only by exercising great care and common sense can you experience the sights and sounds of the great falls in safety. View them from a safe distance. Stay away from the edge.

Southwestern North Carolina

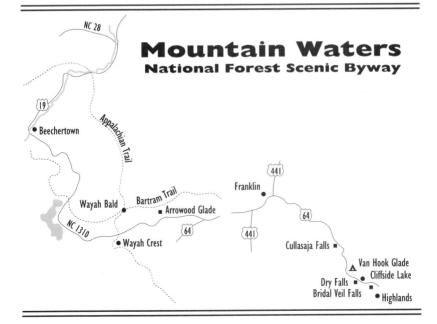

Mountain Waters
National Forest Scenic Byway

There are some beautiful areas in the Great Smoky Mountains, but none more so than a section of the Nantahala National Forest now designated Mountain Waters. From the tiny mountain city of Highlands in the south, the road runs for more than 60 miles northwest almost to Bryson City. Along the way it will take you to visit some spectacular waterfalls, lakes and rivers.

Whitewater Falls Scenic Area (Highlands Region)

Whitewater will take you off the beaten path a little, but the spectacle at the end of the short journey will more than justify the extra driving. The 411-foot falls are the highest unbroken waterfalls in the southeastern US. The river drops over a horizontal distance of only 500 feet. It's an awesome sight and very popular with nature photographers.

When you get to Highlands, take Highway 64 east to Cashiers, then turn south on Highway 107 and drive 10 miles to the state line. From there, drive another mile and take the first paved road to the left.

Silver Run Falls (Highlands Region)

Once again, take Highway 107 south from Cashiers. Go four miles to a graveled pull-off on the left. From there it's a short hike along a woodland path, over the creek by way of a log bridge, to a sandy beach and crystal pool at the foot of the lovely 30-foot falls. The pool is safe for swimming, so be sure to take a swimsuit. Unfortunately, it can also be quite busy, especially over the weekend during the summer months. Photographers should note that Silver Run and its surroundings turn into a magical kingdom of ice and snow in winter.

Bridal Veil Falls (Highlands Region)

Perhaps the most famous of all falls in this area, Bridal Veil is just off Highway 64, about 2½ miles east of Highlands in the Cullasaja Gorge.

The falls cascade down the mountain more than 120 feet and provide a magnificent display.

In summertime you can drive your car right under them – a real thrill for kids and adults as the water splashes all around.

Dry Falls (Highlands Region)

Just a little farther on up Highway 64 from Bridal Veil, 3½ miles from Highlands and 16 miles south of Franklin, Dry Falls is reached by walking from the parking lot along a paved path that takes you right under the rushing waters. On the other side you can view the 75-foot falls and take photographs.

Lower Cullasaja Falls (Highlands Region)

More of a cascade than a waterfall, the waters tumble over 250 feet down the mountain to present a picture more often found in paintings than in real life. The falls are on Highway 64, almost nine miles west of Highlands, and present something of a problem for motorists and tourists alike: some want to move on, while others want to stop and gaze, and so the road often becomes a bottleneck. Parking along the road is limited and, if you can find a spot, you're in for a dangerous walk back along the highway. To leave the road and visit the falls involves a somewhat hazardous hike along an extremely difficult footpath. Best to be satisfied with the view from the road.

Glenn Falls Scenic Area (Highlands Region)

From Highlands, take Highway 106 south for two miles to a sign that points the way left along a gravel road to the Glenn Falls Scenic Area. It's about a mile to the parking lot. From the parking lot, you'll have to hike the steep trail for a mile to the three falls: one of 70 feet, one of 60 feet and one of only 15 feet. The hike is a grand experience in itself. Along the way you'll enjoy magnificent views down into the Blue Valley and the peaks beyond. You might like to take along a picnic. You won't find a better place to enjoy it.

Lower Satulah Falls (Highlands Region)

To visit these falls, drive south from Highlands again, this time on Highway 28 for 2½ miles, where you'll find a pull-off for a view of the falls. Long and narrow, they cascade more than 100 feet down the mountain just across the valley. Photographers will have a great time working the falls and the peaks of Rabund Bald and Scaly Mountain just beyond.

Southwestern North Carolina

Looking Glass Falls (Brevard Area)

Though not really within the scope of Mountain Waters, it would be unforgivable to leave out the most visited of the area's 150 or so waterfalls. Looking Glass is in the Pisgah National Forest, near the Pisgah Ranger District Office, and it's easy to reach. From Highlands, travel east on Highway 64, through Cashiers and Rosman to Brevard. From there, take Highway 276 north for about 5½ miles to a paved parking area by the side of Looking Glass Creek. Leave your vehicle in the parking lot and walk down the steps to the base of the falls. At the edge of the rushing waters you'll enjoy a spectacular view of the 60-foot cascade, up close and personal. You'll even feel the soft mist thrown up as the water hits the rock.

The area gets quite busy on weekends; visit during the week if you can.

Moore Cove Falls (Brevard Area)

While you're at Looking Glass Falls, you might as well take full advantage of the trip and visit Moore Cove. The gravel parking lot is only a mile farther along 276, just before the first bridge. Cross the bridge to a short flight of steps that lead to the head of a beautiful country nature trail. Only a little more than a half-mile in length, it's a bit steep for the first few yards, but soon levels out. At the end of the trail you'll find the falls, a small mountain creek that drops 45 feet before flowing onward through the forest. You can walk under the ledge that leads behind the falls. You can even climb the steep path to the top, but watch out for wet rocks. Moore Cove Falls is great for photography.

Nantahala Lake (Brevard Area)

From Franklin, the byway continues west along Highway 1310, through Nantahala National Forest, and on to Nantahala Lake. On the way, you can take a side trip to Wayah Bald, described earlier in this section. Drive 4½ miles up the gravel Forest Road 69. From 69 the byway – Highway 1310 – follows Jarrett Creek west before turning north along the shore of Nantahala Lake. You are now deep in the remote reaches of Macon County and the national forest, far away from the crowds.

The lake is a big tract of water, the product of a major hydroelectric dam that provides electricity for the Nantahala Power and Light Company. The fishing is good, and you'll certainly find lots of peace and solitude. Be sure to take along whatever supplies you might need, as there are no nearby stores. Access to the lake is at Rocky Branch, just off the highway.

Nantahala River (Brevard Area)

From the lake, the byway continues north through Beechertown, a remote spot on the map, where it meets Highway 19 and stays along the Nantahala River. You are now in whitewater country. The level of the Nantahala is closely controlled by the dam at the head of Nantahala Lake, which means the waters are perfect for rafting. The stretch of road you are now on is one of the busiest sections of its entire 61 miles. Take a few moments at the riverside and watch the fun, or even embark on a wild ride down the river with one of the many rafting companies. You're sure to get wet, but it's an experience you won't forget. See the Information Directory for outfitters.

Byway's End (Brevard Area)

Officially, the Mountain Waters Scenic Byway ends on Highway 19 at the junction with Highway 28, just a few miles south of Bryson City. You are, however, deep in the heart of some of the most scenic river and lake country in the region. You could spend several days here. Bryson City, alone, will provide you with a pleasant day out and a fun ride down the river with the Nantahala Outdoor Center (see *Information Directory*). Or you could turn west along Highway 28 and visit 10,000-acre Fontana Lake that stretches for more than 30 miles east and west, and includes more than 240 miles of scenic shoreline. The Great Smoky Mountains National Park is just to the north and the Nantahala National Forest to the south.

ROBBINSVILLE

Robbinsville is set deep in the Nantahala National Forest just east of Lake Santeetlah on Highway 129, and south of Fontana Lake via Highways 143 and 28. It's also the seat of Graham County, a somewhat remote area where more than 60% of the land is in the national forest.

Once the home of the Snowbird Indians, a part of the Cherokee Nation that lived on the slopes of Snowbird Mountain, it's a land of outdoor opportunity and wonderful scenic vistas. It's also the location of the Nantahala Gorge and the Joyce Kilmer Memorial Forest. Robbinsville has yet to be properly discovered by the touring public. That means you can still find a parking place and the waters of Lake Santeetlah, though quite heavily used by the locals, are, for the most part, quiet and uncluttered.

Joyce Kilmer Memorial Forest

Joyce Kilmer was a poet of some renown. His most famous line was, perhaps, "I think that I shall never see a poem as lovely as a tree." And that line aptly sums up this section of the Nantahala set aside as a memorial to the great poet who died fighting in France during the First World War.

Wherever you may go in the two great forests of western North Carolina, and despite their primordial appearance, logging has been a part of the economy throughout the area for the past several hundred years. With the exception of Joyce Kilmer, no area has escaped the woodsman's axe. The great trees you see are all that remain of the virgin stands discovered by settlers. Many of the trees were here when Hernando De Soto first set foot in the mountains more than 450 years ago; some are more than 150 feet tall, with a 20-foot circumference. But the Joyce Kilmer Memorial Forest is only a part of the whole; a small section, 3,500 acres, of the Joyce Kilmer-Slickrock Wilderness Area. The 14,000-acre wilderness area is untouched forest incorporating more than 60 miles of hiking trails that provide access to its nether regions. To visit, take Highway 129 north out of Robbinsville, turn left onto State Road 1116, and then left again onto Forest Service Road 416.

Hooper's Bald

This area abounds in bald-top mountains like Hooper's. This one, set in the heart of the Nantahala National Forest, is one of the highest. At an elevation of more than 5,000 feet, almost devoid of vegetation except for a light covering of wild grasses, it offers spectacular views and some of the best hiking opportunities in the Great Smoky Mountains. Named for early settlers, Hooper's Bald is a wild and desolate spot high above the great forest that stretches away into the misty distance. If solitude, peace and quiet are what you're looking for, this is the place for you. Hooper's Bald is just off the Cherohala Skyway outside of Robbinsville.

Nantahala Gorge

The Nantahala Gorge, 10 miles east of Robbinsville, is a product of the Nantahala River which flows parallel to Highway 19 from Topton in the south to Wesser in the north. It, too, is a major center for whitewater activity. But more than that, the gorge is a scenic attraction of the first magnitude. Varying in depth from a mere 500 feet to more than 1,500 feet in some places, it's an area of outstanding natural beauty, a mecca for photographers, and a location that most outdoor lovers and sportsmen only dream about. Unfortunately, the river has turned it into something of playground. Throughout the summer, the river is a hive of activity. Thousands of rafters, led by several dozen rafting companies, turn it into a fast-moving logjam of black rubber rafts filled with screaming people. The road, too, is often chock-a-block with vehicles, rafters inside, rafts piled high on top. There are places where you can go to enjoy the river alone, but they are few and far between.

Adventures

■ Boating

 The boating centers of southwestern North Carolina lie, as one might imagine, mostly on the great lakes. Fontana, north of Nantahala National Forest is the most popular, but Nantahala and Thorpe lakes east of Franklin, Hiwassee Lake far to the west, and Chatuge on the Georgia border also provide great opportunities. Some of the lakes are quite remote and, therefore, less busy than their more accessible counterparts.

LAKE CHATUGE

Half in North Carolina, half in northern Georgia, Lake Chatuge is know locally as "The Crown Jewel of the TVA Lakes." And, like all TVA lakes, it was designed and built to produce energy. But the by-product is a vast outdoor playground serviced and maintained in pristine quality by its owners. Easily accessible by a network of free-flowing highways, it's a popular outdoor center, with lots of facilities, including boat ramps, marinas and campgrounds. Boaters, especially will appreciate the stretches of open water, some almost two miles across, and the hidden nooks and crannies that take you away from the maddening crowds. The lake has more than 132 miles of scenic shoreline backed by forest-covered mountain peaks and, in the spring, a profusion of color from the wildflowers blooming on the mountain slopes.

 Lake Chatuge can be quite busy on weekends, especially during the summer months.

The lake can be reached via highways 64, 69 and 175 in North Carolina, and via highways 17, 75 and 76 in northern Georgia. Private boat ramps are provided at several lakeside campgrounds, and public access ramps are located principally on the North Carolina side of Highway 64 on Cabe Road, and at Jackrabbit Mountain Public Campground just off Highway 175 on Philadelphia Road.

FONTANA LAKE

For more than 30 miles Fontana runs east and west through the mountains north of the Nantahala and south of the Great Smoky Mountains National Park. A center for the sightseeing public, as well as boating enthusiasts, it can become very busy at times, especially around the Fontana Village Resort. The resort's sightseeing boats ply the lake back and forth and many other types of watercraft zoom this way and that during the summer. Popular as it is, there seems to be a dearth of public boat ramps. You'll find plenty at the Fontana Village Resort, but other than that there are only two: one at the Cable Cove Campground off Highway 28 south of the lake, and another on Forest Road 2550, near the Tsali Campground off Highway 28 to the east.

LAKE HIWASSEE

Near the far western reaches of the Nantahala National Forest, Lake Hiwassee is one of the quieter boating centers. The lake is more than two miles long, covers some 6,000 acres and offers more than 180 miles of scenic, forest-covered shoreline. Public boat ramps are few and far between. There's one at Hanging Dog Campground, another off Joe Brown Road just west of Murphy, and a third at Hiwassee Village close to the dam. Access to the lake is made either from Murphy (north), or via several access roads that lead off Highway 64 (south), the most notable of which is Highway 294. Unfortunately, if you want to launch your boat, going that way will mean a drive of some 14 miles after you leave Highway 64.

NANTAHALA LAKE

This lake, in the remote regions of Macon County, is large enough and quiet enough for you to get away from the hustle and bustle of city life. Drive the boat into the far reaches of the lake and cut the motor; drift for a while, then lie back, look at the sky and listen to the sounds of the forest. It's quite an experience, and one that is rarely available these days. There are only two public boat ramps on the Nantahala, both of them quite remote. The first is to the north on Dick's Creek Road, off Wayah Road (Highway 1310), the other is on the western side of the lake on Choga Road off Route 2.

SANTEETLAH LAKE

Santeetlah, set close to Robbinsville on Highway 129, is a popular spot for boaters, skiers and Waverunners. It's not a large lake, which means the waters are often crowded. Only on weekends, however, during the peak months of summer, does it become extremely busy. Even then, you can still find a quiet spot to relax and enjoy the scenery and an afternoon in the sun.

There are three public boat ramps. Two are in the Robbinsville area: one at Choah Point off Highway 129, the other in the same area near the ranger station. The third is at the north end of the lake near the dam on Forest Road 416 off Santeetlah Road, 10 miles north of Robbinsville off Highway 129.

■ Camping

As in most areas of the Great Smoky Mountains, camping is a popular pastime. There are a number of national forest recreation areas, several state parks, and some commercial campgrounds. Needless to say, the commercial campgrounds are where you'll find the most facilities. State park campgrounds are often only a little more blessed with facilities than are their national forest counterparts. Your choice will depend upon the type of camping you prefer. If you like to rough it, you won't do better than to go to one of the more remote national forest facilities. If you like to have everything taken care of – hookups, cable TV, etc. – you'll only find what you need at the commercial grounds. For a full listing of campgrounds, see the *Camping Directory* at the back of the book.

■ Craft Hunting & Fairs

 Although there are not many, here are the outstanding crafts sources and fairs you should be aware of.

BRASSTOWN

Brasstown Fall Festival, held at the John S. Campbell Folk School in October. ☎ 828-837-2775.

Cherokee Indian Fall Festival, held on the Cherokee ceremonial grounds in early October, ☎ 800-438-1601.

FRANKLIN

The Bulgin Forge, a blacksmith's shop where you can purchase all sorts of ironwork. 319 West Main Street. ☎ 828-524-4204.

Festival of Festivals, held in late June, ☎ 828-524-3161.

HENDERSONVILLE

Arts & Crafts Fair, held in September, ☎ 828-692-1413.

HIGHLANDS

High Country Arts & Crafts Fair, early June, ☎ 828-525-2112.

MURPHY

Carolina Mountain Arts & Crafts Cooperative. Workshops, demonstrations and sales by local crafts people, ☎ 828-389-6661.

Streets Crafts Show, mid-May, ☎ 828-837-2242.

ROBBINSVILLE

Great Smoky Mountains Heritage Festival, Fourth of July.

■ Fishing

 This region of North Carolina provides opportunities for bass, bluegill, walleye and crappie fishing from shore or boat. But this is also trout country. Almost every tiny lake, fast-flowing river, mountain creek and stream is well stocked with the wily fish so avidly sought by anglers who specialize in their capture. There are rainbow, brown and brook trout almost everywhere in vast numbers. Pick your spot and give it a try. For a full list of trout streams, lakes and rivers, and for a complete listing of North Carolina's current fishing rules and regulations, including bag limits, contact the North Carolina Wildlife Recourses Commission in Raleigh, ☎ 919-733-3633.

NANTAHALA LAKE

Located in the most remote regions of Macon County, Nantahala is popular with anglers who want large expanses of quiet waters. There are only two public boat ramps on Nantahala, both of them fairly remote. The first is north of the lake on Dick's Creek Road, off Wayah Road (Highway 1310). The other is on the western side of the lake on Choga Road off Route 2.

There's plenty of smallmouth and largemouth bass, some white bass, crappie, bluegill and muskie. The waters will rise and fall with the operation at the dam, and the fishing is extremely good.

FONTANA LAKE

Fontana is just south of the Great Smoky Mountains National Park, and north of the Nantahala National Forest. Although there are not many public boat ramps on the lake, it's always busy. There are a couple of ramps in the vicinity of Fontana Dam just off Highway 28, another at Cable Cove, one off Forest Service Road 2550, and another at Evans Knob. Although Fontana is one of the busiest lakes in the region, with more than 10,000 acres and many tiny tributaries to explore, you'll find there's plenty of room to fish, once you get away from the boat dock, the sightseeing boats, Waverunners and ski boats.

The park lake is well stocked with smallmouth, largemouth and white bass, as well as walleye and muskie that on occasion have been known to exceed four feet in length. Of course, there's the inevitable crappie, and even a few trout. The fishing is good.

LAKE CHATUGE

This lake, described in detail under *Boating*, above, offers vast stretches of open water, some almost two miles across, and hundreds of hidden side-waters where you can get away from the crowds. More than 30 species of fish have been caught in the lake. All sizes of smallmouth, largemouth, spotted, white and striped bass, crappie, catfish, bluegill, walleye, muskie, trout and more are among those reported. Needless to say, the fishing is excellent.

See above for directions to Chatuge Lake.

LAKE HIWASSEE

If you like solitude when you go fishing, you'll find it here on the quiet waters of Lake Hiwassee. The fishing is excellent. See above under *Boating* for full details, including directions.

SANTEETLAH LAKE

Located close to Robbinsville on Highway 129, Santeetlah has, over the last few years, gained a reputation as one of the best bass fishing locations in the region. See *Boating*, above, for a full description of the lake, its access points and directions. Smallmouth, largemouth and white bass are plentiful. There's also crappie, sunfish, walleye and catfish.

■ Rock Climbing

Whiteside Mountain in the Highlands District of the Nantahala National Forest offers 10 climbing routes rated from 5.8 through 5.10 – not for beginners. The two-mile-plus loop leads to the top of the mountain, with a second trail on the northwestern side, also leading to the mountaintop. Whiteside Mountain is between Highlands and Cashiers off Highway 64. For more information, ☎ 828-526-3765.

■ Hiking

There are plenty of opportunities for hiking enthusiasts to find something new and exciting. How many miles of woodland and forest trails there are in the area is a subject for debate. Throw in all the trails and Forest Service roads and there must be more than two thousand miles of hiking routes. More than 700 miles of hiking-designated trails lace the Nantahala alone. These range from easy strolls to extremely difficult treks. Most of the good trails are inside the Nantahala National Forest, more are located in the southeastern section of the Pisgah National Forest. If that's not enough, there are the two nationally designated long distance trails that run through the region: the Appalachian Trail (AT) and the Bartram Trail.

With so much available, the question of where to hike is difficult to answer within the pages of a book like this. The following, then, is a listing and short description of some of the most popular trails. There should be something here for everyone.

Note that some of the trails are also open for horseback riding and mountain biking, as indicated below.

APPALACHIAN TRAIL: The AT runs northward out of Georgia, more than 88 miles through the Nantahala National Forest to Fontana Dam and on into the Great Smoky Mountains National Park. For most of its way, it follows the ridges and crests of the mountains, which can make for difficult going in some areas. Fortunately, there are rest areas and shelters along the way at distances of from three to 14 miles apart. The trail is easy to follow, being well marked with white blazes. There are numerous access points along the way, far too many to list here. Let's just say that you can virtually pick your spot and jump right in.

The AT, even in this fairly small region, is far too long to be documented in any detail here, and there are a number of books that do a good job of describing it. They are easily obtained by mail or telephone through any one of the Forest Service District Offices, through the Supervisor's Office in Asheville (see *Information Directory*) or by mail from the **Appalachian Trail Conference**, PO Box 807, Harpers Ferry, WV 25425-0807.

ART LOEB TRAIL: This popular and often busy trail begins in a parking lot one mile west of Highway 276, just inside the Brevard entrance to Pisgah National Forest. From there, it ascends Shut-in Ridge and Chestnut Knob, goes down into the Davidson River Gap near the National Fish Hatchery, then climbs over Cedar Rock Mountain. It crosses the Blue Ridge Parkway into Hayward County, continues over Black Balsam Knob into the Shining Rock Wilderness Area, and then on to Cold Mountain where it intersects the **Cold Mountain Trail**. The going is rarely easy, often strenuous, and sometimes downright difficult. Having said that, if you can manage it, you're in for one of nature's treats. The scenery along the way is spectacular.

BARTRAM TRAIL: The Bartram Trail is a national recreation trail that takes hikers across the Nantahala National Forest from the Nantahala Gorge east and south into Georgia.

William Bartram

The trail is named for William Bartram, a renowned naturalist and explorer who roamed the southern wilderness from Florida to North Carolina more than 200 years ago. Bartram studied the flora and fauna of the wilderness areas and recorded many of his findings in a journal published as the *Travels of William Bartram*.

The trail, blazed with yellow markers, is easy to follow and runs for more than 70 miles through the Nantahala National Forest, following the Mountain Waters Scenic Byway for most of its length. You can join the trail at any one of a number spots, but we recommend you join it in Franklin near the Wayah District Office.

FIRE'S CREEK RIM TRAIL: This is a loop of about 25 miles that's open to hikers and horses. It follows a high, elongated rim around Fire's Creek and features some spectacular views of heath, grassy balds and a mixture of hardwood and softwood forest with rhododendron and wildflowers. The trail is blazed in blue, but you have to look carefully; the blazes are few and far between. Several side trails provide for interesting excursions. Water is scarce, so bring plenty with you. It's a quiet trail.

From Hayesville, take Highway 64 and then NC 1307 to NC 1300. Travel west for a little more than 5½ miles to Forest Road 1344 (there's a Fires Creek sign). From there, drive north to the Fires Creek Parking Area.

HAOE LEAD TRAIL: This 12-mile trail begins at a parking lot 5½ miles along Kilmer Road from Santeetlah Lake, a 10- or 12-mile drive west and then north from Highway 129 in Robbinsville. From the parking lot, the trail ascends Rock Creek Knob and heads west across Jenkins Meadow. It climbs steeply and steadily to Haoe Lookout at an elevation of more than 5,200 feet for a spectacular panoramic view of the surrounding peaks and valleys. From the lookout, the trail descends to a junction with several other trails before it ends on the wilderness boundary near Stratton Bald. Once again, you'll need to be fairly fit if you're going to make it all the way up the mountain to Haoe Lookout. This trail is almost always strenuous.

JOYCE KILMER MEMORIAL TRAIL: This is one for the occasional outdoorsman who is more comfortable taking a pleasant stroll in the morning sunshine than backpacking through miles of wilderness. This little trail – it's less than two miles long – is an easy figure-eight loop that winds through the virgin stands of forest where 400-year-old poplars and hemlocks reach upward to the sky. The forest is named for the soldier poet, Joyce Kilmer, who died in action during the First World War at the age of 31.

From Robbinsville, take NC 1116 (Massey Branch Road), off Highway 129 and drive for two miles to the stop sign. Turn right onto NC 1127 and drive on for 10 miles, then turn left at the signs.

SNOWBIRD BACKCOUNTRY AREA: Hikers have lots of choices here. There are more than 37 miles of trails in the Snowbird Area, ranging from a little more than a mile in length to more than 12 miles, and from easy to extremely difficult. Of these, **Big Snowbird** is the most popular and the most difficult. For more than 10 miles the trail winds its way, following the creek, through some fairly remote areas of the mountains from Junction in the Snowbird Mountains to Big Junction on the Tennessee state line. It's an area where the Cherokee Indians hid out while on the run from General Winfield Scott during the roundup, just before the great exodus along the Trail of Tears. Before the trail ends, you'll cross the creek, always swollen after heavy rains, seven times.

 Watch the weather; the trail becomes impassable after a heavy storm.

From the Cheoah District Office in Robbinsville, turn left onto NC 116. Go for 2½ miles to a stop sign and turn right onto NC 1127. Go two miles to a fork in the road and bear left onto SR 1115. Drive on for two more miles to a point where 1115 turns sharply left – it's just past Robinson's Grocery Store. Make the left turn and continue until you come to a pair of bridges. At the end of the second bridge, turn right onto NC 1120, which becomes gravel Forest Service Road 75, and follow it for about six miles to its end. You'll find the trailheads there, in a former logging camp.

TSALI TRAILS: The Tsali Trail system of four loops winds through mixed hardwood and pine forest on a peninsula that stretches out into Fontana Lake. The loops range from 6½ miles to 12 miles in length and all four are rated by the National Forest Service as most difficult. The trails are also popular with mountain bikers and horseback riders. Even though hikers may use all four trails at any time, bikers and horses are kept separate by alternating the use of the trails. You'll find a schedule posted at the trailheads. Nearby facilities include a bike washing station, a developed campground with showers and flush toilets, a boat ramp, and picnic tables.

From Bryson City, take Highway 19S for nine miles. Turn right onto NC 28 and drive on for 5½ miles, then turn right again onto Forest Road 521 at the sign for the Tsali Recreation Area. The recreation area and trailheads are 1½ miles down this road.

UPPER TELLICO AREA: The Upper Tellico Area is a high-elevation basin formed by the Unicoi Mountains. It is also one of only a few areas in the national forests of North Carolina where off-road vehicles are allowed. The trails are a network of old logging trails and skid trails that range from easy to most difficult. They are open to all users – mountain bikes, all-terrain vehicles, four-wheel-drives – except for one trail that's set aside for use by ATV drivers only. Some badly eroded trails have been closed to off-road vehicles to allow the land to heal and to protect water quality. All trails are open to hikers, who should exercise care and watch out for fast-moving off-road vehicles.

From Murphy, drive north on NC 1326 for almost three miles, then turn right onto NC 1331 and go 5½ miles more. Turn right onto NC 1337 (Davis Creek Road) and go five miles to the top of the mountain and the Allen Gap Staging Area. (NC 1337 becomes gravel Forest Road 420.)

STANDING INDIAN BASIN TRAILS: This outstanding area of great natural beauty is a horseshoe-shaped drainage area formed by the Nantahala and Blue Ridge Mountains with several peaks rising to more than 5,000 feet. Within the area, a network of trails leads hikers to a number of magnificent waterfalls and upward to the mountain peaks. The going is considered moderately difficult to most difficult.

Pickens Nose Trail climbs almost two-thirds of a mile through a forest of mature oak trees to a promontory on Brushy Ridge.

Waslik Poplar Trail, a little more than a half-mile, leads to the nation's second largest yellow-poplar tree.

The Appalachian Trail crosses the mountain for more than 32 miles through this area, and passes through the Southern Nantahala Wilderness. You can use the AT to make several complete loop trails.

More than 16 miles of hiking trails in the area that are also open for equestrian use, and primitive camping for horses and riders is available at Hurricane Creek beyond the Standing Indian Campground, a developed site with showers, flush toilets and picnic tables.

From Franklin, take Highway 64 and drive west for nine miles, then turn left onto old 64 and drive two more miles. Turn right onto Forest Road 67 (it's a gravel road) and drive to Standing Indian Campground, where you'll find several trailheads.

WHITESIDE MOUNTAIN NATIONAL RECREATION TRAIL: A challenging two-mile trail open only to hikers. It's a loop trail rated by the National Forest Service as most difficult. You do have a couple of options, though. From the trailhead, you can take the old road, which begins the hike with a fairly gradual, though strenuous, climb to the summit. Or you can take the right branch and start with a steep climb up a set of stairs. Either way, your efforts will be rewarded by the magnificent vista at the top. South Carolina stretches away into the distance before you. You'll see the headwaters of the Chattooga River more than 2,100 feet below. In spring the surrounding rocky outcrops are a riot of wildflowers, rhododendrons and azaleas. The summit is at an elevation of 4,930 feet. White Mountain, a landmark on the eastern continental divide, has sheer cliffs that rise to more than 750 feet and provide a home for the endangered peregrine falcon that was reintroduced to the area in 1985.

From Highlands, take Highway 64 E five miles and turn right onto NC 1680 (White Mountain Road). Follow the signs to the trailhead.

■ Snow Skiing

This area of North Carolina is not as well blessed with ski resorts as the northwestern portion of the state. In fact, there are only three that are truly outstanding.

CATALOOCHIE SKI AREA

This is Maggie Valley's contribution to skiing in the region. It was the first of North Carolina's commercial ski resorts, having opened for business some 37 years ago, when such a thing was unheard of here. It is more than a mile high which, along with its snow-making capability, allows for a longer season. It's not unusual to ski as late as March. The resort's longest slope rivals even the best of its more famous peers in California, Colorado, or even Europe. From the peak of 5,400-foot Moody Top Mountain, the Omigosh ski run plummets more than 2,200 feet down the mountain to join with its less dramatic namesake, Lower Omigosh, to continue for another 1,800-plus feet for a combined drop of more than 4,000 feet. Together, these two magnificent runs require skill levels from beginner to advanced.

Rarely will you find it less than busy here and sometimes the crowds are intolerable.

Along with its nine excellent slopes, the resort offers a range of facilities, including a ski school and a pro shop where you can rent or buy equipment, including snowboards. There's also a fine mountain lodge where you can get a hot meal or enjoy a warm drink in front of a roaring fire.

The resort is in Maggie Valley on Fie Top Road, ☎ 800-768-3588.

SAPPHIRE VALLEY SKI AREA

This resort bills itself as "a resort for all seasons," and that's exactly what it is. Aside from the winter skiing activities, guests can enjoy organized outdoor activities year-round, including golf, tennis, horseback riding, fishing, swimming and hiking. But it's the skiing that made the resort what it is. Not quite as big as Cataloochie (or as well known or expensive), Sapphire Valley still has a lot to offer. There are slopes for all skill levels, as well as the obligatory ski lodge, pro shop and school. The resort is near Cashiers at 4000 US 64W. ☎ 828-743-1165.

SKI SCALY

This is a family resort just a few miles south of Highlands on Scaly Mountain. And the emphasis really is on family fun and adventure. It's not a place for the international playboy skier, nor is it a place for the rich and famous, or even the experienced skier who wants to show off his skills. The longest slope here is 1,600 feet, and it's dedicated to beginners. The advanced slope, while nice and steep to provide a fairly good run, is only 1,200 feet long. Rates are comparable with the class of resort that it is: moderate. There's a ski school and a pro shop where you can buy or rent equipment. The lodge is grand. Large windows allow parents to remain warm and cozy inside while keeping an eye on the kids as they play outside in the snow. There's also a café that serves hot drinks and food. The resort is at 106 South Scaly Mountain, off Highway 106, ☎ 828-526-3737.

■ Whitewater Rafting

The big center for whitewater rafting here is the **Nantahala River**. Because of the way the water flow through the gorge is controlled, rafting is a viable sport almost all year. It's a fast-moving river, with clear, cold water that rushes and tumbles along, taking rafters on a wild ride of more than nine miles through the Nantahala Gorge and the Nantahala National Forest. It's also one of the busiest spots in western North Carolina. More than a dozen outdoor adventure companies and outfitters fight for the available business. All have competent, though often young, employees to take care of the rafting public, and all are well qualified at what they do.

For a list of rafting companies and outfitters working the Nantahala, check the *Information Directory* at the back of the book.

Shopping

Asheville is central enough to be included in both northwestern and southwestern sections of North Carolina for this book, and it is considered to be the center of shopping for both areas. (See page 141) Other than that, real shopping opportunities are few and far between.

Obviously, there are major shopping areas in the larger towns – Murphy, Franklin, Andrews – but there's little there to distinguish them from any other town. There are just one or two places that deserve a mention.

■ Brevard

Until as recently as 1994, downtown Brevard had little to boast about. However, the arrival of the mega stores – Kmart and Wal-Mart – served to galvanize the old business district. Today, downtown Brevard is a bustling, attractive shopping center with lots to do and see. It's a kind of pedestrian center, only with traffic, which offers a variety of outdoor entertainment on weekends. It's clean, picturesque, and has an atmosphere that promotes a feeling of well-being and good times.

As in most small towns, the business district is centered on Main Street, with shops, stores and restaurants of every type and specialty on both sides, with even more spilling over into the side streets.

Of the specialty shops, there are some particularly worthy of mention: **The Book Nook**, 15 Broad Street, not only sells new books but also has a nice selection of quality used books; **Backcountry Outfitters** can supply you with the stuff you forgot to bring; **Brevard Antique Mall**, 57 E. Main, offers more than 12,000 square feet of quality goodies from times gone by; **D.D. Bulwinkle's**, 38 S. Broad, is one of those shops where you never know exactly what you'll find, but always seem to come away with something.

■ Dillsboro

This is a little town a couple of miles west of Sylva on Highway 19, about 14 miles northeast of Franklin. Sylva is, in itself, a neat place with plenty of good shopping. So why pick out Dillsboro? Well, for one thing it's one of the stops for the Great Smoky Mountain Railroad, which brings in a lot of extra business; but more than that, it's a unique community that has had to compete toe-to-toe with its much larger neighbors to the east. It's had to do just that little bit more to attract visitors, not only of the tourist kind, but from Sylva, too. The shopping center in Dillsboro is not a large one – just two blocks long and three blocks wide – but it's jam-packed with specialty shops.

The Riverwood Shops are a conglomerate of shops developed around the **Riverwood Pewter Shop**, just across the railroad tracks from Front Street, where they still make hand-hammered pewter goods in-house. All stores in Riverwood are outstanding. **The Time Capsule**, for instance, offers all sorts of used, rare goodies: out-of-print books, old maps, prints and so on. Even if you're not going to buy, it's a great place to browse. The **Oaks Gallery**, a cooperative of mountain crafts people more than 80 strong, offers a variety of hand-made items from jewelry to country furniture. **Mountain Pottery** is another type of cooperative where more than 50 of area potters display and sell an assortment of hand-crafted stoneware and porcelain. Of special interest to collectors is **Decoy Ducks**, a small shop where you can sift through hand-crafted ducks, far too nice to use for hunting, as well as other gift items. If you're into camping and the great outdoors, then you'll need to visit **Venture Out**, where you'll find all sorts of outdoor equipment, clothing and supplies.

Bradley's General Store on Front Street is also worth a visit. They carry an extensive line of country gifts and goodies. They also have an old, working soda fountain – a real blast from the past. **Dogwood Crafters** is just around the corner. The goodies you'll find here are far too numerous to list, but you can browse to your heart's content, and it's a rare visitor that leaves empty handed.

∎ Hendersonville

Hendersonville is not a large town, spread out though it might be. At the last count it boasted a population of 7,284, but it is the seat of Henderson County, which has a population of almost 70,000, so you can see why the little town has so much to offer. It, too, has had to compete for business, this time with Asheville just a few miles north, and easily accessible via I-26. Hendersonville, unlike most small towns, never did fall victim to the advent of the large shopping mall. Downtown Hendersonville took all the necessary steps to maintain its independence and its appeal. The result is a downtown shopping district with a difference. All the old buildings have been refurbished; Main Street is lined with so many beautiful trees and blooming shrubs and plants that they require the services of a full-time gardener; park benches have been placed at strategic spots along the street; and there's piped music playing softly from hidden speakers. All this makes for a shopping experience that's truly unique. Unfortunately, that very difference brings drawbacks all its own. The streets are always busy and parking is often a real problem. If you are lucky enough to find a spot on Main Street or one of the side streets, you'll find they are not metered. But you'd better watch out, as the two-hour parking limit is strictly enforced and tickets are scattered among unwary visitors like confetti. If you don't mind starting early, say around 10 am, you can alleviate the problem by parking in one of the several metered areas on Church or King Streets, and there are parking areas on Fifth and Sixth Avenues, too. (Also see page 182.)

■ Highlands

Highlands is, and always has been, something very special. It is located high in the mountains of southwestern North Carolina, where the air is always sweet and crisp. Even when it's raining, which it often is, the little mountain town has more to offer than most of its size.

Main Street is the shopping center for Highlands. Along its length you'll find a variety of unique shops and country restaurants where you can browse away an hour or two, and enjoy a snack and a cup of coffee. As always, it's difficult to separate the one or two outstanding shops from among the many excellent ones, but **Fireside Books, Etc.**, on Main Street is one, as is **Mountain Fresh Foods**, on the corner of Fifth and Main, where you can purchase fresh-baked goods and deli sandwiches that are to die for. **Mirror Lake Antiques** and **Tiger Mountain Woodworks**, where you can find those special hand-crafted goodies, are two more.

If you are a Christmas person, Highlands in December will enchant you. With snow on the ground, the town is difficult to reach. But, if you can, you'll find it a veritable winter wonderland.

■ Waynesville

This little country town of under 7,000 population is set deep in the heart of the mountains, some 30 miles west of Asheville on Highway 19/23. More than a little reminiscent of Hendersonville, Waynesville also has a charming and decidedly inviting downtown business district unaffected by the trend toward out-of-town shopping. Main Street, with its wonderful facade of old buildings, all lovingly restored and refurbished, its brick sidewalks, trees, plants and benches, is only one of the attractions. Here, too, there's always something going on and visitors come from Asheville and other nearby towns, as well as from around the country.

During the summer, the street in front of the courthouse is often blocked off to accommodate dancing, feasting, fairs and festivals. On such occasions, live music played by country and bluegrass bands echoes through the town. It's an altogether unique experience. And for shoppers, the downtown district has more than 50 stores that offer a selection of goods and specialties. Don't miss **Whitman's Bakery & Sandwich Shop** on North Main; their fresh-baked goods are, by themselves, worth the drive. The **Curbside Market** is also a treat, as is the **Mast General Store** with its turn-of-the-century fixtures. Both are on Main Street. For something really different, you might try **The Blue Owl Shoppe & Gallery** on Church Street. They do wonderful things with old prints and pictures. For something to eat and drink, try **O'Mally's Pub**, 295 North Main.

Parking in downtown Waynesville is not the problem it is in many other small mountain towns. There always seems to be room enough for everyone on Main Street, although it might mean a walk in from the outer reaches. If you do happen to visit on a day when parking is at a premium, you can always find room on one of the streets running parallel to Main.

Southwestern North Carolina

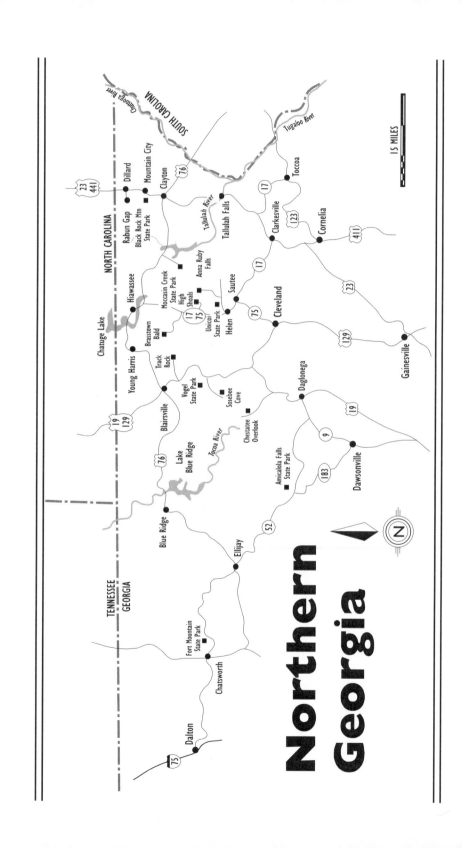

Northern Georgia

Northern Georgia represents the southern boundary of our interpretation of the Great Smoky Mountains. The area we are concerned with is primarily inside the perimeter of the Chattahoochee National Forest, a strip that includes a half-dozen counties on the Georgia/North Carolina border. In the west, it includes Lookout Mountain as far south as Lafayette; to the east it covers most of Rabun County. Once you leave the main arterial highways, with the exception of the Greater Chattanooga area to the west, it's a fairly remote region, incorporating huge tracts of mountainous wilderness, forests and a number of lakes. Georgia is proud of its wilderness areas, and has gone to great lengths to ensure their preservation. At the same time these regions have been opened up not only for outdoor recreation on a grand scale, but to draw tourists in from around the world.

Within the Chattahoochee National Forest, you'll find all sorts of outstanding opportunities to pursue almost every outdoor sport and activity you can think of. There's not much for the urban adventurer in search of shops, but there are plenty of opportunities for sightseeing and casual recreation. For the dedicated outdoorsman, there are hundreds of miles of hiking trails, dozens of backcountry campgrounds, several whitewater rafting and kayaking rivers, and vast lakes for fishing, boating, sailing, skiing or swimming.

There are a dozen state parks scattered throughout the area. These, too, have received a great deal of money and attention from the powers that be in Atlanta. Some of them have purposely been maintained as primitive, backcountry parks; others have been developed to a point where they rival even the finest of holiday resorts. You'll find them all described in the following pages.

Within the Chattahoochee National Forest itself, the Forest Service has not been idle. Compared with other national forests in the east, it is well blessed with recreation areas, wilderness campgrounds, and well-marked trails. Facilities in this forest are rivaled only by those of the Cherokee National Forest in Tennessee. And then there are the tiny mountain communities. Towns like Ellijay, the Apple Capital of Georgia; Helen, a tiny tourist town that might have been lifted right out of Germany's Black Forest and dropped down in the mountains of North Georgia; Clarksville; Dahlonega; Chattsworth; Blue Ridge; Blairsville and Clayton. All are unique.

Northern Georgia and its rivers and mountains were the subject of James Dickey's novel, *Deliverance*, which was subsequently turned into a major motion picture. You'll remember the story was about four men from Atlanta and their terrifying experiences running the rapids.

With the exception of Helen, northern Georgia is not blessed or, as some would say, cursed, with the sort of great tourist attractions one finds in some sections of eastern Tennessee and western North Carolina. There are no flashing colored lights, no fairyland-like attractions, no theme parks, and certainly no clogged and crowded roads; at least, not yet. And Helen is but a very poor cousin when compared to Gatlinburg. Northern Georgia is a kinder, gentler place, packed with adventuring possibilities – a place where the pace is slower, the people friendlier, and the accents soft and lilting.

Getting Here

BY AIR

You have a couple of options here. The easiest way is to fly into Atlanta's **Hartsfield International Airport** ("you can't go anywhere in the South without flying into Atlanta") and then rent a car or RV and drive north. You can also fly into Chattanooga, even though that probably will mean changing planes in Atlanta and then driving south or east. Atlanta is the headquarters for Delta Airlines, and the city is served by almost every other major carrier too. **Chattanooga** is well served by ASA, American, USAir, and a variety of small carriers.

BY ROAD

From Atlanta

 Driving out of Atlanta, depending upon the time of day, can be either the easiest of experiences or hell on earth. It is served by a 16-lane (eight in either direction) super highway, and several four-lane arterial highways.

On weekdays the hours from 7 to 9 am, and 3:30 to 7 pm, see all roads become one solid mass of barely moving cars, vans and trucks. If you arrive at that time, take time out, eat some breakfast or lunch, and then sally forth when the congestion has eased.

Once you do get out onto the highways, you have several choices. You can take I-75 north toward Chattanooga, branching off on any minor state road that leads into the forests and mountains; you can take Highway 19 north to Dahlonega and Brasstown Bald; or you can follow Highway 23 northeast through Gainesville to Toccoa and the Tallulah Gorge. A fourth option is to drive north on I-75 to its intersection with I-575, which you follow to Highway 76. This leads on to Blue Ridge and McCaysville.

From Tennessee

If you're driving in from Chattanooga, you also have a couple of options; both revolve around I-75. You can drive south on 75 to Dalton and then take 76 west through Chatsworth, Ellijay, and so on all the way to Brasstown. You'll find it a very beautiful, though often hazardous, drive through the mountains. The other option is to drive south on I-75 to Ressaca, turn east on GA136, and then proceed to its junction with Highway 76 via Carter's Lake. Either way, you're in for a treat.

From North Carolina

From western North Carolina and the Great Smoky Mountains National Park, you really only have one viable option, Highway 19. From Cherokee, the road runs all the way southwest to Murphy, and from the south into Georgia where it joins Highway 129 and heads on down to Dahlonega and Atlanta, with side roads branching east and west into the mountains along the way.

Northern Georgia

■ Once You Get Here

Here, at the southern end of the chain, the Appalachians are smoothing down – settling, if you will. The mountains are not quite so sharply defined as they are in North Carolina, nor are they as high. Hiking trails tend to be a little easier; the rivers, with the exception of the Chattooga, are not as wild; the lakes, though not quite a big as those in eastern Tennessee, are surrounded by forests and mountains and are just as beautiful as those farther to the north. Chattahoochee National Forest is just as magnificent and as well managed as its more famous cousins to the north. Perhaps the best way to enjoy these mountains is to rent an RV or camping trailer, maybe even a tent, and venture out into the wilderness on your own, making a base for yourself at one of the many well-developed state parks.

 Good hotels outside of Chattanooga and Atlanta are few and far between.

PLANNING

Unless you have six months to spare, it would be impossible to do northern Georgia in a single visit. So it's imperative that you decide what it is you want to do and see, always remembering that just the driving on these backcountry roads will take a great deal of time. Once you have decided upon an itinerary, put it on paper and, within reasonable bounds, try to stick to it. You'll do better, see more, and therefore make the best use of your time.

Most of the things to see and do in northern Georgia revolve either around the mountains and magnificent terrain or the many historic sights. The tiny towns and villages have close links with the past, both pioneer and Native American.

Sightseeing

■ Amicalola Falls State Park

 In the language of a Cherokee Indian, Amicalola means "Tumbling Waters." No other word could better describe the spectacular falls that plunge 729 feet in seven cascades, making it the highest waterfall in Georgia. An eight-mile trail meanders through the 1,020-acre park, leading first to the falls and then on to Springer Mountain and the southern end of the 2,150-mile Appalachian Trail, which runs from Georgia to Maine. The trails within the park and along the Appalachian Trail offer the nature lover a treasure chest full of wildlife, and an opportunity to experience the great outdoors at its very best.

The Park Service offers a full, year-round program of special events, including Spring Wildflowers in April; an extensive schedule of Naturalist Programs in summer; Summer's End Trading Days in August; an Overnight Backpacking Trip in October; and the Fall Leaf Displays, also in October. Other popular activities include fishing, camping, hiking, nature study, bird watching, wildlife photography, and picnicking. For camping information, check the listing in the *Camping Directory* at the back of the book.

The park, 15 miles northwest of Dawsonville, is open from 7 am to 10 pm, and the park office is open from 8 to 5.

Take Highway 53 west out of Dawsonville, and then Highway 183 to Highway 52 east. Amicalola Falls State Park and Lodge, State Route, Box 215, Dawsonville, GA 30534. ☎ 706-265-8888.

■ Black Rock Mountain State Park

Black Rock Mountain State park is set high atop the eastern continental divide close to the Georgia/North Carolina border. At an altitude of more than 3,600 feet, it is the highest state park in Georgia. Named for its great granite cliffs and peaks, the 1,500-acre park offers some of the most spectacular views of the southern Appalachian Mountains. On a clear day, from its seven scenic overlooks, it's possible to see for more than 80 miles, and even as far as Atlanta.

The Park Service offers a schedule of activities and programs that includes Spring Wildflowers in May; Overnight Backpacking in the fall; and a variety of other events and mountain culture programs. Other activities include hiking, which takes in the **Tennessee Rock Trail**, the **Ada-hi Falls Trail**, and the **James E. Edmonds Trail**, as well as various lesser-known trails. Camping, both pioneer and primitive, is available too (see *Camping Directory*). There's also a visitor center where you can

Northern Georgia

find nature guides, raised relief maps and hiking and trail guides. Park Service Rangers are ready to answer you questions and help you to make the most of your visit.

Black Rock Mountain State Park, Mountain City, GA 30562. ☎ 706-746-2141. The park is open from 7 am to 10 pm, and the park office from 8 to 5.

The park is three miles north of Clayton via Highway 441.

■ Blue Ridge

 Blue Ridge is a small mountain community at the southern end of the Blue Ridge Province of the Appalachian Mountain chain, from which it takes its name. With a population of less than 1,400, it's barely a spot on the map. It is, however, set right at the heart of some of the most spectacular country in what we are calling the Great Smoky Mountains: the **Cohutta Mountains in the Unaka Range** and the **Murphy Syncline**, a great depression in the mountains that runs northward from Tate, through Ellijay, to Blue Ridge and beyond.

Blue Ridge is a rural community, devoted mostly to farming and, lately, tourism. It's also an area steeped in Native American history and folklore, being one of the last strongholds of the Cherokee Nation.

Blue Ridge is inside the Toccoa Ranger District of the Chattahoochee National Forest, just east of the vast **Cohutta Wilderness**, a wild area with a great deal to offer outdoor enthusiasts (see *Cohutta Ranger District* in the section dealing with the Chattahoochee National Forest).

■ Cloudland Canyon State Park

 Cloudland Canyon State Park sits high on the western edge of Lookout Mountain and is the westernmost state park covered in this book. It's also one of the most scenic parks in northern Georgia. The canyon itself, cut by Sitton Gulch Creek, varies in elevation from more than 1,800 feet at the highest point to a low of less than 800. Overlooks on the canyon rim provide breathtaking views, and a wooden walkway offers an exciting, though somewhat long and strenuous (even hazardous in winter) climb down to the foot of the waterfall and the canyon floor.

Cloudland Canyon is one of Georgia's busiest parks. Its magnificent views and close proximity to Chattanooga make it attractive, not only to outdoor adventurers, but to casual day-visitors, too. It's also a major camping destination (see *Camping Directory*). Nature lovers flock to the mountaintop park in the spring for the annual show of wildflowers, and hikers will enjoy the more than six miles of backcountry trails. In the fall, the canyon is full of color. The park is a well-known and extremely popular picnic spot (there are lots of tables and an open-air pavilion with grills).

 The Park Service provides several annual special events, including **Crafts in the Clouds** *the third weekend in May (subject to change), a* **Wildflower Program** *during May, and an* **Overnight Backpacking Trip** *in October.*

Cloudland Canyon State Park, Route 2, Box 150, Rising Fawn, GA 30738. ☎ 706-657-4050. The park is open from 7 am until 10 pm and the park office is open from 8 until 5.

Cloudland Canyon State Park is on Lookout Mountain, about 10 miles south of Chattanooga on Georgia Route 136, eight miles east of Trenton and I-59 and 18 miles west of Lafayette.

■ Chattahoochee National Forest

 This is, perhaps, the most visitor-oriented of the four national forests covered in this book. Now a part of a single forest system that includes the Oconee National Forest to the south, the Chattahoochee stretches across northern Georgia like a green ribbon of velvet. The two forests are administered by seven national forest service ranger districts. They are responsible for more than 860,000 acres – 750,000 of which are within the boundaries of the Chattahoochee. More than 500 developed campsites, 200 picnic sites, 10 wilderness areas, six swimming beaches, the Chattooga Wild and Scenic River, several hundred lakes, rivers and streams, and over 500 miles of hiking trails, including 83 miles of the Appalachian Trail, are also covered. To include it all in a single book would be a task of monumental proportions. The following, then, is an overview of each of the seven districts, with some of the most popular attractions and recreation areas. You'll find the address and telephone number for each district in the *Information Directory* under Chattahoochee National Forest.

ARMUCHEE RANGER DISTRICT

Headquartered in Lafayette, this office is responsible for the far western reaches of the forest that run from Summerville in the south, all the way to Ringgold, just outside of Chattanooga, in the north. There are three popular recreation areas within the district.

Hidden Creek

The main feature here is a small creek that's sometimes there, but often isn't. When it does run, the waters are crystal clear. It's a popular spot for hiking, picnicking and camping (see *Camping Directory*).

Take GA 156 southwest from Calhoun for 7½ miles, turn left onto Everatte Springs Road and drive two more miles. Turn right on Rock House Road and go for three miles to Forest Service Road 955. Turn right there and you'll come to the park entrance after about one mile.

Keown Falls & Scenic Area

The focus here is the small but scenic waterfall from which the area gets its name. There's a modest recreation area (no camping) with flush toilets, and a picnic site with tables and grills.

Take GA 136 east from Lafayette. Drive 13½ miles, past Villanow, and turn right onto Pocket Road. The park entrance is just five miles away.

Pocket

This is a small wooded glen surrounding a large spring and a little creek. It was the site of a Civilian Conservation Corps Camp during the 1930s. Today, it's a nice, quiet place where you can go camping (see *Camping Directory*), hiking and picnicking.

Take GA 136 east from Lafayette and drive for 13½ miles, past Villanow, and turn right Pocket Road. From there, drive seven miles to the entrance.

BRASSTOWN RANGER DISTRICT

Lots to see and do here. Centered on Blairsville, this district features some of the Catahoochee's most scenic areas, including the Brasstown Wilderness Area and Brasstown Bald, Georgia's highest mountain.

High Shoals Scenic Area

Two waterfalls, several crystal-clear mountain creeks, and a profusion of wildflowers, rhododendrons and mountain laurels provide a picture of the mountains you just have to see. The scenic area covers 175 acres with a mile-long hiking trail from a parking area on Forest Road 283 to the falls. Day use only; no camping.

From Cleveland, take GA 75 north for 22 miles. Turn right onto Forest Road 283 and drive a mile to the trailhead that will take you to Blue Hole Falls.

Russell/Brasstown Scenic Byway

This is a 38-mile driving loop through some of Georgia's most scenic countryside. Along the way are several scenic overlooks with views of the mountains and valleys. Begin your tour at Helen by taking GA 17/75 and driving north. Turn left on GA 180, and then left again on GA 348. Drive on and turn left on GA 74ALT and proceed on back to Helen.

Brasstown Bald

This is Georgia's highest mountain; it's also one of its most visited. From the summit, some 4,800 feet above sea level, there are breathtaking panoramic views across four states for a distance of almost 100 miles on clear days. Although the Brasstown Wilderness is a section of the Chattahoochee National Forest, the mountain itself is not inside the wilderness area. This is a wild and beautiful region, where the upper slopes are covered with spectacular displays of wildflowers, rhododendrons, mountain laurels and azaleas in the spring, and the foothills with a profusion of color in the fall.

Brasstown Bald Visitor Center

The center helps visitors to better understand the workings of the mountain ecosystem and its surrounding forests. This is done through a series of interpretive programs and exhibits, such as one aptly called "Man and the Mountain," which traces both the human and natural history of the Southern Appalachians. Within the complex, the mountaintop theater offers a series of continuously running video programs, and there are a number of interesting artifacts on display. Perhaps the center's best feature is its outside observation deck, where you can experience the chilling winds and enjoy a 360° view of the countryside. It's an awesome experience, one that's well worth the small amount of effort it takes to visit. There's a small parking fee (at the time of writing it was $1), but entrance to the center, its theater, observation deck, bookstore and gift shop are all free.

The center is open daily from 10 am until 5:30 pm, Memorial Day through October and, depending upon the weather, on weekends during the spring. (It's best to call first, ☎ 706-896-2556.) The observation deck is open year-round.

From Cleveland, take GA 75 north through Helen to GA 180. Turn left, drive for six miles, then turn right onto the GA 180 spur. Three miles more brings you to the Brasstown Bald parking lot. From there, you can hike up the steep, half-mile trail to the center, or you can take the shuttle bus. The hiking trail leads through some of the most stunning scenery in the area.

Sosebee Cove Scenic Area

This 175-acre tract of hardwood forest is set aside as a memorial to Arthur Woody, who served as ranger from 1918 to 1945. Known as the "Barefoot Ranger," he loved this peaceful cove and spent much of his spare time here before negotiating its purchase by the forest service. Along with its wonderful displays of wildflowers, the cove has a healthy stand of yellow poplars.

From Blairsville, take Highways 19 and 129 south for 10 miles and turn west on GA 180. Drive on for two more miles.

Lake Winfield Scott

This is a beautiful, 18-acre lake set high among the mountains of northeast Georgia. Only 10 miles from Blairsville to the north with Helen and Cleveland to the east and south, it's no wonder that the lake is a popular spot for outdoor lovers. Camping is available (see *Camping Directory*), as well as hiking, picnicking, swimming, boating (electric motors only) and, of course, fishing.

From Blairsville, take Highways 19 and 129 south for 10 miles, turn west on GA 180 and drive for seven more miles.

From Cleveland, take Highways 19 and 129 north to GA 180 and follow the directions above.

Coosa Bald Scenic Area

This 7,100-acre scenic area lies in both the Brasstown and Chestate Ranger Districts. It's an area full of botanical diversity, where many species of endangered plants grow and great boulders are evidence of the last great glacial retreat. And it's filled with wildlife: black bears, deer, wild hogs, birds of prey, etc. There are no facilities here, just the natural terrain, some wild and remote streams where the trout fishing is good, and one or two primitive trails. If you're looking for solitude, you'll find it here.

From Blairsville, take Highways 19 and 129 south for 10 miles and turn west on GA 180. The scenic area borders 180 for the next seven miles.

Lake Chatuge

This lake has already been covered extensively under the Southwestern North Carolina *Boating* section (see page 215). There are, however, extensive boating, fishing and other recreational opportunities available on the Georgia side of the state line, including a national forest recreation area with boat ramps and camping facilities (see *Camping Directory*).

From Hiawassee, take Highway 76 north and drive for two miles, then turn left on GA 288 and drive on for about a mile.

CHATTOOGA RANGER DISTRICT

Anna Ruby Falls

The biggest attraction in the Chattooga District is Anna Ruby Falls, two waterfalls that, between them, drop more than 150 feet. In the summertime it's a cool and inviting place; in winter the entire area turns into a wonderland of ice and snow, making it one of the most photographed spots in the state. The recreation area itself features a visitor center and craft shop, two interpretive trails, and a scenic picnic area. There's a small parking fee ($1 at the time of writing). The park can be extremely busy at times, especially on summer weekends.

From Helen, take GA 75 northeast for one mile to Robertstown. Turn right onto GA 356 and drive 1½ miles. Turn left and drive through Unicoi State Park. Follow the signs for 3½ miles to the parking area.

Chattahoochee River Recreation Area

Close to the headwaters of the Chattahoochee, and adjacent to the beautiful Horse Trough Falls and the Mark Trail Wilderness Area, this area is packed with outdoor opportunities. Camping (see *Camping Directory*), hiking, canoeing, picnicking and fishing are all popular.

From Helen, take GA 75 north for 1½ miles and turn left on GA 356. Cross the river and turn right on the paved road next to the Chattahoochee Church and follow it, beyond the point where the pavement ends, for nine miles to the campground.

Dukes Creek Falls

The falls here plummet more than 300 feet into a scenic gorge and can be viewed from a number of strategically located observation points, most of which are reached via a mile-long hiking trail through the forest. Aside from the falls, Dukes Creek itself is a place of great natural beauty, a definite stop for naturalists and bird watchers. Fishing is available, too, and there's a gift shop and a nice, quiet picnic area.

From Helen, take GA 75 north for 1½ miles, then turn left onto GA 356. Drive on for 2½ miles.

COHUTTA RANGER DISTRICT

This district takes in the area north of Chatsworth on the North Carolina and Tennessee borders. Most easily accessed via GA 52, the Cohutta Wilderness is a wild, heavily forested area that provides a natural habitat for the black bear, as well as a number of other exotic species, including wild boar, deer and eagles. It's also the location of a small, scenic river, the Conasauga (see *Canoeing* in the Adventures section, page 263).

Lake Conasauga Recreation Area

At an elevation of more than 3,100 feet, near the top of Grassy Mountain, Lake Conasauga is Georgia's highest lake.

> *The name, Conasauga, is derived from an old Indian word "kahnasagah," which means sparkling water.*

And sparkle they do. Set among the peaks and forests of the Blue Ridge, the lake is one of the most beautiful in the area. It's also one of the most popular recreation areas in the Chattahoochee. With a well-developed campground, boat ramps, good fishing, and excellent picnic facilities, it's no wonder that people from miles around flock to the lake, mostly on summer weekends, but also through the spring and fall.

Activities here include bird watching (see below), camping (see *Camping Directory*), picnicking, swimming, boating (electric motors only), canoeing, fishing, and hiking.

BIRD WATCHING: If you're a bird watcher, you'll love it here. More than 100 species of wild birds make their homes around the lake. These include several species of hawks, owls, woodpeckers, cuckoos, flycatchers, chickadees, titmice, nuthatches, tanagers, grosbeaks, buntings and crossbills.

HIKING: There are a number of nice hiking trails within the Lake Conasauga and Cohutta Wilderness Area, including the Conasauga River Trail (see *Hiking* section later in this chapter).

From Chattsworth, take Highway 441 north for four miles into Eton and turn right at the light. Follow that road until it becomes unpaved Forest Service Road (FSR) 18, and then turn right onto FSR 68 for 10 miles more.

If you are coming from Ellijay, take Highway 52 west for seven miles to FSR 18, where you'll find a sign pointing the way to Lake Conasauga Recreation Area.

Conasauga River

The Conasauga has its origins deep in the Cohutta Wilderness. It's a crystal-clear mountain river that winds its way north through a series of gorges, into the Alaculsy Valley, to eventually join with the Jacks River. The upper section flows through some untouched areas. If you are a canoeist of some ability, you'll want to give it a try (see *Canoeing* section, page 263). Hikers should also investigate the Conasauga.

From Atlanta, take I-75 north to its intersection with Highway 411. Turn north on 411 and to the Conasauga Bridge, just a couple of miles across the Tennessee state line. Continue for a short distance and turn right onto Sheeds Creek Road (the first paved road past the bridge next to a gas station). Another seven miles takes you to a small valley, where you'll find the river, several campgrounds, and a number of hiking trails. The road is unpaved for most of the way.

TOCCOA RANGER DISTRICT

This district has nothing to do with the town of the same name. The Toccoa centers upon the forest in and around the Toccoa River, with its focal point being the Blue RidgeLake.

Blue Ridge Lake

This man-made lake in the heart of the Chattahoochee National Forest, just west of Blue Ridge on GA 60, stretches for more than 10 miles along the Toccoa River. The Toccoa flows north through the lake to Copperhill, Tennessee, where it changes name and becomes the mighty whitewater river and Olympic kayak venue, the Ocoee.

Blue Ridge Lake is a popular spot for anglers and boaters alike, but never as busy as one might expect. It's a fairly remote location compared to the lakes farther to the south: Alatoona and Lanier. It's kept as something of an open secret among watersports aficionados. Even on its busiest days there's plenty of room for everyone to do their thing, be it skiing, swimming or fishing.

Blue Ridge Lake is blessed with two national forest recreation areas: **Blue Ridge Lake** and **Morganton Point**. Both have boat ramps and well-developed campgrounds (see *Camping Directory* listings under Chattahoochee National Forest).

To reach the Blue Ridge Lake Recreation Area, drive east from Blue Ridge on Highway 76 to its junction with Dry Branch Road. Turn right and drive three miles to the entrance.

To use the boat ramp at Morganton Point Recreation Area, drive a little farther on along 76 to its junction with GA 60 and then turn south. Drive three more miles, through Morganton, and look out for the white and green signs that point the way. You'll then turn right onto County Road 616 and drive for a mile. There's another ramp near Lakewood, between the dam and Lakewood Junction.

Deep Hole

This is another recreation area set beside the Toccoa River not far west of the Cooper Creek Scenic Area. It's a fairly remote spot and still not as popular as many wilderness sites have lately become. It's a very pretty area with a nice campground, numerous opportunities for hiking, and some very good river fishing, too.

From Dahlonega, take GA 60 north for 27 miles. An alternative route is to take Highway 76 east from Blue Ridge to its junction with GA 60 at Morganton, and then go south for 16 miles.

Cooper Creek Scenic Area & Recreation Area

Cooper Creek is a remote recreation area with plenty to see and do. It adjoins the beautiful Cooper Creek Scenic Area, a 1,240-acre tract of forest with a number of hiking trails. The region has a partially developed campground (see *Camping Directory*), and more opportunities for hiking, fishing and picnicking. It's a very beautiful stretch with lots of sparkling water and plenty of trout.

From Dahlonega, take GA 60 north and drive 26 miles, then turn right onto Forest Road 4 and continue for six miles. From Blue Ridge, take Highway 76 east to its junction with GA 60 at Morganton and then go south for 17 miles. Turn left onto Forest Road 4 for six miles.

Frank Cross

This creekside recreation area is near the Chattahoochee National Fish Hatchery on Rock Creek. It has just a small campground, but good fishing on the creek. Lovely country and sparkling waters await. If you like to get away from the crowds, this will suit you fine.

From Dahlonega, take GA 60 north for 27 miles. Turn left onto Forest Service Road 69 and go for five miles. From Blue Ridge, take GA 76 to its junction with GA 60, drive south for 15 miles to GA 69 and turn right. Drive on for five miles more.

Northern Georgia

CHESTATEE RANGER DISTRICT

This district is centered on an old gold mining town named Dahlonega. It was during the years 1828-1829 that white settlers first began pouring into the area in search of the yellow metal. There was so much of it that the government built a mint here and, from 1838 to 1861, more than 1.3 million gold coins were struck. The Civil War soon brought an end to that, but gold can still be found in the area.

Desoto Falls Recreation & Scenic Areas

This scenic area covers some 650 acres of rugged, mountainous country ranging in elevation from 2,000 to 3,500 feet. It's exceptionally beautiful, with magnificent views, several lovely waterfalls, and a number of crystal-clear streams and creeks. There's a small, well-developed campground, a half-dozen picnic sites, several hiking trails, and good fishing.

From Dahlonega, take Highway 19 north for 18 miles; or use Highway 129 north from Cleveland for 15 miles.

TALLULAH RANGER DISTRICT

Covering the northeastern corner of the Chattahoochee, this district has a great deal to offer outdoor enthusiasts. The Appalachian Trail, the Chattooga River, the southern section of the Elliott Rock Wilderness Area, and some of the most beautiful mountain scenery in Georgia are all within its boundaries.

Chattooga Wild & Scenic River

The Chattooga is one of the longest free-flowing rivers in the southeastern United States that remains relatively primitive and undeveloped. "Wild and Scenic" is an official designation awarded by the Federal Government to certain unique rivers. For more than 40 miles, the Chattooga serves as the border between Georgia and South Carolina. Wild and scenic applies in more ways than one. True, it's one of the most beautiful rivers in northern Georgia, but it also can be very dangerous. And it's another of those centers for outdoor adventures where the rafting companies ply the waters with their great rubber boats. It's also a popular kayaking destination, and therein lies the danger.

Only canoeists of considerable experience should venture out onto the waters, and then never alone.

The river is most easily reached by traveling northeast on Highway 23. Maps of the river are available from the National Forest Service (see *Information Directory*).

Tallulah River & Colman River

Tallulah River is a forest recreation area; Colman River is a forest scenic area. They are close enough to be counted as one, at least for the purposes of this book. It's an area of old-growth timber, rugged scenery and tumbling waters with lots of hiking and fishing opportunities, as well as a small, secluded campground. Never very busy, it's one of those quiet places where you can relax and perhaps enjoy fresh trout cooked over the grill or a romantic outdoor picnic.

Take Highway 76 west from Clayton for eight miles, then turn right onto an unpaved road and drive four miles more. Turn left on Forest Service Road 70; the campground is a mile farther on.

Willis Knob

Rugged mountain country near the South Carolina state line and spectacular scenery make this recreation area quite popular with outdoor enthusiasts, especially those who enjoy horseback riding. The campground is very small – only eight sites – but there's good fishing on the Chattooga River, lots of hiking and horse trails, and it's never very busy.

From Clayton, go east on Warwoman Road for 11½ miles. Turn right on Goldmine Road – it's a gravel road – and look for signs indicating Woodall Ridge Day Use Parking Area on the left.

Rabun Beach

This is the most well-developed of all the national forest recreation areas in the Chattahoochee. Situated on the edge of 940-acre Lake Rabun, it offers some of the most spectacular mountain scenery in northeast Georgia. There are plenty of opportunities for outdoor recreation, especially hiking, boating, fishing, picnicking and camping (see *Camping Directory*).

Northern Georgia

Take Highway 441/23 south from Clayton and drive seven miles. Here, turn right onto an unmarked county road, drive on for one-tenth of a mile and turn left onto GA 15. Drive for two miles and then turn right onto County Road 10 for another five miles.

■ Chief Vann House State Historic Site

The Chief Vann House is a classic, two-story, brick mansion, called the "Showplace of the Cherokee Nation." It was built by Chief James Vann in 1804 and is decorated with magnificent hand carvings, all painted in natural colors of blue, red, green and yellow. Of the house's many features and antiques, the most outstanding is a fine cantilevered stairway.

Chief Vann is remembered for his contribution to the education of the Cherokee. He was responsible for bringing Moravian missionaries to teach children the Christian way of life. But Vann was still a Cherokee Indian and a polygamist. He had three wives and five children. He was executed in 1809 for killing his brother-in-law in a duel in 1808 and the house, along with Vann's other possessions and business interests, passed on to his son, Joseph.

In 1834 the government seized the property when "Rich Joe" Vann unknowingly violated state law by employing a white man. It was passed into the hands of white owners by way of a land lottery.

The house is open all year-round, Tuesday through Saturday from 9 am until 5 pm, and on Sunday from 2 until 5:30. There's a small admission fee.

Chief Vann House State Historic Site, Route 7, Box 7655, Chatsworth, GA 30705. ☎ 706-695-2598.

■ Dahlonega Gold Museum & Historic Site

For more than 30 years the gold towns of Dahlonega and Auraria in northern Georgia thrived as a river of the precious metal flowed in from the mountains. Gold was discovered in the region in 1828, some 20 years before the great finds in California. From all points of the compass, thousands of hopeful prospectors headed for the diggings deep in the heart of the Cherokee Nation. It was the beginning of the gold rush era.

A Federal Branch Mint was established in Dahlonega and from 1838 to 1861 the plant turned out more than $6 million in gold coins. Today, the old Lumpkin County Courthouse is a museum dedicated to the "good old days" of the nation's first major gold rush. A wide range of exhibits, including a gold nugget that weighs more than five ounces, a 30-minute film entitled *Gold Fever*, and a series of special events, gives the visitor a unique look into the lives and times of the pioneering families that lived, toiled and fought for their very existence in northern Georgia's gold fields.

The museum is open all year, Monday through Saturday, from 9 am to 5 pm and on Sunday from 10 until 5. It is closed on Thanksgiving and Christmas Day. There is a small admission fee, and group rates are available with advance notice.

Dahlonega Gold Museum State Historic Site, Public Square, Box 2042, Dahlonega, GA 30533. ☎ 706-864-2257.

The museum is on the Public Square in Dahlonega, five miles west of GA 400.

▪ Fort Mountain State Park

 High on the top of the mountain is an ancient, 855-foot-long stone wall from which the park gets its name. No one knows for sure how the wall came to be, but some believe it was built in prehistoric times by Indians as a means of fortification against other more hostile tribes. Others think it might have been built as a place to carry out ancient tribal ceremonies. We'll probably never know for sure.

The mountain park, with its abundance of wildlife and the surrounding Chattahoochee National Forest, is a place of outstanding natural beauty, and well worth a visit. The wall is reached by hiking up a long, very steep set of steps and a trail to the top of the mountain.

The park covers more than 1,900 acres and has an extensive range of facilities. There are more than 12 miles of mountain trails, a swimming beach with bathhouse, a miniature golf course, seven picnic shelters and 117 tables.

Northern Georgia

> *The Park Service puts on several annual events, including* **Spring Wildflowers**, **Fort Mountain Mysteries** *in August, and* **Overnight Backcountry Trips** *in October and November.*

Fort Mountain State Park, Route 7, Box 7008, Chatsworth, GA 30705. ☎ 706-695-2621. The park, seven miles from Chatsworth on GA 54, is open from 7 am until 10 pm daily.

■ Hart State Park

Situated as it is on the banks of Lake Hartwell, this park is one of Georgia's most popular outdoor centers and the fair-weather crowd makes it somewhat congested at times. The fishing is excellent and anglers come from miles around for the largemouth and smallmouth bass, black crappie, bream, rainbow trout, and walleye. And, if it's watersports, boating, waterskiing, or swimming that you like, there's probably no better place to do it than on the sparkling waters of this reservoir. Several boat ramps and docks offer easy access to the 56,000-acre lake and it's a rare day in summer when the park and lake are not busy. Facilities include camping, picnicking, hiking, swimming, fishing and boating. The 146-acre park has its own swimming beach and three picnic shelters. There's also a small theater where you can enjoy live music programs.

> *The Park Service puts on a number of annual events, including the* **Labor Day Music Festival** *in September, the* **Memorial Day Weekend Craft Show**, *and the* **Hot Rods of Hart Car Show** *on the 1st Sunday in November.*

Hart State Park, 1515 Hart Park Road, Hartwell, GA 30643. ☎ 706-376-8756. Park hours are from 7 am to 10 pm.

The park is east from Hartwell on Highway 29; turn left on Ridge Road and go two miles.

■ Helen

No coverage of northern Georgia would be complete without a look at the alpine village of Helen. Known throughout the Southeast, much to the locals' displeasure, as the Gatlinburg of northern Georgia, the little mountain town has long struggled to establish an identity of its own. But it's inevitable that Helen should be compared with the much larger mountain city in Tennessee, as both feature an alpine facade. Fortunately, that's where the similarities end. Small as it is, Helen really does have something different to offer, and its visitors remain remarkably faithful, returning year after year. For the past several years commercialism has been steadily on the increase – it's said there are more hotel rooms in Helen than there are permanent residents – but the garish colored lights and high-tech attractions so characteristic of Pigeon Forge and Gatlinburg have not yet made an appearance. Helen is, for the most part, a quiet town with pleasant views of the surrounding countryside, along with gift shops, factory outlets, and some very nice country restaurants and cafés. If you're visiting northern Georgia's mountains, stop by. You'll find the side trip an enjoyable one.

■ James H. "Sloppy" Floyd State Park

This state park was named for James H. Floyd, one of Georgia's most distinguished State Representatives. Sloppy Floyd served in the Georgia House of Representatives from 1953 until his death in 1974. The park is adjacent to the Chattahoochee National Forest. Hiking and fishing are the popular activities, and you can take along your boat – if you can get by without a motor – or rent a pedal boat and spend an afternoon on the quiet water of two small managed lakes. Beyond that, there are a couple of picnic shelters and a playground.

James H. Floyd State Park, Route 1, Box 291, Summerville, GA 30747. ☎ 706-857-5211. The park hours are from 7 am to 10 pm.

The park is three miles southeast of Summerville on Marble Springs Road via Highway 27.

Northern Georgia

■ Lake Chatuge

 Lake Chatuge, half in North Carolina, half in northern Georgia, has already been covered in some detail in the previous chapter. Even so, the lake, built by the Tennessee Valley Authority to produce electricity, is worthy of a mention here. Easily accessible via a vast network of free-flowing highways, both in North Carolina and northern Georgia, it's a popular outdoor center with lots of facilities, including boat ramps, marinas and campgrounds. The lake is blessed with more than 132 miles of scenic shoreline and is set against a backdrop of forest-covered mountain peaks. In the spring, the pastel colors of wildflowers bloom on the mountain slopes.

Private boat ramps are provided at several lakeside campgrounds, and public access ramps are located principally on the North Carolina side of Highway 64 on Cabe Road, and at Jackrabbit Mountain Public Campground, just off Highway 175 on Philadelphia Road.

 Lake Chatuge can be quite busy on weekends, especially during the summer; visit on weekdays, if you can.

The lake can be reached in northern Georgia via Highways 17, 19, 75 and 129 from Atlanta, and then Highway 76.

■ Moccasin Creek State Park

 This park is affectionately known as "the place where spring spends summer." And it's true, for here on the shores of magnificent Lake Burton, among the hills and valleys of northeast Georgia, the unspoiled countryside is literally covered by a blanket of greenery and wildflowers. It's an enchanted setting, threaded throughout with tiny trout streams and backcountry trails, the perfect starting point for high country exploration or a place to simply enjoy the peace and quiet of the mountains, leave your worries behind, and relax.

Boating and fishing are the popular activities here. There's a boat dock and ramp, a playground, a wheelchair-accessible fishing pier, and a fishing stream set aside for senior citizens and children. You can hike the **Moccasin Trail** and the nearby **Appalachian Trail** or you can visit the trout rearing station next to the park.

*Annual Park Service events include the **Georgia Mountain Trout Program and Contest** in June, and the **Lake Burton Arts & Crafts Festival** in July.*

Moccasin Creek State Park, Route 1, Box 1634, Clarksville, GA 30523. ☎ 706-947-3194. The park is open from 7 am until 10 pm.

The park is 20 miles north of Clarksville on Georgia Highway 197.

■ New Echota State Historic Site

 The Cherokee Nation once covered almost all of northern Georgia, western North Carolina, eastern Tennessee and northern Alabama. In 1821 the Cherokees made a remarkable step forward with the invention of a written form of their language. In 1825 they established their capital, New Echota, in northwestern Georgia. It soon became a thriving community and government headquarters for the independent Indian nation, a city complete with a tavern and a bilingual newspaper, the *Cherokee Phoenix*, and all this by 1828. But this new-found prosperity was not to last. The Indians, who had tried to model their government and lifestyles after those of the white man, were gathered together in 1838 and herded west along the Trail of Tears to the reservations in Oklahoma.

Today, New Echota is an historic site where visitors can tour the reconstructed buildings: the Print Shop, the Supreme Courthouse, Vann's Tavern, and the original home of missionary Samuel A. Worcester.

 *The site holds several annual events, including the **Cherokee Festival**, a **New England Christmas**, **Artifacts Identification Day**, and **Gold Panning**.*

New Echota State Historic Site, 1211 Chatsworth Highway NE, Calhoun, GA 30701. ☎ 706-629-8151. The site is open year-round from Tuesday through Saturday, 9 am until 5 pm, and on Sunday from 2 until 5:30.

New Echota is one mile east of I-75, Exit 131, on Highway 225.

■ Rabun Gap

This small spot on the map is famous for the Foxfire books, a product of Rabun Gap Nacoochee School. A young English teacher, Elliott Wigginton, not long out of Cornell University, was unable to make much of an impression upon his students. Exasperated, he set aside the school textbooks and asked the children if they would like to publish a magazine. Soon the children were out interviewing parents and neighbors about local culture, history and living. The first edition of *Foxfire* magazine sold out all 600 copies. From that small beginning came the books and, eventually, national attention for Wigginton and his school. Unfortunately, there the story ends, for Rabun Gap is not Foxfire; there are no souvenirs to buy or sights to see. Rabun Gap is a sleepy community set deep in the heart of the Chattahoochee National Forest, and surrounded by lakes, mountains, creeks, state and national parks, and some fine scenery.

■ Red Top Mountain State Park

Red Top Mountain, near Cartersville, is located at the extreme southern limits of the Appalachian/Great Smoky Mountain Range, but its easy access and extensive facilities make it well worth a mention here. Named for the color of its earth, the 1,950-acre park is on a peninsula of Lake Allatoona and is an extremely popular center for outdoor activities. It's an extensive recreation area criss-crossed by numerous hiking trails that give access to some of northwest Georgia's most spectacular mountain and forest scenery. The terrain is rich in iron-ore and Red Top Mountain once was an important mining district. The fine fishing available on the great lake is, perhaps, the park's main attraction. The abundant wildlife, however, that roams freely throughout forest, and on the mountain, along with an unusual opportunity to explore the great outdoors, make the park a not-to-be-missed get-away, not only for the family, but for business groups and conventions too.

Camping also is a popular activity at Red Top Mountain. There are 172 tent and trailer sites (including 60 walk-in sites) along with all the facilities to make a week in the open air a comfortable experience: water and electric hookups, showers, flush toilets, a dumping station, and a small store where essential supplies can be purchased. There are also 18 rental cottages and a 33-room lodge for those who take home comforts a little more seriously. The lodge also has a restaurant, tennis courts, and a swimming beach on the lakefront.

For the hiker, there are more than seven miles of nature trails. Bird watching, wildlife photography, picnicking, and boating (there's a marina, two boat ramps and five docks) are also popular activities in the park. Water-skiing is popular as well and private boats are permitted on the lake with no restrictions. Fishing, though, is why most of the locals come to the park. The lake is well-stocked with largemouth and smallmouth bass, crappie, bluegill, and catfish.

The park is two miles east of I-75 via Exit 123. It is open daily from 7 am to 10 pm and the park office is open from 8 until 5. For reservations and information, contact Red Top Mountain State Park & Lodge, 653 Red Top Mountain Rd., SE, Cartersville, GA 30120. ☎ 706-975-0055.

■ Tallulah Falls & Gorge

Unfortunately, the falls that once tumbled into the Tallulah Gorge, and from which this community takes its name, are no longer there. They dried up when the Georgia Power Company dammed the river, thus creating Tallulah Lake. The great gorge, however, still remains as the center of the Tallulah Basin, which is rapidly becoming one of Georgia's great outdoor recreation areas. For years hunters have known about Tallulah, and for years they've hunted the black bear, wild hogs and white-tailed deer that make the basin their home. Today, it's not quite the secret the locals and dedicated hunters would like.

Tallulah is a land of deep ravines, sparkling creeks, waterfalls, threaded throughout with hiking and horse trails, many of which connect with the Appalachian Trail.

To visit, take Highway 23 from Atlanta, through Gainesville, and on to Tallulah Falls.

■ Traveler's Rest State Historic Site

Traveler's Rest was the center of Devereaux Jarrett's once thriving plantation. Jarrett was, at that time, the richest man in the Tugaloo Valley and, in order to accommodate the growing numbers of travelers to northwestern Georgia, he expanded the structure and opened it as an inn. It soon became a popular watering hole; the hotel register boasts many a famous name, including John C. Calhoun and Joseph E. Brown, the Civil War Governor of Georgia.

The Traveler's Rest of today is furnished much as it was back in Jarrett's day. Many of the antiques you'll see were made by local craftsmen. In 1866 the house, with its 90-foot-long porch, hand-numbered rafters, and 20-inch-wide paneling, was recognized as a national historic landmark. A very special annual event at the Traveler's Rest is the Old-Fashioned Christmas, held on the 2nd Sunday in December.

Traveler's Rest State Historic Site, Route 3, Toccoa, GA 30577. ☎ 706-886-2256. The site is open all year, Tuesday through Saturday, from 9 am until 5 pm and on Sunday from 2 until 5:30.

Traveler's Rest is six miles east of Toccoa on Highway 123.

■ Tugaloo State Park

Tugaloo is the old Indian name for the river that once flowed freely through the valley. The river is gone now, covered by the lake that came with the construction of Hartwell Dam. The 390-acre Tugaloo State Park occupies a rugged peninsula that juts out into the Hartwell Reservoir. It is surrounded by spectacular scenery and offers some of the finest year-round lake fishing in Georgia.

There are facilities for camping (see *Camping Directory*), as well as volleyball, horseshoes, tennis, and hiking. There's also a swimming beach and bathhouse, a miniature golf course, and two boat ramps.

*Entertainment is provided and includes frequent **Mountain Music** programs and an annual **Harvest Festival** held in October.*

Tugaloo State Park, Route 1, Box 1766, Lavonia, GA 30553. ☎ 706-356-4362. The park is open from 7 am until 10 pm.

It is two miles northeast of Lavonia, close to the South Carolina border. Take I-85 to Exit 58 and go north on Georgia 17; follow the park signs and turn right onto County Road 385. From there, go 1½ miles to Georgia 328 and turn left. Drive for 3.3 miles to the park.

■ Unicoi State Park

 The fairly busy Unicoi State Park is set deep in the mountains of northern Georgia only a couple of miles from the alpine village of Helen. Spectacular views, rugged terrain, fine fishing, excellent opportunities for watersports, and a year-round program of organized activities, as well as its close proximity to one of the area's biggest tourist attractions, draw visitors from all across Georgia. It's also one of the most extensively developed state parks in Georgia.

There are more than 1,000 acres of unspoiled park land and lake, a magnificent 100-room lodge, rental cottages, and a campground, all of which offer visitors a wide range of vacation accommodations. There's also a swimming beach, four lighted tennis courts, a restaurant, and a craft shop.

 The Park Service provides a full schedule of annual and monthly programs for entertainment and education, including special Friday night and Saturday programs held throughout the year.

Unicoi State Park & Lodge, PO Box 849, Helen, GA 30545. ☎ 706-878-2201. The park is open from 7 am until 10 pm and the park office from 8 until 5.

Unicoi is two miles northeast of Helen via Highway 356.

■ Victoria Bryant State Park

 This is one of northern Georgia's smaller state parks. Set in the mountains, it offers outdoor enthusiasts many excellent spots for hiking, picnicking, swimming, golf, and camping (see *Camping Directory*). There are

Northern Georgia

more than five miles of nature trails that meander through the woodlands, and a well-stocked fish pond. There's also a small golf course with a pro shop, clubhouse and driving range.

*A number of annual events are held here, including a **Jr.-Sr. Catfish Rodeo** in April or May; the **Independence Day Bluegrass Festival** held over the July 4th weekend; and **Pioneer Skills Day** the 1st weekend in November.*

Victoria Bryant State Park, Route 1, Box 1767, Royston, GA 30662. ☎ 706-245-6270 (office) or 706-245-6770 (golf course). The park is open from 7 am until 10 pm and the park office is open from 8 until 5.

Victoria Bryant is two miles north of Franklin Springs on GA 327.

■ Vogel State Park

Vogel is one of Georgia's oldest state parks. Located in the Blue Ridge Mountains in the northeast and deep within the confines of the Chattahoochee National Forest, the park is steeped in local folklore: stories of Indian battles and buried gold tickle the imagination. Vogel has 280 acres of rolling parkland, forests and spectacular views, and is arguably one of Georgia's most beautiful state parks. There are more than 17 miles of hiking trails, extensive camping facilities (see *Camping Directory*), rental cottages, a 20-acre lake, a miniature golf course, a swimming beach with a bathhouse, four picnic shelters, rental pedal boats, and a group shelter.

Obviously, there are lots of opportunities for outdoor recreation. The park is a popular place for nature study, bird watching, wildlife photography, picnicking, boating (pedal boats only), and hiking.

*The Park Service puts on an extensive program of annual events and nature-related programs, including a **Wildflower Program** in April, **Old Timer's Day** in August, and several other seasonal festivals.*

Vogel State Park, Route 1, Box 1230, Blairsville, GA 30512. ☎ 706-745-2628. Open 7 am until 10 p.m; the office is open from 8 until 5.

The park is 11 miles south of Blairsville on Highway 19/129.

Adventures

■ Boating

BLUE RIDGE LAKE

 Blue Ridge Lake has two national forest recreation areas: Blue Ridge Lake and Morganton Point. Both areas have boat ramps and well-developed campgrounds (see *Camping Directory* listings under Chattahoochee National Forest).

To reach Blue Ridge Lake Recreation Area drive east from Blue Ridge on Highway 76 to its junction with Dry Branch Road and turn right. Drive on for three miles to the entrance.

To reach Morganton Point Recreation Area, drive a little farther along 76 to its junction with GA 60 and then turn south. Continue for three more miles more, through Morganton, and look out for the white and green signs. You'll then turn right onto County Road 616 and drive for a mile to the recreation area. There is also a ramp near Lakewood, between the dam and Lakewood Junction.

CARTERS LAKE

Unlike most of the great lakes in the Smoky Mountain Region, Carters Lake was constructed by the Army Corps of Engineers rather than the TVA. It's a very pleasant stretch of water (more than 3,500 acres) and is popular with the boating fraternity and anglers, too. There are several campgrounds around the lake (see *Camping Directory*), some with boat ramps, and there are a number of challenging hiking trails. A large area near the dam has been developed as the Blue Ridge Mountain Marina Resort. It too, has boat launching facilities, and you can purchase boating and fishing supplies there. The campgrounds all offer boat ramps. This area is busy during the summer.

The lake is 12 miles south of Chatsworth off Highway 411.

LAKE CONASAUGA

A popular recreation area set high among the peaks and forests of the Blue Ridge at an elevation of more than 3,000 feet. It attracts watersports enthusiasts and anglers, too. With a well-developed campground, boat ramps, good fishing, and excellent picnic facilities, it can become very congested on summer weekends and throughout the spring and fall, when visitors arrive by the thousands to see the color.

From Chatsworth, take Highway 441 north for four miles into Eton and turn right at the light. Follow that road until it turns into an unpaved road, FSR 18, and then turn right onto FSR 68 and drive another 10 miles.

If you are coming from Ellijay, take Highway 52 west for seven miles to FSR 18, where you'll find a sign pointing the way to Lake Conasauga Recreation Area.

RABUN BEACH

A national forest recreation area in the eastern Chattahoochee on the edge of 940-acre Lake Rabun. The main feature here is spectacular mountain scenery, which provides for a very pleasant, though often crowded boating experience. If you like other outdoor activities, such as camping, you'll find plenty of opportunities here. The National Forest Campground is the best developed in the system (see *Camping Directory*).

Take Highway 441/23 south from Clayton for seven miles and turn right on an unmarked county road. Drive one-tenth of a mile and turn left onto GA 15. Drive another two miles, turn right onto County Road 10 and go five miles more.

TUGALOO STATE PARK

A busy boating site, popular for all sorts of watersports including waterskiing (private boats are allowed on the lake) and fishing. There are two boat ramps.

The park is two miles northeast of Lavonia, close to the South Carolina border. Take I-85 to Exit 58 and go north on Georgia 17; follow the park signs and go right onto County Road 385. From there, go 1½ miles to Georgia 328 and turn left. Drive on for 3.3 miles to the park entrance on the right.

UNICOI STATE PARK

Because of its location only two miles from the popular tourist town of Helen, Unicoi State Park is one of north Georgia's busier parks. Watersports enthusiasts of all types come to enjoy the lake, the spectacular views, and rugged terrain. This area is busy during spring, summer and winter.

Unicoi State Park & Lodge, PO Box 849, Helen, GA 30545. ☎ 706-878-2201. The park is open from 7 am until 10 pm.

Unicoi is two miles northeast of Helen via Georgia Highway 356.

■ Camping

If you're a camping enthusiast, northern Georgia will suit your needs extremely well. Whatever your preference, you'll find hundreds of excellent opportunities. These range from wilderness camping at any one of two dozen well-developed national forest campgrounds, to 11 state parks where the facilities rival, and often exceed, those at their larger commercial competitors, to a large number of commercial operations where the facilities range from basic to luxurious. You'll find all of the state and national forest campgrounds listed, along with some of the commercial establishments, in the *Camping Directory*.

Camping in this region has been approached by the powers that be with a great deal of enthusiasm. It's long been recognized in Atlanta that the mountains and forests are important resources. Authorities have gone out of their way to make these places attractive to camping enthusiasts. If you've never tried a state park or wilderness campground, you won't find a better place to get your feet wet, metaphorically speaking.

■ Canoeing

CONASAUGA RIVER

The Conasauga is a crystal-clear mountain river that flows north through a series of gorges, into the Alaculsy Valley, to eventually join the Jacks River. The upper section of the river flows through some wild areas and is very scenic. If you are a canoeist of some ability, you'll want to give it a try.

Most of the rapids along the way are Class I and Class II, with one section of Class III. The river is runnable for most of the winter and spring when water levels are at their peak. During summer, however, there's often not enough water to float even a rubber raft. In the depths of winter the waters are icy; a full wetsuit is essential. The river is also quite remote, and help is not likely to happen along just when you might need it. Don't venture out alone.

■ Craft Hunting & Fairs

 Northern Georgia is more country-craft oriented than any other location in the Great Smoky Mountain region. Down every road, in every small town, you'll find tiny shops, roadside stands, and many festivals and crafts shows. Half the fun of this addictive pastime is in the hunting. What follows is but a small representation of what awaits you.

BLUE RIDGE

Fannin County Fair. Held in mid-August, this fair features all the traditional country exhibits, including mountain crafts, livestock, local produce and country foods.

BLAIRSVILLE

Blairsville Sorghum Festival. This early October festival focuses on the production of molasses, but also features a number of mountain crafts exhibitors from around northern Georgia, along with square dancing, rock throwing and greasy pole climbing.

CHATSWORTH

Vann House Days. An annual event in mid-July that features demonstrations and exhibits of Indian crafts, including Indian finger weaving, carding and spinning.

CLARKSVILLE

Serendipity. This is a stained glass studio and shop where customers can choose from a variety of ready-made art glass, or order custom pieces, such as lamps and windows. Located on Highway 69, ☎ 706-947-3643.

Chattahoochee Mountain Fair. This annual event is held on the Habersham County Fairground in August. Basically a country fair, it features all sorts of agricultural exhibits, along with a large number of crafts and carnival rides.

CLAYTON

Granny's Hilltop Crafts. You'll find this neat little shop on Highway 441 three miles south of Clayton. It's full of hand-crafted goodies from toys to textiles to food, including jams and jellies.

ELLIJAY

Possum Holler Country Store. Located east of Ellijay on GA 52, this country store is packed with interesting goodies, especially local crafts and antiques.

Apple Festival. Ellijay is the Apple Capital of Georgia. Held the second week of October, the Apple Festival is the highlight of Ellijay's year. The fair, one of the largest in northern Georgia, features more than 100 crafts exhibitors from as far away as Tennessee and even Kentucky.

HELEN

Tekawitha. A neat shop on South Main Street in Helen, it's a member of the Indian Arts and Crafts Association and, as such, is packed with all sorts of interesting, Native American, hand-crafted bits and pieces: wall hangings, carved goods, jewelry, etc.

Helen Arts Council Craft Show. Held annually the last weekend in October at the Helen Pavilion, this show features the work of local and regional crafts people. Demonstrations, exhibits and sales.

HIAWASSEE

Georgia Mountain Fair. One of the largest annual fairs in northern Georgia, this 12-day event starts the first Wednesday in August and brings some 200,000 visitors to Hiawassee. More than 75 crafts people display and sell their goods, which include everything from hand-made pottery to country furniture. In addition, live Bluegrass music, country dancing, demonstrations of soap-making, blacksmithing, rope making, quilting, and board splitting make it interesting for everyone. Held at the Hiawassee fairgrounds.

Northern Georgia

RABUN GAP

Hambridge Center. A community for the arts, the Hambridge Center is an estate of more than 600 acres where qualified artists, composers and writers can go for peace and quiet. Visitors are welcome. Batty's Creek Road in Rabun Gap, three miles west of Highway 23/441. ☎ 706-746-5718.

Rabun Gap Crafts. An interesting little craft shop operated by the Rabun Gap-Nacoochee School, featuring wood carvings, pottery and hand-made dolls and toys. Open Monday through Saturday, March through December. Highway 23/441.

SAUTEE

The Country Store. This is not a craft shop, but is well worth a visit. The restored drug store features an ice cream parlor and original soda fountain. Skylake Road off GA 255.

UNICOI STATE PARK

Fireside Arts & Crafts Festival. Held in mid-February, this festival features local crafts people and their goods. Demonstrations, workshops and sales. For more information contact the park. ☎ 706-878-2201.

■ Fishing

BLUE RIDGE LAKE

 One of the Tennessee Valley Authority's finest and best managed lakes, Blue Ridge, just west of the town of the same name, is set in the heart of the Chattahoochee National Forest. Not a busy lake, but a mecca for sport fishermen nonetheless. Blue Ridge is the only lake in Georgia where anglers can hunt the mighty muskellunge, ("muskie" for short), a fierce member of the pike family that can grow up to four feet in length. For those who have the patience to hunt it, the rewards can be great; some of the largest muskie on record have been caught in the area. As for the rest of them, smallmouth bass, bluegill, crappie, walleye and catfish are all present in goodly quantities. The fishing is good to excellent. Morganton Point Recreation Area, also on the lake, offers a boat ramp, too.

See above under *Adventures, Boating* for directions.

CARTERS LAKE

The fishing here is good, but you'd best go in the early morning on weekdays; it gets crowded with recreational craft during the summer, especially on weekends. Lots of small fish, some bass and catfish. The lake is on Highway 411, 12 miles south of Chatsworth.

JAMES H. FLOYD STATE PARK

Floyd has 250 acres of parkland on the edge of the Chattahoochee National Forest, plus two small lakes totalling 51 acres and two boat ramps. The lakes are kept well stocked with bass, crappie, bluegill, bream and channel catfish. You can use your own boat, but will only be allowed the use of an electric motor. The fishing is fair.

The park, open from 7 am to 10 pm, is three miles southeast of Summerville on Marble Springs Road via Highway 27. ☎ 706-857-5211.

LAKE HARTWELL

See *Tugaloo State Park*, below.

LAKE CONASAUGA

Georgia's highest lake, set among the peaks and forests of the Blue Ridge, is one of the most beautiful fishing spots in the area. It's also one of the most popular, and not only for anglers. With a well-developed campground, boat ramps, good fishing, and excellent picnic facilities, it's no wonder that people from miles around flock to the lake. It is very congested on summer weekends, and throughout the spring and fall.

It's a heavily fished lake, but it is kept well stocked and you should be able to enjoy some fine sport. There are stories of some very large bass that lurk in the deepest areas. Walleye, crappie, bream, catfish and rainbow trout are also present in goodly numbers. The fishing is good.

For information, contact the National Forest Service, Cohutta Ranger District, 401 Old Ellijay Road, Chattsworth, GA 30705, ☎ 706-695-6736.

From Chatsworth, take Highway 441 and drive north for four miles into Eton. Make a right at the light. Follow that road until it turns into an unpaved road, FSR 18, and then turn right onto FSR 68. Drive on for 10 miles to the lake.

If you are coming from Ellijay, take Highway 52 west for seven miles to FSR 18, where you'll find a sign pointing the way to Lake Conasauga Recreation Area.

CONASAUGA RIVER

A very picturesque wilderness river, inaccessible over much of its length, with good bank fishing if you can get to the water. If you like solitude along with your sport, Conasauga is the place.

Follow directions given above for Lake Conasauga.

RABUN BEACH

Good fishing on a 940-acre lake in the heart of the national forest is only one of the many outdoor activities available here. Lake Rabun's spectacular mountain scenery, well-developed campground (see *Camping Directory*), numerous hiking trails, boating and watersports opportunities, and picnic sites make it a very popular destination. Unfortunately, it's too small for one to ever get very far away from the crowds. Anglers will only find peace and quiet in the early mornings and, perhaps, on weekdays. Fishing is good, with bass, crappie, beam and catfish all present in fair numbers.

Take Highway 441/23 south from Clayton and drive seven miles. Turn right onto an unmarked county road, drive on for one-tenth of a mile and turn left onto GA 15. Drive two miles, turn right onto County Road 10 and go five miles more.

TUGALOO STATE PARK & HARTWELL RESERVOIR

Hartwell Reservoir, next to this park, was formed when Hartwell Dam was built. Surrounded by spectacular scenery, it offers fine year-round lake fishing. It's kept well stocked with bass, and there's plenty of crappie and catfish. There are two public boat ramps and a dock. The lake gets very busy at times, but the fishing is excellent.

The park, two miles northeast of Lavonia, close to the South Carolina border, is open from 7 am until 10 pm.

Take I-85 to Exit 58 and go north on Georgia 17; follow the park signs and turn right onto County Road 385. Go 1½ miles to Georgia 328 and turn left. Drive on for 3.3 miles to the park entrance on the right. ☎ 706-356-4362.

UNICOI STATE PARK

Because Unicoi is only a couple of miles from Helen it can get very busy. Other than anglers, watersports enthusiasts of all types come to enjoy the spectacular views and rugged terrain. The lake is well known for its bass, crappie, bluegill, and catfish.

The park, open from 7 am until 10 pm, is two miles northeast of Helen via Georgia Highway 356.

■ Hiking

There are many hundreds of hiking trails in northern Georgia, some very famous, others barely known even to locals. To include them all would require a book of monumental proportions. What follows, then, is a sampling of the more exciting or interesting trails. Some are for experienced hikers in the best of physical condition; others are for the casual walker who might enjoy an afternoon stroll among wildflowers. Whatever your preference, you're sure to find something here.

AMICALOLA FALLS STATE PARK

In the Cherokee Indian language, Amicalola means "tumbling waters." For more than 700 feet, in seven cascades, the waters crash down the mountain in a spectacular display.

It's no wonder that the Park Service is proud of their charge, and they've made it as accessible as possible by providing three excellent hiking trails, one of which intersects with the southern end of the 2,150-mile Appalachian Trail.

APPALACHIAN TRAIL APPROACH: This is an eight-mile trail that meanders through the 1,020-acre park from the visitor center, northward to a scenic overlook of the falls, and then on to Springer Mountain and its intersection with the southern end of the AT.

AMICALOLA FALLS TRAIL: This quarter-mile walk is exceptionally scenic. It leads from a parking area beside the creek, near the reflection pool at the end of the park road, to a steep and rocky path that climbs uphill alongside the cascading waterfalls to end at an observation deck. It's magnificent and a must for photographers.

WEST RIDGE LOOP: From the parking area near the visitor center, you walk the scenic trail beside the creek to its intersection with the loop, a distance of about 350 yards. From there you can turn either left or right and walk the mile-long trail through lovely parkland. This pleasant walking trail is suitable for everyone.

Amicalola State Park, 15 miles northwest of Dawsonville, is open from 7 am to 10 pm.

Take Highway 53 west out of Dawsonville, and then Highway 183 to Highway 52 east.

CARTERS LAKE

HIDDEN POND TRAIL: A half-mile trail that crosses the creek by way of a 20-foot bridge and a large beaver pond via a structure that's more than 200 feet long. There's an observation platform at the end of the trail suitable for bird and beaver watching. The trailhead is near the entrance to the Carters Lake Management Area on Highway 136, off Highway 441.

CLOUDLAND CANYON STATE PARK

Backpacking is the way to go in Cloudland's backcountry. More than five miles of trails, each one intersecting another, travel through some beautiful wilderness territory. Lots to see and enjoy: views, wildflowers and birds. Camping is allowed on the trail, but you'll need a permit from the park office.

WEST RIM LOOP TRAIL: For almost five miles this trail winds its way along the canyon rim and back again. In the spring the way is lined with rhododendrons and azaleas. In the winter the views overlooking three gorges are breathtaking. When the early morning mist lies low in the rift, and the tips of the mountains show above it like rocky islands in sea of white cotton wool, it bestows an aura you will long remember. The going is fairly easy for most of the way.

WATERFALL TRAIL: Just a third of a mile, this pleasant walk takes you to two waterfalls. It's a little strenuous at times.

COHUTTA WILDERNESS

There are more than 95 miles of hiking trails within the Cohutta Wilderness. All are well maintained, well blazed and easy to follow. In some areas, however, bad weather can make hiking very difficult, if not impossible. Heavy rains can cause water levels to rise quickly and turn the Jacks and Conasauga rivers into raging torrents, which are often impossible to cross. If you are planning to walk in the rain, be sure to file a route plan with someone you know. Take along plenty of fresh water and something to eat. You never can tell when your half-day hike will turn into an overnight ordeal. Camping is permitted throughout the wilderness, except on the trails themselves and at the trailheads. Here's a sample of what's available. For more information, contact the Cohutta Ranger District Office (see *Information Directory*).

CONASAUGA RIVER TRAIL: From a trailhead at Betty Gap to a parking area on FSR 17, the trail winds its way through the Cohutta Wilderness, following the Conasauga for a little more than 13 miles. This is a great hike, very picturesque, often wet and wild, but also quite popular. There's a large tent campground along the way at Bray Field, just beyond the trail's junction with the Panther Creek Trail.

From Ellijay, go west on GA 52 for two-thirds of a mile to FSR 90 and north to FSR 68. Turn north and go to the intersection with FSR 64 at Potato Patch Mountain, turn right and drive to the trailhead at Betty Gap.

CHESTNUT LEAD TRAIL: From a trailhead on Forest Road 68, Chestnut winds north through the forest for almost two miles to intersect the Conasauga River Trail, at which point you have several options. You can return the way you came; turn right and hike to the Conasauga Trailhead on FSR 64 and then turn west and return to Forest Road 68; or you can turn left and hike on along the Conasauga to its end at FSR 17.

From Ellijay go west on GA 52 for two-thirds of a mile to FSR 90 and north to FSR 68. Turn north and go to the intersection with FSR 64 at Potato Patch Mountain, bear left on 68 and drive 1½ miles to the trailhead on the right.

PANTHER CREEK TRAIL: Panther Creek can be accessed only by hiking into the wilderness on one of the other trails. The shortest route is from the Crandall Access on FSR 17. From there, you'll follow the Conasauga River Trail to its intersection with the Panther Creek Trail, just south of Bray Field. The trail then heads east to a junction with the East Cowpen Trail. It's a popular hike that takes in a high waterfall along the way. Be sure to take your camera.

From Ellijay go west on GA 52 for two-thirds of a mile to FSR 90 and north to FSR 68. Turn north and go to the intersection with FSR 64 at Potato Patch Mountain, bear left on 68 and drive to FSR 17. Turn right. The parking area is 2½ miles farther.

EAST COWPEN: From a trailhead in a parking area at Three Forks, Cowpen meanders northward to another trailhead on FSR 51. The route follows Old GA 2, now closed, up hill and down, with several interesting stops along the way. It's a great hike and highly recommended.

From Ellijay, go west on GA 52 for two-thirds of a mile to FSR 90 and north to FSR 68. Turn north and go to the intersection with FSR 64 at Potato Patch Mountain, turn right onto 64 and drive on for about four miles to the trailhead on the left.

JACKS RIVER TRAIL: Experienced and dedicated hikers should put this trail on their "must do" list. It's a hike to remember and talk about. For more than 16 miles the Jacks Trail follows the river, crossing and recrossing it some 40 times, through the Cohutta Wilderness, past Jacks River Falls, through Horseshoe Bend to its end on FSR 221 near Conasauga. Often wet, always picturesque and sometimes difficult, this is one of the most popular trails in the wilderness. Be sure to wear appropriate hiking shoes, and take along your camera.

From Chatsworth, take Highway 441 and drive north for about four miles to Eton. From there, continue north on 441 to Cisco. Turn right at Greg's General Store and go east until you hit FSR 16. Turn left and follow 16 to the Tennessee state line. You'll find the trailhead just over the line on your right.

From Blue Ridge at the intersection of Highway 76, take note of your mileage and drive north on GA 5 for 3.2 miles to the intersection with Old FSR 2. Turn left onto Old GA 2 and drive on until your odometer reads 13.3 and the pavement ends. You should see a Cohutta Wildlife Management Area sign for Watson's Gap. Turn right onto FSR 22 and drive on to the trailhead at Dally Gap.

FORT MOUNTAIN STATE PARK

There are four hiking trails within the boundaries of Fort Mountain State Park. You can obtain detailed maps with directions at the park office.

The park is seven miles from Chatsworth on GA 52.

OLD FORT TRAIL: This is both the best-known and the most popular of the four park trails. From the entrance, take the park road all the way to the picnic area at the north end of the park; the trailhead is just to the right.

The trail leads upward via a series of wooden steps and earthen plateaus to the top of the mountain and the old wall from which the park takes its name. Of the wall itself, there's not too much to see. The view from the top, however, west of the tower, is outstanding and well worth the long and strenuous climb. If you're taking children to the top, be sure to keep an eye on them once you arrive. There are a number rocky outcrops that are very tempting to small and inquisitive minds.

BIG ROCK NATURE TRAIL: This is a small but attractive trail just west of the park lake. For about three-fourths of a mile it loops through the rugged terrain and wildlife habitats on the slopes of the mountain. Be sure to take along your camera, for the trail leads past an overlook affording a magnificent view of Gold Mine Creek, which cascades down the mountain more than 400 feet.

LAKE LOOP TRAIL: A really nice, fairly easy walk of a little more than a mile suitable for almost everyone. It leads around the shores of the 17-acre Fort Mountain Lake.

GAHUTI TRAIL: A long, looping trail of more than eight miles that takes you around the outer perimeter of the park to a number of scenic overlooks of the surrounding countryside and the Cohutta Wilderness. There are a few primitive and limited-use campsites along the way. The trail is an excellent backpacking experience that never takes you too far away from Park Service personnel and help if you need it. The trailhead leads from a parking area at the north end of the park.

Northern Georgia

Shopping

Northern Georgia is not, by any stretch of the imagination, a center for outstanding shopping. Helen does offer some unique opportunities, but for fine goods, top-notch stores, and variety, the locals all go to one of two places: Atlanta or Chattanooga, the former being the most popular. Here and there across the region you'll find some out-of-the-way antique stores, and there are always the crafts and gift shops around almost every corner.

Camping Directory

There are, essentially, three types of campgrounds in the Great Smoky Mountains: commercial, state park and national forest. You will find them listed in this directory alphabetically by region.

The three types of campgrounds vary significantly. Commercial grounds offer much more in the way of recreational activities and amenities but are short on open space, while state and national grounds, some of which cover thousands of acres, go much further toward making camping a real outdoor experience. Most national grounds are short on the basic comforts, such as electricity and running water; state parks usually offer more.

As this book focuses on adventuring, you'll find the outdoor-experience type of campgrounds are covered in a bit more detail than the commercial grounds that offer all the comforts of home.

All contact numbers are given in the *Information Directory* at the back of this book.

■ Wilderness Camping

SOUTHEASTERN TENNESSEE

Cherokee National Forest

Most of the campsites in the Cherokee National Forest can accommodate tents or trailers; none have hookups for electrical or septic services. For more information and detailed maps showing exact locations and directions, contact the appropriate Ranger District Office listed in the *Information Directory* under Cherokee National Forest. Fees shown are per campsite, per night.

Hiwassee Ranger District

Quinn Springs: not gated; piped water; flush toilets; showers; drinking water; picnic tables and grills; open from April 1 through November 1; $8; family sites with electricity, $10; double sites, $20.

Lost Creek: gated; hand-pumped water; vault toilets; picnic tables and grills; fishing; open April 1 through November 1; $5.

Ocoee Ranger District

Chilhowee: not gated; piped water; flush toilets; cold water showers; watchable wildlife; picnic table and grills; swimming beach; fishing; open from April 1 through November 1; $10.

Parksville Lake: not gated; piped water; hot showers; flush toilets; picnic tables and grills; open from March 18 through November 16; $10; family sites with electricity $10; double sites $20; tent $8.

Thunder Rock: not gated; hand-pumped water; vault toilets; picnic table and some grills; open all year; $8.

Sylco: not gated; vault toilets; drinking water; open all year; no charge.

Tumbling Creek: isolated; not gated; hand-pumped water; vault toilets; picnic tables and grills; recommended for tents only; open all year; no charge.

Tellico Ranger District

Indian Boundary (three locations): gated; piped water; flush toilets; hot showers on loop A; group camping available; $10; fees for group camping rise in increments of $5 for each additional five persons; open March 31 through October 2.

Spivey Cove: gated; hand-pumped water; flush toilets; open March 31 through the last big game hunt of the year; $8.

Holly Flats: gated; hand-pumped water; flush toilets; open all year; $8.

Gig Oak Cove: gated; hand-pumped water; flush toilets; open March 31 through the last big game hunt of the year; $8.

State Line: not gated; hand-pumped water; flush toilets; open all year; $8.

Davis Branch: not gated; hand-pumped water; flush toilets; open all year; $8.

McNabb: gated; group camping; open all year; $25.

UPPER EAST TENNESSEE

Cherokee National Forest

Nolichucky Ranger District

Horse Creek: gated; piped water; flush toilets; swimming; open April 21 through October 16; $7.

Old Forge: gated; hand-pumped water; fishing; open April 7 through October 16; $7.

Round Mountain: gated; hand-pumped water; open April 14 through October 16; $7.

Paint Creek: gated; hand-pumped water; fishing; open April 7 through November 16; $6 & $10.

Houston Valley: gated; piped water; flush toilets; open April 14 through November 16; $7.

Unaka Ranger District

Rock Creek: gated; piped water; hot showers; flush toilets; group camping available; open May 5 through October 2; $5 & $10; fees for group camping rise in increments of $5 for each additional five persons.

Limestone Cove: gated; piped water; flush toilets; open May 5 through October 2; call for rates.

Dennis Cove: gated; piped water; flush toilets; open May 5 through last big game hunt of the season; call for rates.

Watauga Ranger District

Carden's Bluff: gated; piped water; flush toilets; open April 21 through October 10; $10.

Backbone Rock: gated; piped water; flush toilets; open April 21 through October 10; $8 & $16 (double sites).

Camping Directory

Jacob's Creek: gated; piped water; flush toilets; hot showers; open April 21 through October 10; $10.

Low Gap: gated; limited facilities; open all year; no fee.

Little Oak: gated; piped water; flush toilets; hot showers; open April 21 through December 4; $10.

Great Smoky Mountains National Park

Reservations: Highly recommended where applicable. Most of the more popular campgrounds are booked up for months in advance. Write Ticketmaster, PO Box 2715, San Francisco, CA 94126. For maps showing exact locations, and backcountry camping permits, you'll need to contact the park direct, either in writing or by telephone (see *Information Directory*).

Abrams Creek: North Carolina side; primitive; 16 sites in an area of exceptional beauty. No reservations; first-come, first-served.

Baslam Mountain: Tennessee side; developed; 161 sites in an area where there's lots to see and do. Bicycling; hiking; photography. Extremely popular, so make a reservation.

Big Creek: North Carolina side; primitive; nine sites located on the eastern edge of the park in an area of exceptional natural beauty. No reservations; first-come, first-served.

Cades Cove: Tennessee side; developed; 161 sites in an area where there's lots to see and do. Bicycling; hiking; photography. Extremely popular, so make a reservation.

Cataloochee: North Carolina side; primitive; 27 sites on the eastern edge of the park; away from the crowds and fairly quiet; historic area, quite beautiful and excellent for photography. No reservations; first-come, first-served.

Cosby: Tennessee side; developed; 175 sites in an area where there's lots to see and do, including Ramsey Cascade, the highest waterfall in the park. Bicycling; hiking; photography. Quiet, but popular. No reservations; first-come, first-served.

Deep Creek: North Carolina side; developed; 119 sites close to Bryson City, Indian Creek Falls, Toms Branch Falls and Juneywhank Falls. Bicycling; hiking; photography. Fairly quiet. No reservations; first-come, first-served.

Elkmont: Tennessee side; developed; 320 sites in an area of exceptional natural beauty, and where there's lots to see and do. Bicycling; hiking; photography. This campground is the closest one to Gatlinburg and is extremely popular. Be sure to make a reservation.

Look Rock: Tennessee side; developed; 92 sites in an area of great natural beauty on the extreme western side of the park. Quiet. Bicycling; hiking; photography. Rarely full, so you should have no trouble finding a site. No reservations; first-come, first-served.

Smokemont: North Carolina side; developed; 140 sites close to Mingus Mill and the Oconoluftee Pioneer Farmstead. Bicycling; hiking; photography. Fairly popular, so it's best to make a reservation.

NORTHWESTERN NORTH CAROLINA

Blue Ridge Parkway

None of the campgrounds on the parkway accepts reservations. They operate strictly on a first-come, first-served basis. There are a number of commercial campgrounds just off the parkway at many of the exits, and certainly at most of the small communities along the way. You'll find many of them listed by their individual community elsewhere in this directory. The five listed here are operated by the Superintendent of the Blue Ridge Parkway.

For more information, detailed maps, and brochures you can write or telephone the Blue Ridge Parkway Superintendent (see *Information Directory*).

The fee for overnight camping is $8 per site, which includes the use of the fireplace and table. Your stay at any one site will be limited to 14 days. Some of the campgrounds have dumping stations, some don't, so make sure you off-load beforehand. Camping regulations are posted at the campsites, but you can obtain a copy of them at any of the visitor centers.

Daughton Park: This is a small campground in a very large park with room for about 100 tents and 25 RVs. It's at Mile Marker 239 and is open May through October.

Julian Price Memorial Park: This campground is at Mile Marker 297, close to Blowing Rock and Moses H. Cone Memorial

Park. A very popular spot; arrive early to secure a site. There's room for 129 tents and 68 RVs.

Linville Falls: A smaller campground near Mile Marker 316. Takes 50 tents and 20 RVs. Very popular. Try to arrive in the morning to ensure that you get a site.

Crabtree Meadows: This is one of the smaller and less busy parkway campgrounds. There's room for 71 tents and 22 RVs. North of Mile Marker 339.

Mount Pisgah: A half-mile north of Mile Marker 408. Open May through October. 70 tents and 70 RVs. A very popular spot, so be sure to arrive early in the day.

Pisgah National Forest

Wilderness camping in the Pisgah is a primitive pastime. Ten campgrounds; none have service hookups and only two have showers. But that's what camping in the boonies is all about, isn't it? The outdoor experience is the essential ingredient. Backcountry campers will put up with a lot of hardship for their sport and bragging rights. They'll certainly find it in the Pisgah.

Black Mountain: Located at the foot of Mount Mitchell. Incorporates four developed areas for family camping. Two scenic hiking trails: one of five miles will take you up Mount Mitchell to a shelter; the Black Mountain Crest Trail leads north from Mount Mitchell almost to Burnside.

A nice campground in one of the best areas. Facilities include 46 sites, drinking water, flush toilets, but no showers. Open from mid-April through October.

From Burnsville, take Highway 19E for five miles. Turn right onto Highway 80 and go 12 miles more. Turn right onto Forest Service Road 472 and drive on for three more miles.

Boone Fork: 16 campsites; one of the smallest campgrounds in the Pisgah National Forest and facilities to match its size. Drinking water and vault toilets, but no showers. Open April through October. No fee.

From Lenoir, take Highway 90 North for seven miles. Turn left onto Highway 1368 and go three miles more, then turn right onto Forest Road 2005 (it's a gravel road). Drive two miles.

Carolina Hemlocks: Not far from Black Mountain Campground, this is also an attractive facility, but not quite as large. Drinking water; 32 sites; flush toilets; no showers. Open from mid-April through October.

From Burnsville, take Highway 19E for five miles, then turn right onto NC 80 and drive another 12 miles. Turn right onto Forest Road 472 and drive nine miles to the campground.

Curtis Creek: Very primitive. If you are the dedicated woodsman or woman, this is the one for you. Tents only; no water; vault toilets; no showers; no charge. Open April through October.

From Old Fort, take Highway 70 and drive east for a little more than 1½ miles. Turn north on Forest Road 482.

Davidson River: This is the largest of the Pisgah Forest's campgrounds, and one of the most extensively developed. There are 161 sites; comfort stations; flush toilets; showers; fresh water. The rate is $11 per unit per night. Open year-round.

From Brevard, take Highway 64 and head north for 3½ miles, then turn left onto Highway 276 and continue for another 1½ miles.

Lake Powhatan: The second largest of the national forest campgrounds in the Pisgah, and just as extensively developed. There are 98 sites; comfort stations; showers; flush toilets; fresh water. Cost per unit per night is $10. Open most of April through November.

From Asheville, take NC 191 and drive south for four miles. Turn right onto Forest Road 3484 and drive another 3½ miles.

Mortimer: Very basic backcountry camping with almost no facilities. There are 23 sites and vault toilets, but no showers. It will cost you $5 per night to rough it here, and you can do it all year-round.

From Lenoir, take NC 90 and drive north to Collettsville. Continue southwest on NC 1337 to NC 1328 and turn right.

North Mills River: Also very basic; 28 sites with almost no facilities (there are flush toilets). Charge per night is only $5. The campground is open most of April through November.

From Asheville, take NC 191 south for 13½ miles. Turn right onto Forest Road 478 and drive on for five miles.

Rocky Bluff Recreation Area: Facilities include 30 sites, flush toilets and drinking water, but no showers. While the focus at Rocky Bluff is on camping, there are also a number of other outdoor activities, including an easy one-mile trail that loops through the forest giving access to a variety of vegetation. There's also a second trail, an easy three-fourths of a mile, that will take you along the banks of the creek to some of best scenery in the area. Camping at Rocky Bluff will cost $5 per night. Open from May 1st through October.

From Hot Springs, take Highway 209 south for three miles. The campground is on Spring Creek.

Sunburst: This is the smallest of the developed campgrounds in the Pisgah. There are only 14 sites, but flush toilets and drinking water are available. The rate is $4 per night per unit. Open March through October.

From Waynesville, take Highway 276 east for seven miles. Turn right onto NC 215 and drive another eight miles.

SOUTHWESTERN NORTH CAROLINA

Nantahala National Forest

Nine primitive forest campgrounds provide only the barest of facilities. Those campgrounds, however, provide access to and shelter in some of the most beautiful, rugged terrain in the Smoky Mountains.

Hanging Dog: The third largest of the forest campgrounds in the Nantahala. Facilities are limited. Flush toilets; 68 campsites; no showers. Open May through October. The rate per unit is $4 per night.

From Murphy, take NC 1326 and go northwest for five miles.

Jackrabbit Mountain: On a peninsula that projects out into Lake Chatuge, this is the largest national forest campground in the Nantahala and it is the most developed. The 103 sites have access to a comfort station with flush toilets, fresh water and showers. The rate is $8 per unit per night. Open May through October.

From Hayesville, take Highway 64 east for six miles. Turn right onto NC 175 and continue for 2½ miles, then turn right onto NC 1155.

Standing Indian Mountain: With 84 sites this is the second largest of the forest campgrounds in the Nantahala. It is fairly well developed, with access to a bathhouse with flush toilets, fresh water and showers. The rate per unit per night is $10. Open April through mid-December.

From Franklin, take Highway 64 west and drive for nine miles. Turn left on Old 64 and follow the signs.

Horse Cove: A 17-site forest campground. Flush toilets and fresh water, but no showers. $7 per night. Campground is open year-round.

From Robbinsville, take Highway 129 north for one mile, turn left onto NC 1116, drive 3½ miles to NC 1127 and turn right. From there, go 12 miles to Forest Road 416 and turn right.

Hurricane Creek: Not far from Standing Indian, Hurricane Creek means primitive in every sense of the word. Vault toilets are the only thing available. There's no charge for camping. Open year-round.

From Standing Indian, take Forest Road 67 and drive for two miles. The tent campsite is on the right.

Cheoah Point: This is another very primitive campground. Seventeen campsites; vault toilets; no showers. It will cost you $7 per night. Open from mid-April through October.

From Robbinsville, take Highway 129 and drive north for seven miles. Turn left at the sign, then drive a mile to the campground.

Cable Cove: This primitive campground has 26 sites and vault toilets; beyond that, nothing. The rate is $7 per night. Open from mid-April though October.

From Fontana Village, take NC 28 and drive east for a little more than 4½ miles. Turn left onto Forest Road 520 and drive another 1½ miles.

Tsali Wilderness

This campground is about the closest thing to a commercial campground you're likely to find in the Nantahala, and that's not saying you'll find any luxuries. The 41 sites have access to a comfort station with flush toilets, showers and fresh water. A very pleasant site. The charge is $16 per night. Open from mid-April through October.

From Bryson City, take Highway 19 and drive south for nine miles, then turn right onto NC 28 and drive on for 5½ miles. Turn right onto Forest Road 521 (a gravel road) and go another 1½ miles to the campground.

Van Hook Glade: Another very primitive forest campground with almost nothing to offer in the way of facilities. There are 20 sites, but no showers. Flush toilets and fresh water are available. The rate per night is $10. Open May through October.

From Highlands, take Highway 64 west for four miles and turn right at the sign.

NORTHERN GEORGIA

Chattahoochee National Forest

The Forest Service in the Chattahoochee has gone much further in its efforts to develop wilderness camping areas than it has within the three other national forests in this book. There are more of them, and they've been developed to a much greater degree while still maintaining reasonable fees. The facilities are more extensive and, for the most part, less primitive. One campground, Rabun Beach, even has water and electrical hookups.

Camping here is still very much a wilderness experience. Now the major part of a single forest system that includes the Oconee National Forest to the south, the Chattahoochee is administered through seven ranger districts that are responsible for 750,000 acres and more than 400 developed campsites. The following, then, is an overview of what's available for campers in the Chattahoochee. You'll find the address and telephone number for each district listed in the *Information Directory* under Chattahoochee National Forest. The telephone number for camping reservations in all north Georgia wilderness areas is ☎ 877-444-6777.

Armuchee Ranger District

Headquartered in Lafayette, this office is responsible for the far western reaches of the forest that run from Summerville in the south all the way to Ringgold, just outside of Chattanooga, in the north. There are three popular recreation areas within the district, but only two have camping facilities.

Hidden Creek: Forest camping on a small campground, the main feature of which is a small creek that's dry more often than it is wet. It's also a popular spot for hiking and picnicking. Facilities are sparse. There are 16 sites, but no flush toilets or showers. Vault toilets and fresh drinking water are available, and there are several nice, quiet hiking trails. No fee.

Take GA 156 southwest from Calhoun for 7½ miles, then turn left onto Everette Springs Road and drive on for two more miles. Make a right on Rock House Road and go for three miles to Forest Service Road 955. Turn right there and drive another mile to the entrance.

Pocket: Forest camping in a small wooded glen that surrounds a large spring and a small creek. A nice, quiet, well-developed campground with lots of possibilities for hiking and picnicking. There are 27 sites, flush toilets and fresh drinking water, but no showers.

Take GA 136 east from Lafayette and drive for 13½ miles, past Villanow. Turn right on Pocket Road and drive seven miles to the entrance.

Brasstown Ranger District

Lots to see and do here. Centered on Blairsville, this district includes some very scenic areas, including the Brasstown Wilderness Area and Brasstown Bald, Georgia's highest mountain. There are seven recreation areas within the district; two have camping facilities

Lake Winfield Scott: Mountain and lakeside camping. This is a beautiful campground 10 miles from Blairsville to the north; Helen and Cleveland are east and south. An extremely popular area for outdoor lovers, offering hiking, picnicking, swimming, boating (electric motors only) and fishing. This is one of the best developed recreation areas in the Chattahoochee system, with 36 developed campsites, a comfort station with flush toilets, hot showers and fresh water.

From Blairsville, take Highways 19 and 129 south for 10 miles. Turn west on GA 180 and drive for seven more miles.

From Cleveland, take Highways 19 and 129 north to GA 180. Turn left there and drive seven more miles.

Lake Chatuge: Lakeside camping with extensive opportunities for boating, fishing and other recreational opportunities. Facilities include 30 developed campsites, a comfort station with flush toilets, hot showers and fresh water. There are several boat ramps in the area.

From Hiwassee, take Highway 76 north for two miles, then turn left on GA 288 and drive another mile.

Chattooga Ranger District

This district is responsible for six national forest recreation areas. Only three of them have camping facilities.

Andrews Cove: A very small campground in the forest beside a beautiful, crystal-clear mountain stream. Just 10 campsites, flush toilets, fresh drinking water, hiking trails and opportunities for trout fishing. No showers.

From Cleveland, take GA 75 and drive north for 14 miles.

Chattahoochee River Recreation Area: Wilderness camping near the headwaters of the Chattahoochee River. Lots of recreational opportunities, including hiking in the Mark Trail Wilderness Area, canoeing, picnicking and fishing. The campsites have access to flush toilets, but there are no showers. Can be busy in season.

From Helen, take GA 75 north for 1½ miles and turn left on GA 356. Cross the river and turn right on the paved road next to the Chattahoochee Church. Follow that road, beyond the point where the pavement ends, for nine miles to the campground.

Lake Russell: Lakeside camping with great views over Chenocetah Mountain and a large, grassy beach. One of northern Georgia's best developed campgrounds, and one of its busiest. There are 42 campsites, a comfort station with flush toilets, hot showers and fresh drinking water. There's also a large group campsite (reservations only). Lots to see and do with access to a number of nearby hiking trails, opportunities for boating, swimming and fishing. Altogether a very pleasant campground. For group camp reservations, ☎ 706-754-6221.

Take Highway 441/GA 365 north from Cornelia to the Clarksville exit on GA 197. Turn right onto Old 197 and right again at the second stop sign onto Dick's Hill Parkway. Go four-fifths of a mile, turn left onto Forest Road 59 (Lake Russell Road) and drive two more miles to the lake.

Cohutta Ranger District

This district has responsibility for an area north of Chatsworth bordering the North Carolina and Tennessee borders. Most easily accessed via GA Highway 52, the Cohutta Wilderness is a beautiful, heavily forested area that provides a natural habitat for the black bear, as well as wild boars, deer and eagles. It's also the location of a small river, the Conasauga (see *Canoeing* in the *Adventures* section). There are just two recreation areas in the district and only one has camping facilities.

Lake Conasauga Recreation Area: Mountain and lakeside camping at an elevation of more than 3,100 feet, near the top of Grassy Mountain, on Georgia's highest lake. Set among the peaks and forests of the Blue Ridge, this is a beautiful site. It's also very popular. The campground is well developed with 35 sites, a comfort station, flush toilets and fresh drinking water, but no showers. There are three wilderness hiking trails, boat ramps, good fishing, and excellent picnic facilities. Often very busy on summer weekends, and also through the spring and fall.

From Chatsworth, take Highway 441 and drive north for four miles into Eton. Turn right at the light. Follow that road until it turns into an unpaved road, FSR 18, and then turn right onto FSR 68. Drive on for about 10 miles more.

From Ellijay, take Highway 52 west for seven miles to FSR 18, where you'll find a sign pointing the way to Lake Conasauga Recreation Area.

Toccoa Ranger District

This ranger district has nothing to do with the town of the same name. It centers upon the forest in and around the Toccoa River, with its focal point being Lake Blue Ridge.

There are seven recreation areas in this district, which covers a large mountainous region in north-central Georgia to the east of Blue Ridge and south of the Tennessee/North Carolina border. Six have camping facilities.

Lake Blue Ridge: Lakeside camping on a large, well-maintained area within the confines of the Chattahoochee National Forest.

Although there's no dumping station, the 55 sites are provided with a comfort station that has flush toilets and hot showers. Trailers and RVs are permitted, but there are no water or electrical hookups. Facilities include a boat ramp, four picnic areas and several hiking trails.

Take Highway 76 east to its junction with Dry Branch Road and turn right. Drive on for about three miles to the entrance to the Blue Ridge Recreation Area.

Morganton Point Recreation Area: Just across the lake to the east of Lake Blue Ridge Recreation Area, Morganton Point offers similar lakeside facilities. There are 37 sites with access to a comfort station flush toilets and fresh drinking water.

From Blue Ridge, take Highway 76 to its junction with GA 60 and turn south. Drive through Morganton and look out for the white and green signs that show the way to Morganton Point Recreation Area. Turn right onto County Highway 616 and drive on for about a mile.

Deep Hole: Mountain and riverside camping on the banks of the Toccoa River near the Cooper Creek Scenic Area. It's a very small campground, quite remote, and not as popular as many wilderness sites, but a very pretty spot with opportunities for hiking and good river fishing. Just eight campsites with access to flush toilets and fresh drinking water.

From Dahlonega, take GA 60 north for 27 miles. An alternate route is to take Highway 76 east from Blue Ridge to its junction with GA 60 at Morganton, and then go south for 16 miles.

Cooper Creek Scenic Area & Recreation Area: Riverside and forest camping in a remote recreation area with plenty to see and do. The campground is adjacent to the beautiful Cooper Creek Scenic Area, a 1,240-acre tract of forest with a number of hiking trails, some of which follow the creek and its tributaries. There are 17 campsites with access to flush toilets and fresh drinking water, but no hot showers. Plenty of recreational opportunities, including hiking and picnicking.

From Dahlonega, take GA 60 north for 26 miles. Turn right onto Forest Road 4 and continue for six miles. From Blue Ridge, take Highway 76 east to its junction with GA 60 at Morganton. Head south for 17 miles, turn left onto Forest Road 4 and continue for six miles.

Frank Cross: Another creekside recreation area near the Chattahoochee National Fish Hatchery on Rock Creek. It's just a small campground, but has good fishing, lovely country and sparkling waters set far away from the crowds. Just 11 campsites with access to flush toilets and fresh drinking water. Unfortunately, there are no hot showers.

From Dahlonega, take GA 60 and drive north for 27 miles. Turn left onto Forest Service Road 69 and go for five miles. From Blue Ridge, take GA 76 to its junction with GA 60 and drive south for about 15 miles to GA 69. Turn right. Drive on for five miles more.

Mulky: This is yet another small creekside campground on the banks of Cooper Creek. Only 10 campsites, but they do have access to flush toilets and fresh water; no hot showers. Opportunities for hiking and picnicking, as well as great trout fishing.

From Dahlonega, take GA 60 north for 26 miles, then turn right onto Forest Road 4 and continue for about six miles more.

From Blue Ridge, take Highway 76 east to its junction with GA 60 at Morganton. Go south for about 17 miles, turn left onto Forest Road 4 and continue for six miles.

Chestatee Ranger District

Centered on the old gold mining town of Dahlonega, this district has five recreation areas. Three have camping facilities. Gold can still be found in the area.

Dockery Lake: Wilderness camping beside a three-acre trout lake. Not much in the way of facilities, just 11 campsites, picnic sites, flush toilets and fresh water; no hot showers. There are some nearby hiking trails and the lake is open for fishing.

Take GA 60 from Dahlonega and drive north for 12 miles. Turn right onto Forest Service Road 654 and drive one mile.

Desoto Falls Recreation & Scenic Areas: Scenic mountain camping on 650 acres of rugged country ranging in elevation between 2,000 and 3,500 feet. Very beautiful with magnificent views, several waterfalls, and a number of crystal-clear streams and creeks. The campground is small, secluded, and well developed. There are 24 campsites with a comfort station, flush toilets, hot showers, and fresh water. There's also a half-dozen picnic sites, several hiking trails, and lots of good fishing.

From Dahlonega, take Highway 19 north for 18 miles, or you can take Highway 129 north from Cleveland for 15 miles.

Waters Creek: Creekside forest camping on a very small, rather primitive campground. Nice and secluded with good fishing and hiking. Just eight sites with access to flush toilets and fresh water, but no showers.

From Dahlonega, take Highway 19 and drive north for 12 miles. Turn left onto Forest Service Road 34 and drive on for another mile to the campground.

Tallulah Ranger District

This district covers a large tract of wilderness at the northeastern corner of the Chattahoochee. It's an area with extensive opportunities for outdoor recreation. The Appalachian Trail, the Chattooga River, the southern section of the Elliott Rock Wilderness Area, and beautiful mountain scenery all lie within its boundaries. Of its nine recreation areas, five have camping facilities.

Tallulah River: Forest camping in an area of old-growth timber, rugged scenery and tumbling waters with lots of hiking and fishing. The campground is small, secluded and never too busy. There are 17 campsites; no water, electric hookups or showers; flush toilets; fresh drinking water. Trout fishing is a popular activity.

Take Highway 76 west from Clayton for eight miles, then turn right onto an unpaved road and drive another four miles. Turn left on Forest Service Road 70, the campground is a mile farther on.

Tate Branch: A remote campground at the junction of the Tallulah River and Tate Branch. Exceptional fall color and mountain scenery. There are 19 campsites with access to flush toilets and fresh water. Unfortunately, there are no hot showers, but there are a number of hiking trails and the river offers outstanding fishing.

From Clayton, take Highway 76 west for eight miles. Turn right onto an unmarked county road and drive four more miles, then turn left onto Forest Service Road 70. Go four miles to the recreation area.

Rabun Beach: A well developed site. It offers lakeside camping on 940-acre Lake Rabun, with spectacular mountain scenery and plenty of opportunities for outdoor recreation, especially hiking, boating, fishing and picnicking. Facilities include 80 campsites with water and electrical hookups, a comfort station with flush toilets, fresh drinking water, hot showers, four picnic sites, several hiking trails, and a boat ramp.

> *Rabun Beach is also one of the busier camp-grounds, so be sure to book your site well in advance.*

Take Highway 441/23 south from Clayton and drive seven miles. Turn right onto an unmarked county road and drive one-tenth of a mile. Turn left onto GA 15. Drive two miles and turn right onto County Road 10; then drive five more miles.

Sandy Bottom: A small forest recreation area with a few undeveloped campsites and access to flush toilets and fresh water. There are no showers, but there are a number of picnic sites and opportunities for good fishing.

From Clayton, take Highway 76 and drive west for eight miles. Turn right onto an unmarked county road, drive four more miles, then turn left onto Forest Service Road 70 and go four miles to the recreation area.

Willis Knob: Rugged mountain country near the South Carolina state line and spectacular scenery make this spot very popular with outdoor enthusiasts, especially those who enjoy horseback riding. The campground is very small (only eight sites), but there's good fishing on the Chattooga River, lots of hiking and horse trails, and the campground itself is never very busy.

From Clayton, go east on Warwoman Road for 11.6 miles. Turn right there on Goldmine Road – it's a gravel road – and look for signs indicating Woodall Ridge Day Use Parking Area on the left.

Carters Lake Area

Carters Lake, a 3,500-acre man-made stretch of quiet water, was constructed by the Army Corps of Engineers. It's a very popular spot for boating, fishing, hiking and, with four campgrounds, camping, too. A large area near the dam has been developed as the Blue Ridge Mountain Marina Resort. It has boat launching facilities, and you can purchase boating and fishing supplies. The following is a listing of the four campgrounds. For additional information and reservations, contact the Resource Manager's Office, also listed below.

Harris Branch Park: Group camping only. There's a shelter with six tables and a large grill, 10 tent sites, fresh water and two comfort stations. There's also a public beach on the lakeshore. Gates open 9 am until 9 pm. Closed October through March.

Doll Mountain Park: Lakeside camping on 65 sites, 28 of which have water and electric hookups. There are two comfort stations with flush toilets, hot showers, and a dumping station. At the time of writing, the fee for a site with hookups was $10 per night; $8 without. Premium sites with full hookups cost $16 per night. Gates open 9 am until 10 pm. Closed October through March.

Ridgeway Park: A small, primitive campground with little in the way of facilities: 22 sites; pit toilets; two boat ramps. Accessible by dirt road only. No Charge.

Woodring Branch: A smaller campground than Doll Mountain, but better developed. All 31 campsites have water and electric hookups; there's also a comfort station with extensive facilities and a boat ramp. At the time of writing, the fee for a site with hookups was $10 per night; $8 without. Gates open 9 am until 10 pm. Closed October through March.

Information: You can contact the Resource Manager at Carters Lake, PO Box 86, Oakman, GA 30732. For reservations, ☎ 877-444-6777.

The lake is 12 miles south of Chatsworth off Highway 411.

■ State Park Camping

TENNESSEE

Tennessee has an extremely active and comprehensive state park system. They have gone to great lengths to make the campgrounds competitive with their commercial counterparts. Most campgrounds covered in this section have some, if not all, of the facilities you would expect at a commercial campground: water and electrical hookups; bathhouses; flush toilets; hot showers; dumping stations. Some even have on-site stores for basic supplies. Many of the parks listed below also have rental cabins, rustic holiday cottages, and lodges with extensive facilities.

Camping, Lodging & Rental Fees

These vary from park to park, but generally range from $10 to $20 per night for RV sites, and from $10 to $15 per night for tent sites. A non-refundable deposit of $5 may be required to reserve a campsite.

Modern and Rustic Cabins: For specific rates and reservations you'll have to call the resort directly but, to give you an idea, rates range from a low of $60 per night, plus tax, to a high of $97 per night, with a two-night minimum stay. A deposit equal to one night's rent is required upon making a reservation. Charges may made by personal check or by credit card: Visa or MasterCard.

Boat Rental: Offered at most parks where water-related activities are available. Fees range from $8 per half-day to $20 for a full day, depending upon the park. Canoe, rowboat, and paddleboat rentals range upward from $5 per hour.

Senior Citizens residing in Tennessee aged 62 and older are eligible for a 50% discount on camping facilities.

SOUTHEASTERN TENNESSEE

Harrison Bay State Park, Chattanooga: Lakeside camping just a few miles north of Chattanooga. The 1,200-acre park, along with more than 40 miles of Chickamauga Lake shoreline, provides outstanding recreational and camping opportunities.

There are 190 tent and trailer camping sites; 135 of them have water and electrical hookups, and all feature picnic tables and grills. Other facilities include several bathhouses with hot showers and restrooms. There's also a camp store selling camping and fishing supplies.

A group camp provides accommodations for up to 144 persons. It has a dining room and a kitchen, both fully equipped for food preparation and serving. Other facilities include group cabins, a bathhouse with hot showers and restroom facilities, a recreation shelter, and a large playing field. The group camp is available during the summer months and can be rented on a weekly basis only.

The park has its own boat ramps, but a full-service marina nearby in one of the best protected harbors on Chickamauga Lake provides other essential services. It has several boat launching ramps, marine supplies and fuel. Fishing supplies, bait, waterskiing equipment, and rental boats can be obtained at the marina store.

Harrison Bay also has a swimming pool with adequate space for sunbathing, a children's pool, a concession stand, a shelter, playground, as well as a number of well-shaded picnic areas with tables and grills.

The park can get extremely crowded during the summer months, the boat ramps very busy, and the swimming pool packed.

Harrison Bay State Park, 8411 Harrison Bay Road, Harrison, TN 37341. ☎ 423-344-6214. Camper quiet time is 10 pm.

From Chattanooga, take Highway 58 and drive north for eight miles, then follow the signs.

UPPER EAST TENNESSEE
Greeneville

Davy Crockett Birthplace State Park: State park camping close to the Nolichucky riverbank, on 73 modern sites, all with water and electrical hookups. There's a bathhouse, public restrooms, a dumping station, three picnic pavilions, scenic picnic sites with tables and grills, boat access to the river, a hiking trail and a swimming pool.

Open May through October from 8 am until 10 pm, and November through April from 8 am until 6 pm.

Davy Crockett Birthplace, Route 3, Box 103A, Limestone, TN 37681. ☎ 423-257-2167. The park is 3½ miles from Limestone off Highway 11E.

Kingsport

Warrior's Path State Park: Facilities include 95 modern camping sites with tables, grills, water and electric hookups, modern bathhouses, and a snack bar. A camp store provides groceries, camping, picnic, and recreational supplies.

There's a recreation center, an 18-hole golf course, a full-service marina on Lake Fort Patrick Henry, boat launching facilities, tennis courts, overnight accommodations for horses, and more than nine miles of hiking trails, bicycle trails, and bridleways.

Warrior's Path State Park, Box 5026, Kingsport, TN 37663. ☎ 423- 239-8531. Open from 8 am until 10 pm. The camper quiet time is 10 pm.

The park is on State Route 36. From I-81, take Exit 59.

Knoxville

Big Ridge State Park: Facilities here are extensive, and include a variety of overnight and long-stay accommodations. There are 19 rustic vacation cabins for rent April through October, each able to accommodate up to six persons with two double beds and a hide-a-way sofa bed, all in one large living area. All cabins have fireplaces, screened-in porches, and are equipped for light housekeeping with linen service, and cooking and dining utensils provided. And, because Big Ridge is supposed to provide a genuine opportunity for solitude, you will not find televisions or telephones in any of the cabins.

Other facilities include 56 full-service camping sites on the shores of Norris Lake, all with water and electrical hookups, picnic tables and grills. The campground is served by two nearby bathhouses with hot showers and restrooms.

There's a group campsite with a capacity for up to 120 persons in 18 bunkhouses (each sleeps six to eight persons). The group area also has two bathhouses with hot showers and restrooms, along with a large kitchen complete with utensils and all equipment necessary for preparing and serving meals.

There are a couple of tennis courts, several boat launching ramps, a snack bar, a gift shop, a visitors center, and a laundromat.

Big Ridge State Park, Maynardville, TN 37807. ☎ 865-992-5523. The park is open during the summer from 8 am until 10 pm, and from 8 am until sundown during the winter.

Big Ridge is 25 miles north of Knoxville on State Highway 61, 12 miles east of I-75.

Panther Creek State Park

Panther Creek, just six miles west of Morristown, offers more than 1,440 acres of lush parkland, unlimited opportunities for recreation, and spectacular views.

Facilities include 15 vacation cabins, all equipped for housekeeping with appliances plus cooking and serving utensils. There are

50 fully-equipped campsites with water and electrical hookups, and a camp laundromat and gift shop. Recreational facilities include a picnic area with table and grills, a public restroom, several tennis courts, hiking trails, boat launching facilities into the nearby lake, and a playground for the children.

The park is open during the summer months from 8 am until 10 pm, and from 8 am until sundown during the winter. The camper quiet time is 10 pm.

Panther Creek State Park, 2010 Panther Creek Road, Morristown, TN 37814. ☎ 423-723-5073. The park is west of Morristown and I-81, off US 11E.

Roan Mountain State Park

With one of the highest peaks in the Cherokee National Forest and one of nature's most magnificent spring shows – more than 700 acres of rhododendrons – Roan Mountain State Park is one of the most attractive state-operated campgrounds in this region of Tennessee.

Facilities include 20 vacation cabins, each with accommodations for up to six people, and all fully equipped for housekeeping with appliances, cooking and serving utensils, and linen service. For more hardy campers there are 87 modern camping sites on two grounds, each with a table, grill, and water and electric hookups. There are 20 more camping sites set aside for tent campers only. All the sites are well served by three modern bathhouses, all with hot showers and restroom facilities. There's also a dumping station for those campers with self-contained rigs.

The park is open the year-round from 8 am until 10 pm. The camper quiet time is 10 pm.

Roan Mountain State Park, Route 1, Box 236, Roan Mountain, TN 37687. ☎ 423-772-3303. The park is on the Tennessee/North Carolina border, off US 19E on State Highway 143.

NORTHERN GEORGIA

Camping is a big part of Georgia's state park economy, and it's been organized on a grand scale. Facilities include not only tent, trailer and RV sites, but walk-in, "Pioneer," and group camps. Most tent, trailer, and RV sites are served with electrical and water hookups, cooking grills, and picnic tables. All campgrounds have modern comfort stations and dump sites. Many have laundry facilities and stores selling camping supplies. Most of Georgia's campgrounds are extremely busy throughout the year and are available on a first-come, first-serve basis. However, each has a number of sites that can be reserved in advance.

Tent, RV, & Trailer Campgrounds: All campgrounds are open from 7 am to 10 pm. Registration at the park office is required no later than 8 pm and before setting up camp. Late arrivals must pay the camping fee the following morning. MasterCard and Visa are accepted. Check-out time is 1 pm. Occupancy is limited to 14 days at each campsite.

Two-day reservations are accepted for a limited number of camp-sites. A non-refundable deposit of two nights' camping fees must be paid within seven days of making the reservation. Bookings may be made in person or by telephone up to three months in advance.

Pioneer campsites have drinking water and primitive sanitary facilities. A small per-person charge for advance reservations is required. Pioneer campsites will not accommodate RVs or trailers.

Group camps and lodges for organized groups are available at several of the parks. These may include sleeping quarters, kitchens, dining rooms, assembly rooms, activity areas, and swimming facilities. Rental fees vary from park to park and reservations are required.

Rental Cottages: These are available at nearly all of Georgia's state parks. They are fully equipped with stoves, refrigerators, kitchen and dining utensils, bed linens, blankets, and towels. All cottages are heated and most are air conditioned. Many have porches or decks and wood-burning fireplaces or stoves (firewood is not provided).

Reservations are taken at the individual parks up to 11 months in advance. A one-night deposit is required within seven days of booking. Reservations are not confirmed until a deposit is received and will be canceled if one is not received. From June 1st to Labor Day, reservations for less than one week are not accepted unless they are made less than one month in advance and are for at least two days.

From Labor Day until May 31st, a minimum two-day reservation is required and one-night occupancy is allowed only with an additional surcharge. MasterCard and Visa are accepted.

Check-in time is 4 pm to 10 pm. The park must be notified if you intend to arrive late and registration is not allowed after 10 pm, except in an emergency. Reservations are not held after 11 am of the second day and deposits will be forfeited unless the park has been notified of your late arrival. Check-out time is 11 am

Deposits may be refunded if a 72-hour notice is given; a cancelation fee will be deducted from the deposit. Unused portions of a reservation period may be refunded when minimum occupancy requirements have been satisfied. A deposit receipt is required for a refund.

Maximum occupancy for the cottages varies. Occupation of a cottage is limited to 14 nights. Cottages are not available for church or civic groups, fraternities, sororities, schools groups, family reunions, youth groups, etc. A responsible adult must accompany all guests under 18 years of age.

Lodges: These are available at Amicalola Falls and Unicoi State Parks. Some offer rooms with special features such as sleeping lofts for children, suites with separate bedrooms, and private porches. Handicapped-equipped and non-smoking rooms are available at all lodges. Children under 12 years of age stay free when accompanied by an adult in the same room. Each room has a television, telephone, and individual climate control. A limited number of port-a-cribs are available. There are no rollaway beds or cots. Maximum occupancy is four in double rooms and six in loft rooms. Check-in time is 4 pm. Check-out time is 11 am.

Meeting Facilities: For group getaways, conferences and meetings, state park lodges offer modern facilities, golf courses, tennis, swimming, hiking, nature trails, plus fishing and boating. The Park Service also provides interpretive programs and special events throughout the year. The lodges are fully equipped and staffed to handle meeting and group functions for 150 to 400 persons. Complimentary audio-visual equipment is available upon request. Each lodge has a full-service restaurant, dining, and catering facilities. Diners may choose à la carte or buffet-style breakfasts, lunches and dinners. Catering is available on-site for banquets, receptions, and a variety of meetings and hospitalities. Group reservations can be made up to five years in advance and the Lodge Conference Coordinators can be called upon to assist in the planning of meetings, receptions, and banquets.

Lodge reservations are accepted up to 11 months in advance. Reservations are confirmed upon receipt of an advance deposit, which can be paid in the form of a check, cash, credit card, or a credit card guarantee. Cancellations are allowed up to 4 pm on the arrival date with no penalty. Guaranteed reservations are held unless cancelled before the cut-off time. However, reservations not canceled and non-arrivals will be charged one night's lodging plus tax. MasterCard, Visa, American Express, and Diners Club are accepted.

User Fees & Overnight Accommodations Rates

Cottages Daily. One-bedroom, Sunday through Thursday $50; Friday and Saturday, $65. Two-bedroom, Sunday through Thursday, $65; Friday and Saturday, $69. Three-bedroom, Sunday through Thursday, $69; Friday and Saturday, $79. Will-A-Way two-bedroom: handicapped persons Sunday through Thursday, $39; Friday and Saturday, $39. All others, Sunday through Friday, $59; Friday and Saturday, $69. There is a $15 surcharge for one-night visits, and a $10 handling fee per unit for cancelations. There is a $10 discount Sunday through Thursdays, December 1st through March 31st for senior citizens (65 & over).

Lodges. Amicalola Falls Lodge: Double/King room, December 1st through March 31st, $55; April 1st through November 30th, $65. Junior Suite/King Loft, December 1st through March 31st, $74; April 1st through November 30th, $79. Executive Suite, December 1st through March 31st, $90; April 1st through November 30th, $100.

Unicoi Lodge: Double Room/Loft Weekdays, December 1st through March 31st, $39; April 1st through November 30th, $59. Double Room/Loft Weekends, December 1st through March 31st, $49; April 1st through November 30th, $59.

Lodge rates are based upon single occupancy and, while they are correct at the time of this writing, they are subject to change without notice. Each additional adult is $10. Children under 12 years of age stay free when accompanied by an adult in the same room.

Campsites. Tent, trailer, RV campsites, $16; senior citizens 65 and over, $10. Walk-in campsites and Squirrel's Nest, $10. Pioneer Campsites per person, $1 (supervised groups only, $15 minimum). Primitive camping per person, $3.

Group camps: $3 per person, per day. Each camp has a minimum occupancy and a one-week minimum stay during June, July, and August. There is a $10 handling fee for cancelations and a cleanup/damage deposit is required. Camp facilities vary, but typically include dormitory sleeping quarters, restrooms/showers, kitchen, and a dining area. Call the individual park for details.

Golf. Weekdays, unlimited play, $18, senior citizens 65 and older, $13; weekends and holidays, 18 holes only, $18, senior citizens 65 and older, $13; high school and college teams (per person, per round), $5; (twilight – Tuesday through Sunday), $10. Rates for nine holes of golf per person can be obtained by calling the park. Golf carts (powered), $15 per 18 holes of golf. Golf carts (pull), $5 per 18 holes of golf. An annual greens pass valid at all parks can be purchased for $300 per individual or $500 per family. Senior citizen passes may be purchased at a cost of $300 for an individual and $400 for a husband and wife. High school and college team passes may be purchased for $500. The fee per round of miniature golf is $1.50 per person.

Rental Fishing Boats & Canoes. One hour, $3. Four to eight hours, $8 to $12.

Motorboat & one tank of gas: four hours, $20; eight hours, $30. Reservation fee (cottage users no charge), $8.

Amicalola Falls State Park

A 1,000-acre state park campground at the foot of the spectacular 729-foot waterfall from which the park takes its name. Lots to see and do for the outdoor adventurer, including a year-round program of special events and activities. There are hiking and backpacking trails, opportunities for fishing, nature study, bird watching, wildlife photography, and picnicking.

Camping facilities are limited to 17 tent and trailer sites, but there are 14 rental cottages and a 57-room lodge with a restaurant and meeting facilities. For the family camper, there are three playgrounds, five picnic shelters, and a rustic walk-in lodge.

There's also a comfort station, hot showers, flush toilets and laundry facilities.

Amicalola Falls State Park and Lodge, State Route, Box 215, Dawsonville, GA 30534. ☎ 706-265-8888. The park is 15 miles northwest of Dawsonville. Take Highway 53 west out of Dawsonville, and then Highway 183 to Highway 52 east.

Black Rock Mountain State Park

State park camping at its highest level, literally. The park is located in the eastern section of the Southern Appalachians at an elevation of more than 3,600 feet, making it the highest state park in Georgia. The views are spectacular, the terrain wild and desolate, and the facilities excellent.

Fifty-three tent and trailer sites; 11 primitive walk-in campsites; 10 rental cottages; a visitor center; two picnic shelters; and a 17-acre lake. All are set on more than 1,500 acres of mountain parkland.

Black Rock Mountain State Park, Mountain City, GA 30562. ☎ 706-746-2141. The park is open from 7 am to 10 pm and the park office from 8 am to 5 pm. The park is three miles north of Clayton, Georgia, via US 441.

Cloudland Canyon State Park

Mountain camping on the rim of the gorge. Magnificent views, wildflowers, rhododendrons and azaleas, and lots of facilities. Very busy from spring through fall (be sure to book well in advance), and very popular with day-visitors and tourists.

Facilities include 2,120 acres of rugged and scenic parkland, 75 tent and trailer sites, a 40-bed group camp, 16 rental cottages, a winterized group shelter, a swimming pool, tennis courts, and 30 walk-in campsites. There are more than six miles of backcountry trails, picnic tables and grills, and an open-air pavilion (also with tables and grills).

Cloudland Canyon State Park, Route 2, Box 150, Rising Fawn, GA 30738. ☎ 706-657-4050. The park is open from 7 am until 10 pm and the park office is open from 8 until 5.

Cloudland Canyon State Park is on Lookout Mountain about 10 miles south of Chattanooga on Georgia Route 136, eight miles east of Trenton and I-59, and 18 miles west of Lafayette.

Fort Mountain State Park

Mountaintop camping on a secluded but well-developed campground with lots of facilities, including 70 tent and trailer sites, 15 rental cottages, a comfort station with hot showers and flush toilets, more than 12 miles of mountain hiking trails, a swimming beach, and a miniature golf course.

Popular activities include hiking, boating (pedal boats for rent; no private boats), and picnicking (there are seven shelters and 117 tables).

This is a very popular campground and is almost always fully booked. Be sure to make your reservations as early as possible.

Fort Mountain State Park, Route 7, Box 7008, Chatsworth, GA 30705. ☎ 706-695-2621. The park is open from 7 am until 10 pm daily. Park office hours are 8 until 5. The park is seven miles from Chatsworth on GA 52.

Hart State Park

Lakeside camping on a 145-acre park beside vast Lake Hartwell. Extremely busy during spring and summer, but lots of facilities, including 65 campsites, a comfort station, two rental cottages, a swimming beach, and three picnic shelters. The fishing is excellent, and there are opportunities for most other watersports. A unique additional attraction is the Cricket Theater, where you can enjoy live music programs.

Hart State Park, 1515 Hart Park Road, Hartwell, GA 30643. Call ☎ 706-376-8756. Park hours are from 7 am to 10 pm and the office is open from 8 until 5. Hart is east from Hartwell on US 29; turn left on Ridge Road and go two miles.

James H. "Sloppy" Floyd State Park

More than 250 acres of parkland on the edge of the Chattahoochee National Forest. Facilities include 25 tent and trailer sites with water and electrical hookups, a pioneer campsite with fresh water and pit toilets, two lakes totaling about 51 acres, a playground, two boat ramps, pedal boat rentals and two picnic shelters.

James H. Floyd State Park, Route 1, Box 291, Summerville, GA 30747. ☎ 706-857-5211. The park hours are from 7 am to 10 pm and the park office is open from 8 until 5. The park is three miles southeast of Summerville on Marble Springs Road via US 27.

Moccasin Creek State Park

Mountain camping on 32 acres of quiet, secluded parkland, surrounded by the peaks, valleys and mountain creeks of the southern Blue Ridge.

Facilities include 53 tent and trailer sites with water and electric hookups, a boat dock and ramp, a playground, a wheelchair-accessible fishing pier, and an open-air pavilion.

Moccasin Creek State Park, Route 1, Box 1634, Clarksville, GA 30523. ☎ 706-947-3194. The park is open from 7 am until 10 pm, and the park office hours are from 8 until 5. Moccasin is 20 miles north of Clarksville on Georgia Highway 197.

Red Top Mountain State Park

Red Top Mountain State Park boasts an extensive campground with all the modern conveniences. Set on almost 2,000 acres of forest and mountain parkland, its facilities include 172 tent and trailer sites, including 60 walk-in sites. All of the RV/trailer sites have water and electric hookups. There are showers, flush toilets, picnic tables and grills. There's also a large outdoor swimming pool, a dumping station, and a small store where essential supplies can be purchased. There are also 18 rental cottages and a 33-room lodge for those who take their home comforts a little more seriously. The lodge also has a restaurant that's open to visitors and campers, lighted tennis courts, and a swimming beach on the lakefront. Other facilities include a marina, two boat ramps and five docks, more than seven miles of nature trails. Popular activities include hiking, bird watching, wildlife photography, picnicking, fishing, boating, and waterskiing. Private boats are permitted on the lake with no restrictions. The lake is well-stocked with largemouth and smallmouth bass, crappie, bluegill, and catfish.

The park is two miles east of I-75 via Exit 123. It is open daily from 7 am to 10 pm and the park office is open from 8 am until 5 pm. For reservations and information contact Red Top Mountain State Park & Lodge, 653 Red Top Mountain Rd., SE, Cartersville, GA 30120. ☎ 706-975-0055.

Tugaloo State Park

A busy lakeside campground with 120 tent and trailer sites, all with water and electric hookups, and comfort stations with flush toilets and hot showers. There are 20 rental cottages, tennis courts, nature trails, a swimming beach and bathhouse, miniature golf, and two boat ramps. Activities include volleyball, horseshoes, and all sorts of watersports, such as waterskiing and fishing (private boats are allowed on the lake).

The park is open from 7 am until 10 pm, and the park office hours are from 8 until 5. Tugaloo is just a couple of miles northeast of Lavonia, close to the South Carolina border. Take I-85 to Exit 58 and go north on Georgia 17; follow the park signs and go right onto County Road 385. From there, go 1½ miles to Georgia 328 and turn left. Drive on for 3.3 miles to the park entrance on the right.

Unicoi State Park

Mountain and lakeside camping on more than 1,000 acres of unspoiled parkland with spectacular views, rugged terrain, and fine fishing, all only two miles from Helen. There are opportunities for all watersports, and a year-round program of activities.

Facilities include 84 tent and trailer sites with water and electric hookups; a comfort station with fresh water, flush toilets and hot showers; and 30 rental cottages. For corporate campers, if ever there was such an animal, there's a 100-room lodge and conference center with a buffet-style restaurant, a swimming beach, four lighted tennis courts, and a craft shop.

Unicoi State Park and Lodge, PO Box 849, Helen, GA 30545. Call ☎ 706-878-2201 (office & group reservations) or 706-878-2824 (individual reservations). The park is open from 7 am until 10 pm and the park office is open from 8 until 5. This is one of Georgia's busiest locations, so be sure to book early.

Unicoi is two miles northeast of Helen via Highway 356.

Victoria Bryant State Park

Mountain camping on a small campground in the heart of northern Georgia's backcountry. Facilities include 25 tent and trailer sites with water and electric hookups, flush toilets, hot showers and fresh drinking water. There's also a dumping station, five miles of hiking trails, three playgrounds, a nine-hole golf course, a swimming pool, five picnic shelters, two pioneer campsites, and a fishing pond. The golf course has a clubhouse, pro shop and driving range.

Victoria Bryant State Park, Route 1, Box 1767, Royston, GA 30662. ☎ 706-245-6270 (office) or 706-245-6770 (golf course). The park is open from 7 am until 10 pm and the park office is open from 8 until 5. Victoria Bryant is two miles north of Franklin Springs on Georgia Highway 327.

Vogel State Park

Mountain and forest camping in one of Georgia's oldest state parks. Located in the Blue Ridge Mountains in the northeast, deep inside the Chattahoochee National Forest, the park offers 280 acres of parkland, along with spectacular views and rugged countryside. Facilities include 110 tent and trailer sites, all with water and electric hookups, along with a pioneer campsite, comfort stations with fresh drinking water, flush toilets and hot showers, 36 rental cottages, a 20-acre lake, 17 miles of hiking trails, a miniature golf course, a swimming beach with a bathhouse, four picnic shelters, a group shelter, and rental pedal boats.

Along with all the above, the park provides plenty of opportunities for outdoor recreation, including nature study, bird watching, wildlife photography, picnicking, and boating (pedal boats only).

Vogel State Park, Route 1, Box 1230, Blairsville, GA 30512. Call ☎ 706-745-2628. Park hours are from 7 am until 10 pm and the park office is open from 8 until 5. Vogel is 11 miles south of Blairsville on US 19/129.

■ Commercial Camping

SOUTHEASTERN TENNESSEE

Chattanooga

Chattanooga West/Lookout Mountain KOA: This is of those campgrounds at the tail end of the Smokies, but close enough to civilization to make life comfortable. The site is blessed with an exceptional view of the mountains, as well as an excellent range of facilities and recreational opportunities. There are 150 sites and six one-room Kamping Kabins. Of the regular campsites, 45 have full hookups; 75 have water and electric; 30 have no hookups; 100

are pull-throughs. The bathhouse has flush toilets and hot showers, there's a laundromat, sewage disposal facilities and a full-service store for groceries, camping supplies, and LP gas by weight or meter. There's a recreation room, pavilion, swimming pool, playground, and all the usual court games.

Rates for campsites range from $15 to $19; the Kamping Kabins are $28 per night for two persons, extra adults are $3 per night extra. ☎ 706-657-6815.

From the junction of I-14 and I-59, go south on 59 for two miles to Exit 3 at Slygo Road. Go west on Slygo for 2½ miles and follow the signs.

KOA-Chattanooga South: A wooded campground on rolling hills with lots of facilities, both for camping and recreation. There are 152 sites and seven Kamping Kabins. Of the campsites, 60 have full hookups, 86 water and electric only, and six tent sites have no hookups; 67 of them are pull-throughs. Six of the Kabins are one-room units, the other has two rooms. Other facilities include flush toilets, hot showers, a laundromat, and sewage disposal facilities. There's also a store selling groceries, camping and RV supplies, ice and LP gas by weight or meter. Security is handled by on-site staff. There's a recreation room, a pavilion, swimming pool, a playground and all the usual court games. The staff conducts a program of group activities.

Rates for campsites range from $14.50 to $19.50 for two persons. For a one-room Kamping Kabin the rate is $30 per night for two persons, and $35 per night for the two-room unit. The KOA discount card is honored. ☎ 706-937-4166.

From the junction of I-75 and Highway 2 (Exit 141), go one-tenth of a mile west on Highway 2.

Best Holiday Trav-l-Park: Close to Chattanooga. A large campground with extensive facilities set on a level site with plenty of shade. Facilities include 171 campsites; 89 with full hookups; 64 with water and electric only; and 18 with no hookups; 130 are pull-throughs. The campground has a full-service store where you can buy groceries and camping supplies, as well as LP gas by weight or meter. There are also three bathhouses with flush toilets, hot showers, sewage disposal facilities, a recreation hall, pavilion with coin games, swimming pool, wading pool, playground, several court games, and planned group activities handled by an on-site recreation director. Rates begin at $16.50 for two persons.

From the I-75, Exit 1 in Chattanooga, turn right at the top of the ramp and then left at the second light onto Mack Smith Road. Drive a half-mile to the campground.

Shipp's Yogi Bear Jellystone Campground & RV Center: A large, well-appointed campground with shady lakeside sites close to Chattanooga with easy access to I-75. Facilities include 225 sites; 95 have full hookups, 130 have water and electric only, and 50 are pull-throughs. Cable and telephone hookups are available. There are two bathhouses with all the usual amenities, a laundromat, a 12-acre fishing lake, a large club house, and rental canoes and pedal boats. There's also a grocery store. For recreation you have all of the sights and sounds of Chattanooga close at hand, hiking trails, planned group activities, along with court games. Rates begin at around $15.

Shipp's Campground & RV Center, 6728 Ringgold Road, Chattanooga, TN 37412. ☎ 423-892-8275. From I-75 Exit 1, take Highway 41 and go a half-mile southeast.

Cleveland

Cleveland KOA: This is the campground with easiest access to the Ocoee River and the southern section of the Cherokee National Forest. Both are less than 10 miles away on Highway 64.

This wooded campground is just outside Cleveland with shaded sites and easy access to I-75. Facilities include 87 sites (14 have full hookups; 49 have water and electric only; and 15 are pull-throughs). Telephone hookups are also available. The bathhouse has all the usual facilities, including hot showers. The are several Kamping Kabins, as well as a grocery store selling LP gas by meter or weight. There's a game room, swimming pool, a playground and court games. Rates begin at $16.

KOA Chattanooga North/Cleveland, PO Box 3232, Cleveland, TN 37320. ☎ 423-472-8928. From I-75 Exit 20, go west for a half-mile, turn right and follow the signs.

UPPER EAST TENNESSEE

Gatlinburg

Crazy Horse: A picturesque campground on rolling countryside with level sites – some creekside, some shaded, some open. Extensive modern facilities include 225 sites: 93 have full hookups; 132

water and electric only; and 61 are pull-throughs. Rental cabins and trailers are also available. Three modern bathhouses provide 22 hot showers and flush toilets, and there are three laundromats. There's also a full-service store for groceries, camping supplies, and LP gas by weight or meter. Extensive recreation facilities include a heated swimming pool, a large recreation hall and playground, a 500-foot waterslide, a small theater, and a number of creekside picnic tables. Rates on request.

Crazy Horse Campground and RV Resort, 4609 E. Parkway, Gatlinburg, TN 37738. ☎ 800-528-9003. From Exit 440 of I-40, go to Highway 321 and turn right.

Twin Creek Campground: This smaller camping resort, surrounded by forest and close to the Great Smoky Mountains National Park, has extensive modern facilities both for camping and recreation. These include 75 sites – some creekside – all with full hookups, cable TV, telephone and large wooden decks. There's a big heated pool, a whirlpool, bathhouses with hot showers, and a full-service store where LP gas is available. There's a recreation hall, coin games, a playground, creek fishing, hiking and planned group activities. All the attractions of Gatlinburg and the mountains are close at hand.

Rates on request. No Tents.

Twin Creek Campground, Route 4, Box 824, Gatlinburg, TN 37738. ☎ 865-436-7081.

Townsend

Townsend is a small mountain town in the heart of the Smokies, far enough away from the big cities to be unspoiled, yet close enough to Gatlinburg and Knoxville to provide easy access to shopping and all the attractions.

Little River Village Campground: Just minutes away from Cades Cove in the Great Smoky Mountains National Park, this campground on the river offers extensive facilities for camping, recreation and the great outdoors. Of the 122 sites, 67 have full hookups; 25 water and electric only; and 22 are pull-throughs. Tents, trailers and RVs are available for rent. The bathhouses are handicapped-accessible and have hot showers and flush toilets. There's a laundromat, a full-service store, and sewage disposal. LP gas is available by weight or meter. There's a large swimming pool, a recreation room and pavilion, a big playground, and the staff offers planned group activities. Beyond all that, there's the river where you can go boating or swimming, and the Great Smoky Mountains National Park, Tuckaleechee Caverns, and Gatlinburg are close at hand.

Rates begin at around $15 per night for two persons.

Little River Village Campground, 8533 State Highway 73, Townsend, 37882. ☎ 423-448-2241. From the junction of Highways 321 and 73 in Townsend, go one mile east on 73.

Lazy Daze Campground: Just a half-mile from the Townsend entrance to the Great Smoky Mountains National Park, this campground on the banks of the Little River is also close to Gatlinburg, Pigeon Forge and Dollywood. Facilities include 75 sites (65 have full hookups) with cable TV and telephone; seven are pull-throughs. The bathhouse has hot showers and flush toilets, and there's a full-service store where you can get LP gas by weight or meter. There's a recreation room, pavilion, coin games, a swimming pool, court games, and the Little River for swimming and fishing. Rates start at around $16.50 for two persons.

Lazy Daze Campground, 8428, Highway 73, PO Box 214, Townsend, TN 37882. ☎ 865-448-6061. From the junction of Highways 321 and 73 in Townsend, go a half-mile east on 73.

Pigeon Forge

Fort Wear Campground: An open campground with level sites and extensive facilities close to the action at Pigeon Forge, Gatlinburg and the Great Smoky Mountains National Park. Facilities include 150 sites, of which 125 have full hookups and 12 are pull-throughs. Rental cabins and RVs are also available. The bathhouses have all the usual amenities. There's a laundromat, sewage disposal facilities, a grocery store, recreation room with coin games, a swimming pool, wading pool, creek fishing, the usual court games, and a playground. Local tours are offered. Rates start around $12 per night.

Fort Wear Campground, 2630 Sequoia Road, Pigeon Forge, TN 37863. ☎ 865-428-1951; 800-452-9835. From the junction of Highways 441 and 321, go almost a mile west on 321.

Pigeon Forge KOA: On the banks of the Pigeon River in Pigeon Forge, this is one of the best appointed KOAs in the franchise system. Extensive facilities include 190 sites, of which 92 have full hookups; 88 water and electric only; 100 are pull-throughs. Kamping Kabins are also available. Beyond accommodations, the list of amenities goes on and on and includes three bathhouses, laundry facilities, a Jacuzzi, playgrounds, game rooms, souvenir shop and store, cable TV, and more.

The campground is within walking distance of the shops, only five blocks from a municipal golf course, and just five miles from Gatlinburg and the Great Smoky Mountains National Park; Dollywood is just a mile down the road. Rates begin at around $25 per night for two persons.

Pigeon Forge KOA, PO Box 210, Pigeon Forge, TN 37868. ☎ 800-367-7903. From the junction of Highway 441 and Dollywood Lane in the center of town, take Dollywood Lane and go east for a quarter-mile, then turn north onto Cedar Lane.

Newport

Newport/I-40/Smoky Mountains KOA: Not far from Pigeon Forge and Gatlinburg, this campground, in the heart of the Smokies, has 73 large, shaded open sites. Thirty-three have full hookups and 45 are pull-throughs. There are a limited number of Kamping Kabins available, as well as a small grocery store, full-service bathhouses, a laundromat, and sewage disposal facilities. LP gas is available by weight or meter. For recreation, there's a fully equipped pavilion, a recreation room with coin games, a swimming pool, playground, pond fishing and court games. Rates begin at around $15 per night for two persons.

Newport/I-40 KOA, 240 KOA Lane, Newport, TN 37821. Call ☎ 423-623-9004. From I-40 Exit 432B, drive two miles east on Highway 25E, then follow the signs for another quarter of a mile.

Sevierville

Riverside Campground & Resort: As the name implies, this resort campground is situated on the banks of the French Broad River, which is a big part of its personality. Extensive facilities include 165 sites, 130 of which have full hookups and free cable TV. There are flush toilets, hot showers, sewage disposal, boat ramps to the river, and a general store where LP gas can be purchased by weight or meter.

The river offers fishing and boating and there's a swimming pool, a fully equipped pavilion, a recreation room, and a playground. There's also a municipal golf course close by, and Gatlinburg and the Great Smoky Mountains National Park are both just up the road.

Rates begin at around $12 per night for two persons.

Riverside Campground & Resort, 4280 Boyds Creek Highway, Sevierville, TN 37876. ☎ 865-453-7299. From Exit 407 on I-40, go four miles south on Highway 66, then a quarter-mile west on Boyds Creek Highway.

NORTHWESTERN NORTH CAROLINA

Asheville

Bear Creek RV Park: High on a hilltop with level ground, this campground has 90 large sites, all with full hookups (45 are pull-throughs). Other facilities include full-service bathhouses, sewage disposal, a laundromat, grocery store, and RV supplies.

There's a 5,000-square-foot clubhouse, a recreation room, swimming pool, and nearby hiking trails. You can also rent bicycles. Rates start at around $17.50.

Bear Creek RV Park & Campground, 81 S. Bear Creek Road, Asheville, NC 28806. ☎ 800-833-0798.

From the junction of I-40 at Exit 47, go west for a quarter of a mile to Bear Creek Road, then west again to the campground.

Blowing Rock

Mine Branch Family Campground: A smaller campground with cool wooded sites midway between Boone and Blowing Rock. There are 66 sites, 23 of which have full hookups (five are pull-throughs). There's a full-service bathhouse, a limited grocery store, a laundromat, a recreation room, a playground and several outdoor games courts. A number of hiking trails are nearby. You will be in the heart of the Blue Ridge.

Rates start out around $14 per night for two persons.

Mine Branch Campground, Route 1, Box 398, Blowing Rock, NC 28605. ☎ 704-264-2170. From the junction of Highways 321 and 105, drive three miles southwest on 105.

Boone

KOA Boone: In the high country close to all the attractions. Facilities include 118 level, open sites with views over the mountains; 78 have full hookups and 100 are pull-throughs. Other facilities include bathhouses with hot showers and flush toilets, a laundromat, sewage disposal, and a grocery store. Recreational facilities include a swimming pool, game room and hall, a playground, and a mini golf course.

Rates start at around $18 for two persons.

Boone KOA, Route 2, Box 205, Boone, NC 28607. ☎ 704-264-7250.

Glendale Springs

Raccoon Holler: A large campground in the woods on the Blue Ridge Parkway with 175 sites, of which 117 have full hookups and six are pull-throughs. Facilities include full-service bathhouses, a grocery store, sewage disposal, and LP gas available by weight or meter.

Good recreation facilities include a large hall, lake fishing and swimming, and several nearby hiking trails. Rates start at around $14 for two persons. ☎ 910-982-2706.

From the junction at Mile Marker 257.8 on the Blue Ridge Parkway, take CR 1630 and go three-quarters of a mile west.

Linville Falls

Bear Den Campground: A mountainous campground close to the Blue Ridge Parkway with 144 sites, of which 17 have full hookups, 127 water and electric, and 11 are pull-throughs. Full-service bathhouses, grocery store, sewage disposal, and a laundromat

Extensive recreational facilities include a pavilion, recreation hall, lake swimming, boating and fishing, a playground, several hiking trails and the usual court games.

Rates start at $16 per person.

Bear Den Family Campground, RFD 3, Box 284, Spruce Pine, NC 28777. ☎ 704-765-2888. From the junction of the Blue Ridge Parkway and Highway 221, go seven miles south on the parkway to Mile Marker 324.8, then a half-mile east on Bear Den Mountain Road.

SOUTHWESTERN NORTH CAROLINA

Bryson City

Deep Creek Tube Center & Campground: Creekside camping close to the Blue Ridge Parkway in a mountain valley. This is a small campground with 23 sites, all of which have full hookups. There are cabins and RVs available for rent, a handicapped-accessible full-service bathhouse, a laundromat and a grocery store.

Recreation is centered on the creek, where you can go swimming, fishing and tubing, a playground, sports field, and court games. Rates begin at around $15 for four persons.

Deep Creek Tube Center & Campground, West Deep Creek Road, Bryson City, NC 28713. ☎ 704-488-6055. From the 2nd Bryson City exit on Highway 75, go northwest for three-quarters of a mile, then two blocks east on Main Street. Go a quarter-mile north on Everette, two blocks east on Depot Street, and 1¼ miles northeast on Deep Creek, then follow the signs.

Cashiers

Singing Waters Camping Resort: Creekside camping on 74 wooded sites, of which 42 have full hookups and six are pull-throughs. Facilities include rental tents, cabins, RVs and TVs, full-service bathhouses, a grocery store, and sewage disposal. There's a large pavilion with coin games, river fishing and swimming, several nearby hiking trails and lots of court games.

Rates start at around $16 for two persons.

Singing Waters Camping Resort, Highway 107 and Trout Creek Road, Tuckasegee, NC 28783. ☎ 704-293-5872.

From the junction of Highways 64 and 107, go 9½ miles north on 107, then one mile east on Trout Creek Road.

Cherokee

KOA-Cherokee Great Smokies: A very large campground on 35 acres of park land close to the mountains and the Great Smoky Mountains National Park. Facilities include 420 sites (200 have full hookups, and 60 are pull-throughs). There are also 65 Kamping Kabins with a choice of one or two rooms. Several bathhouses provide hot showers and there are handicapped-accessible restrooms. Sewage disposal is available, and there's a full-service general store. Security is provided by a guard at the gate.

Recreation facilities are extensive. Three tribal trout ponds are re-stocked twice a week and you can fish with a bag limit of 10 fish for only $4 a day. There's a swimming pool, a fully-equipped pavilion, bike rentals, hiking trails and group activities with a recreation director.

Rates start at around $16 for two persons.

Cherokee KOA, Box 39, Cherokee, NC 28719. ☎ 800-825-8352.

From the junction of Highways 19 and 441 in town, go two miles north on 441, then 4½ miles north on Big Cove Road.

Franklin

Cullasaja River Campground: Riverside camping on the banks of the Cullasaja on 75 sites, 52 of which have full hookups; 15 are pull-throughs. Facilities are extensive and include cable TV and telephone hookups, full-service bathhouses, a grocery store, and sewage disposal.

Recreation centers on the river where you can go rafting, swimming and fishing, but there's also pavilion, court games and a recreation room. Rates start at around $16 for two persons.

Cullasaja River Campground, 801 Highlands Road, Franklin, NC 28743. ☎ 800-843-2795.

From the junction of Highways 64 and 441, go east for five miles on 64.

Hendersonville

Lakewood RV Resort: A terraced campground with 87 sites, all with hookups; seven are pull-throughs. RVs are limited to 38 feet maximum length. Full-service bathhouse, handicapped-accessible restroom facilities, laundromat, and grocery store. There's a lounge, recreation hall, swimming pool, fishing on the pond, planned group activities and court games.

Rates begin at $16 for two persons.

Lakewood RV Resort, PO Box 1836, Hendersonville, NC 28739. ☎ 704-397-6641.

From Exit 22 on I-26, take Upward Road east for a quarter-mile, then go north for the same distance on Ballinger Road.

Murphy

Riverbend Campground: A smaller riverside campground with 62 shaded sites (30 have full hookups and 19 are pull-throughs). Full-service bathhouse, laundry, sewage disposal. There's a swimming pool, river fishing, and court games.

Rates start at $12 for two persons. ☎ 704-837-6223. PO Box 606, Murphy, NC 19129.

From the junction of Highways 64 and 19, take 19 and go northeast for four miles.

NORTHERN GEORGIA

Northern Georgia is not as well blessed with commercial campgrounds as are other nearby regions. Those listed below are among the best and, while this is not a recommendation for any or all of them, we feel sure that you won't be disappointed by the facilities or the service you receive.

Blairsville

Canal Lake Campground: A small but scenic lakeside campground with 24 semi-shaded sites on level ground and good recreational facilities. Of the 23 sites, 14 have water and electrical hookups, 10 have no hookups and there's only one pull-through. There are flush toilets, hot showers, restroom facilities for the handicapped, and a small grocery store for basic supplies.

Recreational facilities include a pavilion, recreation room, a boat dock and the opportunity to go swimming, boating, waterskiing or fishing. There are also horseshoe and volleyball courts.

Rates start at around $10 per night, per vehicle.

Canal Lake Campground, 1035, Canal Lake Road, Blairsville, GA 30512. ☎ 706-745-1501.

From the junction of Highways 76 and 19, go north for two miles on 19, then turn left onto Pat Colwell Road and drive another mile to Canal Lake Road. Go for about a half-mile to the campground.

Clarksville

Appalachian Camper Park: A well-managed campground on rolling woodland with 48 shaded sites, of which 15 are pull-throughs, 10 have full hookups and 38 have water and electric hookups only. Facilities include flush toilets, hot showers, sewage disposal, a laundromat, and a convenience store selling ice and wood.

There's a swimming pool, a playground, lake fishing, hiking trails, and a selection of court games. Rates start at around $12.50 per night per site.

Route 2, Box 2144, Clarksville, GA 30523. ☎ 706-754-9319.

From the junction of Alt Highway 17/US 441 Bypass, drive one mile north on US 441.

Cleveland

Turner Campsites: A level campground with open sites on the banks of a mountain stream. Facilities include 120 sites, 52 of which are pull-throughs (115 have full hookups and five have water and electric only). There are flush toilets and hot showers, and campers have access to a laundromat and a sewage disposal.

For recreation, there's a fully equipped pavilion and opportunities for river swimming and fishing, boating and hiking. There's also a playground and a sports field. No pets. No tents.

Rates start at around $15 per night for two persons.

Route 3, Box 3460, Cleveland, GA 30528. ☎ 706-865-4757.

From the junction of Highways 75 and 129, drive 10 miles northwest on 129 and turn onto Highway 129. The campground is 200 feet south of the intersection.

Dillard

Dillard's Resort: A scenic campground close to the mountains with wonderful views. Not too big, Dillard's has good facilities and some opportunities for recreation. Facilities include 58 sites, of which 30 have full hookups, and 28 have none. There are flush toilets, hot showers, and a laundromat. Tents are available. There's the river and a pond (both good for fishing), several hiking trails, and a variety of court games. Rates start at around $12 for two persons.

PO Box 160, Dillard, GA 30537. ☎ 706-746-2714.

From the junction of Highways 246 and 23/441, go south on 23/441 for three-quarters of a mile.

Hiawassee

Bald Mountain Park: A very large, well-appointed campground beside a mountain stream with good facilities and even better recreational opportunities. There are 400 sites (12 are pull-throughs). Sixty-three have full hookups; the others have water and electric hookups only. Cable TV and telephone hookups are available at extra cost. Other facilities include flush toilets, hot showers, a laundromat and sewage disposal. There's also a grocery store for essentials, as well as RV and camping supplies. There's a restaurant, a fully equipped pavilion, an Olympic-size swimming pool, boat dock, rental pedal boats, mini-golf, a playground, fishing, hiking and planned group activities. Some of the above activities may involve an extra charge.

Rates start at $12.50 per night.

Bald Mountain Park Campground, Hiawassee, GA 30546. ☎ 800-253-6605.

From the junction of Highways 76 and 75/17, go northwest on 76 for a quarter-mile, then west on Highway 288 for the same distance. Turn south onto Foudder Creek Road and drive four miles to the campground.

Brasstown Village Resort: A smaller campground with excellent facilities on a shaded, level site beside a mountain creek. There are only 40 sites, eight of which have full hookups, 23 have no hookups. There are flush toilets, hot showers, a laundromat, tables, patios, grills, and sewage disposal. You can easily access Brasstown Bald and the wilderness area from here. There's a recreation hall/pavilion and opportunities for creek fishing, hiking, field sports and court games.

Rates start at around $14 per vehicle.

☎ 706-896-1641.

From the junction of Highways 76 and 17/75, go south on 17/75 for 6½ miles to Highway 180. Go 2½ miles west on 180 to the campground.

Georgia Mountain Campground & Music Hall: Another large, well-appointed campground in a county park. Facilities include 226 sites, of which only 11 have full hookups; the rest have water and electric only. There are flush toilets, hot showers, a boat ramp, a playground, six tennis courts, a sports field and several hiking trails nearby. Sewage disposal is available. The campground is gated and there's a guard on duty.

There's a pavilion, lake swimming, boating, planned group activities through the services of an on-site recreation director, and a variety of court games. The Music Hall features live entertainment with stars coming in from Nashville.

Rates are available by calling the office.

Georgia Mountain Park Campground & Music Hall, PO Box 444, Hiawassee, GA 30546. ☎ 706-896-4191.

From the junction of Highways 76 and 75/17, go northwest on 76 for a quarter of a mile, then west on Highway 288 for the same distance. Turn south onto Foudder Creek Road and drive three miles to the campground.

Mountain City

Mountain City RV Park: A small campground in the center of Mountain City on Highway 441 with good facilities for its size and location. There are 30 sites; 12 are pull-throughs; 26 have full hookups, and four have no hookups. Hot showers, flush toilets, and picnic tables are available. There are no supplies on site, but shops are within walking distance. Rates start at around $12 per night, per vehicle. ☎ 706-746-6985.

Ringgold

KOA-Chattanooga South: A wooded campground on rolling hills with lots of facilities, both for camping and recreation. There are 152 sites and seven Kamping Kabins. Of the sites, 60 have full hookups, 86 water and electric only, and six tent sites have no hookups; 67 of the sites are pull-throughs. Six of the Kabins are one-room units, the other has two rooms. Other facilities include flush toilets, hot showers, a laundromat, and sewage disposal facilities. There's also a store selling groceries, camping and RV supplies, ice and LP gas by weight or meter. Security is handled by on-site staff.

There's a recreation room, a pavilion, swimming pool, a playground and all the usual court games. The staff conducts a program of group activities.

Rates for campsites range from $14.50 to $19.50 for two persons. For a one-room Kamping Kabin the rate is $30 per night for two persons, and $35 per night for the two-room unit. The KOA discount card is honored. ☎ 706-937-4166. Route 5, Box 12, Ringgold, GA 30752.

From the junction of I-75 and Highway 2 (Exit 141), go one-tenth of a mile west on Highway 2.

Rossville

Best Holiday Trav-l-Park: Close to Chattanooga. This is a large campground with extensive facilities set on a level site with plenty of shade. Facilities include 171 campsites, 89 with full hookups, 64 with water and electric only, and 18 with no hookups (130 are pull-throughs). The campground has a full-service store for groceries and camping supplies, as well as LP gas weight or meter. There are also three bathhouses with flush toilets, hot showers, and sewage disposal facilities. There's a recreation hall, pavilion with coin games, swimming pool, wading pool, playground, several court games, and planned group activities handled by an on-site recreation director. Rates begin at around $16.50 for two persons.

From Exit 1 on I-75 in Chattanooga, turn right at the top of the ramp and then left at the second light onto Mack Smith Road. Drive a half-mile to the campground.

Sautee (Helen)

Sleepy Hollow Campground: A small campground close to Helen with level sites in a nice country setting on the lakeshore. There are 67 sites, 30 of which have full hookups and 17 have water and electric. The bathhouse has flush toilets and hot showers, and there's a grocery store when you can purchase the essentials and some camping supplies. Sewage disposal is also available.

For its size, the campground has extensive recreational opportunities, including a pavilion, boat dock and ramp, a sports field and several hiking trails. All of the usual court games are available, as well as badminton and basketball. There's also a playground for the kids. Rates begin at around $14 per vehicle.

Sleepy Hollow Campground, Route 1, Box 1324, Sautee, GA 30571. ☎ 706-878-2618.

From the junction of Highways 17 and 255, drive 2½ miles north on 255, then turn north onto Skylake Road and drive another 2½ miles to the campground.

Tallulah Falls

Terrora Park: This is a very appealing terraced mountain campground in the Tallulah Gorge area with lots to see and do. There are only 50 sites. None have full hookups, but they do have water and electric; 12 are pull-throughs. The bathhouse has flush toilets, hot showers, and handicapped-accessible restrooms. There's a laundromat and ice is available. There is no store, but shops are not too far away in Tallulah Falls. Sewage disposal facilities are available, too.

Aside from the obvious advantages of the wilderness, the falls, and the Tallulah Gorge, the campground offers a pavilion, lake swimming, fishing, a playground, hiking trails and court games.

Rates start out at around $12 per vehicle. ☎ 706-754-6036. PO Box 12, Tallulah Falls, GA 30573.

From the gorge bridge on Highway 441, take 441 north for a half-mile, then head southeast for another half-mile on Rock Mountain Road.

Trenton

Chattanooga West/Lookout Mountain KOA: This campground is right at the tail end of the Smokies. It is blessed with an exceptional view of the mountains, as well as excellent facilities and recreational opportunities. There are 150 sites and six one-room Kamping Kabins. Of the regular campsites, 45 have full hookups; 75 have water and electric; and 30 have no hookups; 100 are pull-throughs. The bathhouse has flush toilets and hot showers, and there's a laundromat, sewage disposal facilities and a full-service store selling groceries, camping supplies, and LP gas by weight or meter.

A recreation room, pavilion, swimming pool, playground, and court games should keep you occupied.

Rates for campsites range from $15 to $19. Kamping Kabins are $28 per night for two person; extra adults are $3 per night each. Call ☎ 706-657-6815. Box 490, Trenton, GA 30752.

From the junction of I-14 and 59, go south on 59 for two miles to Exit 3 at Slygo Road. Go west on Slygo for 2½ miles and follow the signs.

Accommodations Directory

Accommodation Rates		
Inexpensive	below $40 per night	$
Moderate	$41 to $75	$$
Expensive	$76 to $99	$$$
Luxury	$100 and up	$$$$

■ Southeastern Tennessee

CHATTANOOGA

Chanticleer Inn, 1300 Mockingbird Lane, Lookout Mountain, GA 30750. ☎ 606-820-2015. Three miles from the foot of the mountain. Pool. Complimentary breakfast. $$

Days Inn Airport, 7015 Shallowford Road, Chattanooga, TN 37421. ☎ 423-855-0011. Close to Interstate 75 north of the city. Pool. Complimentary coffee. $$

Econo Lodge, 1417 St. Thomas, Chattanooga, TN 37412. ☎ 423-894-1417. North of the city at Exit 1 on Interstate 75. Pool, restaurant, complimentary breakfast and coffee. $

Hampton Inn, 7013 Shallowford Road, Chattanooga, TN 37421. ☎ 423-855-0095. Pool, restaurant, exercise room, complimentary breakfast. $$

King's Lodge, 2400 West Side Drive, Chattanooga, TN 37404. ☎ 423-698-8949. Close to Lookout Mountain and city center. Pool, restaurant, bar. $$

Super 8, 20 Birmingham Hwy, Chattanooga, TN 37419. ☎ 423-821-6820. Close to Lookout & Raccoon mountains. Restaurant, complimentary coffee. $

CLEVELAND

Budgetel Inn, 107 Interstate Drive NW, Cleveland, TN 37311. ☎ 423-339-1000. Pool, complimentary coffee and breakfast. $$

Holiday Inn-North, 2400 Executive Park Drive, Cleveland, TN 37312. ☎ 423-472-1504. Just off Interstate 75 at Exit 25. Pool, restaurant. $$ to $$$

Quality Inn Chalet, 89 Georgetown Road, Cleveland, TN 37311. ☎ 423-476- 8511. At Exit 25 on Interstate 75. Pool, restaurant. $$

■ Upper East Tennessee

GATLINBURG

Alpine, River Road & Cottage Drive, Gatlinburg, TN 37738. ☎ 423-436-5651. Close to center of town. Pool, free coffee. $$

Comfort Inn Downtown, 200 East Parkway, Gatlinburg, TN 37738. ☎ 800-221-2222. Pool, restaurant. $$$

Jack Huff's Motor Lodge, 204 Cherokee Orchard Road, Gatlinburg, TN 37738. ☎ 423-436-5171. Close to all the attractions. Pool, complimentary coffee. $$

Midtown Lodge, 805 Parkway, Gatlinburg, TN 37738. ☎ 423-436-5691. Two miles to ski center. Pool, restaurant opposite. $$$

River Edge Motor Lodge, 665 River Road, Gatlinburg, TN 37738. ☎ 423-436-9292. Close to Great Smoky Mountains National Park. Pool, complimentary coffee. $$

JOHNSON CITY

Days Inn, 2312 Brown's Mill Road, Johnson City, TN 37601. ☎ 423-282-2211. Close to city. Restaurant, pool, complimentary breakfast, bar. $$

Fairfield Inn by Marriott, 207 E. Mountcastle, Johnson City, TN 37601. ☎ 800-228-2800. Close to Interstate 81 feeder. Restaurant, complimentary coffee. $

KINGSPORT

Ramada Inn, 2005 La Masa Drive, Kingsport, TN 37660. ☎ 423-245-0271. Easy access to Interstate 81. Restaurant, bar, pool, tennis courts. $$

∎ Northwestern North Carolina

ASHEVILLE

Forest Manor Motor Lodge, 866 Hendersonville Road, Asheville, NC 28803. ☎ 704-274-3531. On Highway 25, one mile south of Interstate 40, Exit 50. Heated pool, complimentary breakfast, tennis privileges. $$ to $$$

Best Western-Central, 22 Woodfin Street, Asheville, NC 28801. ☎ 704-253-1815. One block off Interstate 240 at Merrimon Avenue exit. Heated pool, café, health club privileges. $$

Howard Johnson-Biltmore, 190 Hendersonville Road, Asheville, NC 28803. ☎ 704-274-2304. Close to Biltmore Estate. Pool, café. $$ to $$$$

Pisgah View Ranch, Route 1, Candler, NC 28715. ☎ 704-667-9100. 13 miles from the Enka-Candler exit off Interstate 40. Resort. Heated pool, playground, tennis, hiking trails, recreation room, lawn games. $$ to $$$

Quality Inn-Biltmore, 115 Hendersonville Road, Asheville, NC 28803. ☎ 800-228-5151. Close to Biltmore Estate. Pool, free coffee, café, bar. $$$

BLOWING ROCK

Blowing Rock Inn, Box 265, Blowing Rock, NC 28605. ☎ 704-295-7921. On Main Street. Heated pool, free coffee. $$

Cliff Dwellers Inn, Box 366, Blowing Rock, NC 28605. ☎ 704-295-3121. One mile south of Blue Ridge Parkway and the exit for

Highway 321. Close to the shops. Heated pool, coffee in rooms, café nearby. $$ to $$$

Meadowbrook, Box 2005, Blowing Rock, NC 28605. ☎ 704-295-9341. On north Main Street three miles from ski center. Free continental breakfast, dining room, bar, entertainment. $$$$

BOONE

Econo Lodge, Route 6, Box 46, Boone, NC 28607. ☎ 704-264-4133. Three miles south of the city on Highway 105. Indoor pool, free coffee, free continental breakfast, café nearby. $$

Mountain Villa, US 321 S, Boone, NC 28607. ☎ 704-264-6166. One mile south on Hwy 321. Pool, whirlpool, free coffee, adjacent café. $$

LINVILLE

Pixie Motor Inn, Box 277, Linville, NC 28646. ☎ 704-733-2579. At the junction of Highways 221 and 105. Seven miles to ski center. $

■ Southwestern North Carolina

BRYSON CITY

Hemlock, Drawer EE, Bryson City, NC 28713. ☎ 704-488-2885. Four miles northeast of the city on Highway 19. Games room, lawn games. $$$$

CHEROKEE

Best Western-Great Smoky Mountains Inn, Box 1809, Cherokee, NC 28719. ☎ 704-497-2020. One mile north of the city on Highway 441. Pool, wading pool, playground, café. $$

Craig's, PO Box 1047, Cherokee, NC 28719. ☎ 704-497-3821. One miles east of the city on Highway 19. Pool, playground, café. $$

Pioneer, Box 397, Cherokee, NC 28719. ☎ 704-497-2435. One mile south of the city on Highway 19. Heated pool, café opposite. $$ to $$$

FONTANA DAM

Fontana Village Resort, NC Highway 28, Fontana Dam, NC 28733. ☎ 704-498-2211. On Highway 28. Indoor/outdoor pool, wading pool, sauna, playground, supervised children's activities, lighted tennis, café, snack bar. $$ to $$$$

HIGHLANDS

Highlands Inn, Box 1030, Highlands, NC 28741. ☎ 704-526-5036. On Main Street. Free continental breakfast. $$$

WAYNESVILLE

Windsong, 120 Ferguson Ridge Drive, Clyde, NC 28721. ☎ 704-627-6111. Mountainside lodge with themed décor. Heated pool, free full breakfast, tennis. $$$

■ Northern Georgia

DAHLONEGA

Days Inn, 1065 South Chestatee Street, Dahlonega, GA 30433. ☎ 706-864-2338. In town. Pool, complimentary full breakfast and coffee. $$

DALTON

Best Western, 2106 Chattanooga Road, Dalton, GA 30720. ☎ 706-226-5022. On Interstate 75 at the Rocky Face exit. Pool, playground, restaurant. $$

HELEN

Comfort Inn, Edelweiss Street, Helen, GA 30545. ☎ 706-878-8000. In town. Pool, complimentary breakfast. $$$

Heidi, Box 507, Main Street, Helen, GA 30545. ☎ 706-878-2689. Four blocks from town center. Pool. $$

Accommodations Directory

Information Directory

■ Fish & Wildlife Agencies

Here is a website with links to all agencies that manage fish & wildlife resources in the US:
http://bluegoose.arw.r9.fws.gov/NWRSFiles/InternetResources/USStateAgencies.html

■ Blue Ridge Parkway

Superintendent, Blue Ridge Parkway
700 Northwestern Bank Building
Asheville, NC 28801
☎ 704-298-0398

■ Fishing

Tennessee Wildlife Resource Agency
Ellington Agricultural Center
PO Box 40747
Nashville, TN 37204
☎ 615-781-6500

North Carolina Wildlife Resources Commission
Transaction Management
1709 Mail Service Center
Raleigh, NC 27699-1709
☎ 919-662-4370

Georgia License and Boat Registration Unit
2189 Northlake Parkway, Building 10, Suite 108
Tucker, GA 30084
☎ 770-414-3333

■ Great Smoky Mountains National Park

GENERAL INFORMATION

Great Smoky Mountains National Park
107 Park Headquarters Road
Gatlinburg, TN 27738
☎ 423-436-1200

HORSEBACK RIDING

Cades Cove Riding Stables
RDF 1, PO Box 2885
Walland, TN 37886
☎ 423-448-6286

Cosby Stables
Route 2
Newport, TN 37821
Mail only

McCarter's Riding Stable
Gatlinburg, TN 37738
☎ 423-436-5354

Smokemont Riding Stables
PO Box 72
Cherokee, NC 28719
☎ 704-497-2373

Smoky Mountains Riding Stables
PO Box 728
Gatlinburg, TN 37738
☎ 423-436-5634

■ Cherokee National Forest

Forest Supervisor
2800 N. Ocoee Street
Cleveland, TN 37320
☎ 423-476-9700

Hiwassee Ranger District
274 Highway 310
Etowah, TN 37331
☎ 423-263-5486

Nolichucky Ranger District
121 Austin Avenue
Greeneville, TN 37743
☎ 423-638-4109

Ocoee Ranger District
USDA Forest Service
Route 1, Box 348-D
Benton, TN 37307
☎ 423-338-5201

Tellico Ranger District
USDA Forest Service
PO Box 339
Tellico Plains, TN 37385
☎ 423-253-2520

Unaka Ranger District
1205 N. Main Street
Erwin, TN 37650
☎ 423-743-4452

Watauga Ranger District
Route 9, Box 2235
Elizabethton, TN 37643
☎ 423-542-294

■ Pisgah National Forest

Forest Supervisor
North Carolina Section
PO Box 2750
Asheville, NC 28802
☎ 704-257-4200

Supervisor Nat'l Forests
Pisgah National Forest
PO Box 2750
Asheville, NC 28802
☎ 704-258-2850

French Broad Ranger Dist.
PO Box 128
Hot Springs, NC 28743
☎ 704-622-3202

Grandfather Ranger Dist.
Route 1, Box 110-A
Nebo, NC 28761
☎ 704-652-2144

Pisgah Ranger Dist.
1001 Pisgah Highway
Pisgah Forest, NC 28768
☎ 704-877-3350

Toecane Ranger Dist.
PO Box 128
Burnsville, NC 28714
☎ 704-682-6146

■ Nantahala National Forest

Supervisor National Forests
PO Box 2750
Asheville, NC 28802
☎ 704-258-2850

Cheoah Ranger District
Route 1, Box 16A
Robbinsville, NC 28771
☎ 704-479-6431

Information Directory

Highlands Ranger District
Route 1, Box 247
Highlands, NC 28741
☎ 704-526-3765

Tusquitee Ranger District
201 Woodlands Drive
Murphy, NC 28906
☎ 704-837-5152

Wayah District Ranger
8 Sloan Road
Franklin, NC 28734
☎ 704-524-6441

■ Chattahoochee National Forest

Forest Supervisor
US Forest Service
508 Oak Street NW
Gainesville, GA 30501
☎ 404-536-0541

Armuchee Ranger District
806 E. Villanow Street
PO Box 465
LaFayette, GA 30728
☎ 706-638-1085

Brasstown Ranger District
1881 Highway 515
PO Box 9
Blairsville, GA 30512
☎ 706-745-6928

Chattooga Ranger District
PO Box 196, Burton Road
Clarksville, GA 30523
☎ 706-754-6221

Chestatee Ranger District
1015 Tipton Drive
Dahlonega, GA 30533
☎ 706-864-6173

Cohutta Ranger District
401 Old Ellijay Road
Chatsworth, GA 30705
☎ 706-695-6736

Tallulah Ranger District
825 Highway 411 South
PO Box 438
Clayton, GA 30525
☎ 706-782-3320

Toccoa Ranger District
E. Main Street, Box 1839
Blue Ridge, GA 30513
☎ 706-632-3031

Oconee Ranger District
348 Forsyth Street
Monticello, GA 31064
☎ 706-468-2244

■ Hiking Clubs

Nantahala Hiking Club
173 Carl Slagle Road
Franklin, NC 28734
☎ 304-535-6331

Appalachian Trail Conference
799 Washington Street
Harpers Ferry WV 25425
☎ 304-535-6331

The AT Conference is the umbrella organization for all the hiking clubs on the eastern seabord, including the clubs that maintain the Appalachian Trail from Maine to Georgia.

■ Rivers & Lakes

Army Corps of Engineers
Tennessee Valley Authority (TVA)
☎ 423-632-2264

■ Whitewater Outfitters & Adventures

SOUTHEASTERN TENNESSEE

Ocoee River

Ocoee Inn Rafting
Highway 64 East
Route 1, Box 347
Benton, TN 37307
☎ 800-272-RAFT

Quest Expeditions
Highway 64
Ocoee, TN 37361
☎ 800-277-4537

Rolling Thunder River
Company (Ocoee River)
Box 88
Almond, NC 28702
☎ 704-488-2030

Ocoee Outdoors
Highway 64
Ocoee, TN 37361
☎ 800-533-7767

Southeastern Expeditions
Route 1, Box 375
Ocoee, TN 37361
☎ 800-868-7238

Sunburst Adventures
Welcome Valley Road
Benton, TN 37307
☎ 423-338-8388

Information Directory

Wildwater Limited
Box 309
Longcreek, SC 29658
☎ 800-451-9972

UPPER EAST TENNESSEE
(Gatlinburg & Pigeon Rivers)

Rafting in the Smokies
Pigeon River Outdoors
PO Box 592
Gatlinburg, TN 37738

USA RAFT (Nantahala Exp.)
11044 Highway 19W
Bryson City, NC 28713
☎ 828-488-3316; 800-USA-RAFT

(Nolichucky River)

USA RAFT (Nantahala Expeditions)
11044 Highway 19W,
Bryson City, NC 28713
☎ 828-488-3316/800-USA-RAFT

NORTHWESTERN NORTH CAROLINA
(French Broad, Nolichucky & Pigeon Rivers)

French Broad River Adventures
Carolina Wilderness
PO Box 488
Hot Springs, NC 28743
☎ 800-872-7437

USA RAFT (Nantahala Exp.)
11044 Highway 19W
Bryson City, NC 28713
☎ 828-488-3316
☎ 800-USA-RAFT

Great Smokies Rafting company
13077 Highway 19 West
Bryson City, NC 28713
☎ 800-581-4772

Rolling Thunder River
Company (Nantahala River)
Box 88
Almond, NC 28702
☎ 704-488-2030

SOUTHWESTERN NORTH CAROLINA

USA RAFT
(Nantahala Expeditions)
11044 Highway 19W
Bryson City, NC 28713
☎ 828-488-3316/
800-USA-RAFT

Carolina Outfitters Rafting
(Nantahala only)
12121 Highway 19W
Bryson City, NC 28713
☎ 800-468-7238

Wildwater Rafting
13077 US 19/74
Bryson City, NC 28713
☎ 800-872-4681

NORTHERN GEORGIA
(Helen)

Cool River Tubing Co.
Edelweis Drive
Helen, GA 30545
☎ 706-878-COOL

(Chattooga River)

Southeastern Expeditions
Chatooga Outpost
Route 3, Box 3178E
Clayton, GA 30525
☎ 800-868-7238

Wildwater Limited
Box 309
Longcreek, SC 29658
☎ 800-451-9972

High Country Outfitters
PO Drawer J
Bryson City, NC 28713
☎ 828-488-3153

Nantahala Outdoor Ctr
USA RAFT (Nantahala Exp.)
11044 Highway 19W
Bryson City, NC 28713
☎ 828-488-3316
☎ 800-USA-RAFT

Index

248, 288-289, 328; Cohutta District, 244-246, 286, 328; information, 328; Oconee District, 328; sightseeing, 239-249; Tallulah District, 248-249, 289-290, 328; Toccoa District, 246-247, 287-288, 328

Chattahoochee River, 244; camping, 285

Chattanooga: accommodations, 319-320; commercial camping, 304-305; fishing, 69; shopping, 84-85; sightseeing, 47-57

Chattooga River, rafting, 331

Cherokee: accommodations, 322; camping, 312; sightseeing, 94-95, 193-196

Cherokee National Forest: camping, 31-32, 275-277; hiking, 74-82, 125-131; Hiwassee District, 58, 276, 326; information, 326-327; Nolichucky District, 88-89, 277, 326; Ocoee District, 57-58, 276, 326; sightseeing, 57-59, 87-89; Tellico District, 58-59, 276, 327; Unaka District, 88, 277, 327; Watauga District, 89, 277, 327

Chickamauga National Battlefield, 50

Chief Vann House Historic Site, 250

Chilhowee Lake, fishing, 69-70

Clarksville, Georgia: camping, 314; craft hunting, 264

Clayton, Georgia, craft hunting, 265

Cleveland, Georgia, camping, 314

Cleveland, Tennessee: accommodations, 320; camping, 306; shopping, 85

Climate, 15-16

Clinch River, fishing, 121

Clingmans Dome, 96-97

Cloudland Canyon State Park: camping, 300; hiking, 270; sightseeing, 238-239

Cohutta Wilderness, hiking, 270-272

Colman River, 249

Commercial campgrounds, 27-28, 304-318; fees, 31-32; Northern Georgia, 313-318; Northwestern North Carolina, 309-311; Southeastern Tennessee, 304-306; Southwestern North Carolina, 311-313; Upper East Tennessee, 306-309

Conasauga River: canoeing, 263-264; fishing, 268; sightseeing, 245-246

Copper Hill, 68-69

Country music, birthplace of, 112

Craft hunting, 44; Northern Georgia, 264-266; Northwestern North Carolina, 165-167; Southwestern North Carolina, 218; Upper East Tennessee, 120-121

Cullowhee, North Carolina, 196-197

Dahlonega, Georgia: accommodations, 323; gold museum and historic site, 250-251

Dalton, Georgia, accommodations, 323

Davy Crockett Birthplace, 104-105

Dillard, Georgia, camping, 314-315

Dillsboro, North Carolina, 228, 230

Dollywood, 108

Douglas Lake, fishing, 122

Driving tips, 17-18; safety, 22-23

Elizabethton, Tennessee, 89-90

Ellijay, Georgia, craft hunting, 265

Erwin, Tennessee, 90, 92

Fall color, 33-34, 67-69

Fish and wildlife agencies, 325

Fishing, 41-42, 325; Great Smoky Mountains National Park, 101-102; Northern Georgia, 266-269; Northwestern North Carolina, 167-168; Southeastern Tennessee, 69-73; Southwestern North Carolina, 219-220; Upper East Tennessee, 121-124

Flat Rock, North Carolina, 197-198

Flora and fauna, 6-12, 102; fall color, 33-34, 66-68; spring wildflowers, 34

Fontana Dam: accommodations, 322-323; sightseeing, 198

Fontana Lake: boating, 163, 216; fishing, 167, 219

Forbidden Caverns, 109-110

Forest fires, 25

Fort Loudoun Lake: boating, 61-65; fishing, 70

Fort Mountain State Park: camping, 300-301; hiking, 272-273; sightseeing, 251-252

Fort Patrick Henry Lake, fishing, 123

Four Loudoun Historic Park, 60

Franklin, North Carolina: camping, 312; craft hunting, 218; sightseeing, 198-203

French Broad River: canoeing, 65, 117; fishing, 122; rafting, 330

Gatlinburg: accommodations, 320; commercial camping, 306-307; craft hunting, 120-121; park entry, 95; rafting, 330; sightseeing, 92-94

Gems and mining, 199-201, 203

Geography, 3-6

Glendale Springs, camping, 310

Gliding, 40

Grandfather Mountain, 154-155

Great Smoky Mountains: accommodations, 319-323; camping, 275-318;